ABOVE THE LAW

ABOVE THE LAW

PAUL PALANGO

M&S

Canadian Cataloguing in Publication Data

Palango, Paul, 1950-
Above the law : the crooks, the politicians, the Mounties, and Rod Stamler

Includes index.
ISBN 0-7710-6929-4

1. Stamler, Rod.   2. Commercial crimes –
Canada.   3. Corporations – Canada – Corrupt
practices.   4. Political corruption – Canada.   5. Royal
Canadian Mounted Police.   I. Title.

HV6771.C3P3   364.1'68'0971   C94-930637-1

The publishers acknowledge the support of the Canada Council, the Ontario Arts Council, and the Ontario Ministry of Culture, Tourism and Recreation for their publishing program.

Typesetting M&S, Toronto

Printed and bound in Canada on acid-free paper.

McClelland & Stewart Inc.
The Canadian Publishers
481 University Avenue
Toronto, Ontario
M5G 2E9

1 2 3 4 5   98 97 96 95 94

For Cheryl
who has stood by me for twenty-two years
and kept me in touch with the real world.

Contents

"They look upon Fraud as a greater Crime than Theft, and therefore seldom fail to punish it with Death; For they alledge, that Care and Vigilance, with a very common Understanding, may preserve a Man's Goods from Thieves; but Honesty hath no Fence against Superior Cunning; And since it is necessary that there should be a perpetual Intercourse of buying and selling, and dealing upon Credit; where Fraud is permitted or connived at, or hath no Law to punish it, the honest Dealer is always undone, and the Knave gets the Advantage."

Jonathan Swift
Gulliver's Travels, 1726

"When I visit a country, I don't examine whether the laws are good, but whether they are executed, because there are good laws everywhere."

Baron de la Brède et de Montesquieu
De L'Esprit des Lois, 1748

Preface

I first heard of Rod Stamler in the spring of 1974, during my first week as a student reporter at my home-town newspaper, *The Hamilton Spectator*. At that time, Stamler was an inspector with the Royal Canadian Mounted Police and was investigating criminal wrongdoing within the Hamilton Harbour Commission. I was fascinated. Here was a police officer more familiar with sharp pencils and bottom lines than with guns and high-speed chases.

From that day, I casually followed his career from afar. I finally met him in 1989, at a book launch for my friend and former colleague, Victor Malarek. By then, Stamler was assistant commissioner in the RCMP, in charge of its Economic Crime Directorate, and was being touted by some as the next commissioner. But shortly after I met him, he suddenly resigned from the force and joined a forensic accounting firm in Toronto. He is currently a partner in another generation of that firm, Lindquist, Avey, Macdonald and Baskerville.

In 1990, I left the *Globe and Mail* after thirteen years' service. As Metro Toronto and then national editor from 1986 to 1990, I had been responsible for the supervision of most of the so-called investigative stories published, the best known probably being the Patti Starr affair. During the summer of 1991, I was working on contract as researcher for the CBC program, "the fifth estate."

One story I was looking into involved a mysterious financial transaction in a Middle Eastern country. Someone suggested that Rod Stamler would know who could help me track down the principals. Stamler agreed to meet me, but by the time I arrived at his Toronto office a few days later, I was less interested in the Middle Eastern mystery than in hearing what Stamler had to say on another matter. I was curious about what appeared to be the demise of good cops and civil servants. It seemed as if a weird plague had struck in the late 1980s and cut down a swath of right-minded people.

At first we talked about the Canadian news media, a natural common ground, as Stamler had always respected the work of reporters. This attitude was not at all what I expected from a senior police officer. He wondered why there were so few good, effective reporters left in Canada.

I told him that it was my belief that investigative reporting, as it applies to the coverage of institutions, the political process, and big business, is largely frowned upon by newspaper owners and managers in Canada. There are a number of reasons for this, not the least of them being a fundamental misunderstanding, even among reporters, of what investigative reporting is. It is not police work or even quasi-police work, but rather the uncovering of new stories. As simple as that concept might seem, it is considered dangerous by some, such as former *Hamilton Spectator* publisher John Muir who, after ridding his paper of its crack investigative reporters and editors in the early 1970s, said, "Nobody elected the press to do anything." Or, as media baron Conrad Black said more recently, "The role of the press is to chronicle, not initiate." But investigative reporters are not chroniclers, nor do they accept conventional wisdom – that would be a betrayal of their instinctive curiosity. That's what Stamler said he liked about good reporters – their curiosity and determination to get at the truth. Our talk turned to the current state of the RCMP and in particular the behaviour of the force during the reign of the Mulroney government. The discussion led to my question about what had happened to the good, effective cops. Stamler clearly had an opinion, but wasn't ready then to express it. Still, I was sure he saw a similarity in my description of the fate of investigative reporters.

Ever since the victory of Brian Mulroney's Tories in the 1984 federal election, Canadians had been treated regularly to tales of impropriety, possible corruption, and police investigations involving members and friends of the government. There were rumours about offshore dealings, Swiss bank accounts, and multi-million-dollar kickbacks. An entire magazine, *Frank*, was built on the pervasive whiff of government scandal. Over the years, some people had been charged and even jailed, but most of their crimes appeared to be relatively minor expense-account fiddles and petty indiscretions masquerading as major crime. It seemed that the most contentious cases, those with the potential to inflict great political damage, rarely attracted the full attention of the police. The few cases that did seemed prone to fizzling out in one courtroom or another. Meanwhile, protestors such as Glen Kealey, a former businessman and Tory, were telling anyone who would listen that the fix was in and that the government was controlling police investigations. What was really going on?

No matter how many stories I edited or read about Canadian politics, especially those alleging corruption within the Mulroney government, I was left with the sense that something was missing. The stories and books seemed too neat, too focused on a particular event or time-span or term of office. Somewhere along the line it struck me that if anyone knew the story about Ottawa that no one was telling, it had to be Stamler, who as a police officer had a unique view into the closets of the political and business élite. My impression was that he had been singularly successful in tackling big, politically difficult cases of fraud and corruption in the 1970s, the kind of investigations and prosecutions that have been rare ever since.

I suggested to Stamler that his biggest cases should be re-counted for the sake of history, adding that if Canadians could understand why he'd been successful then, we might begin to understand why the police seemed so unsuccessful in investigating the scandals that permeated the Mulroney government.

"You're absolutely right," Stamler replied. "What happened in the 1970s is the key to understanding why the police are so ineffective today."

That statement triggered this book.

Soon I was immersed in researching arcane and long-forgotten events and people from the 1960s and 1970s. As white-collar crime was my initial focus, I was surprised by how much time I spent studying the Quebec separatist movement. At one point I was reminded of an incident in 1970 during the height of the October crisis that symbolized for me how little Canadians sometimes know about the inner workings of their own country.

I was a journalism student at Carleton University in Ottawa at the time and was disconcerted, along with other Ottawans, by the armed soldiers patrolling the city ever since the War Measures Act had been invoked. British diplomat James Cross and Quebec Labour Minister Pierre Laporte were being held hostage by the Fédération de libération du Québec. On the evening of October 17, I decided to go with a friend to the 9:00 p.m. showing of the film *Catch 22* at the Nelson Theatre on Rideau Street. As I was waiting in line, I saw Prime Minister Pierre Trudeau, sporting a purple ascot, and his date, Madeleine Gobeil, leave the cinema, accompanied at a discreet distance by two plain-clothes Mounties. While they waited at the curb for Trudeau's limousine to arrive, a number of people waiting in line for the movie walked up to him to chat and shake his hand. I didn't. I was surprised, and even more later that evening, when I saw Trudeau, dressed in black, on television lamenting the murder of Pierre Laporte, whose body had just been found stuffed in the trunk of a parked car. If this was a dire terrorist threat to the nation, how come the

prime minister had so little obvious security? I could only conclude that the crisis was not as serious a threat as we'd all been led
to believe. An eager student, I tried to place my little story with
the press, which could not have been less interested.

Now in 1991, I was researching a story that in some ways
sprang directly from that time. In the wake of the October crisis,
the RCMP's Security Service had burned a barn and broken into
Parti Québécois headquarters; the McDonald Commission had
been set up to investigate; and I was starting to realize just how
the commission's recommendations had really affected the
RCMP's ability to do its job.

Stamler had agreed to co-operate with me to the extent of giving me access to copies of his old court briefs, hand-written notes,
and other documents. These I supplemented with at least sixty
hours of formal interviews with him, which generated as many
questions as answers. The only condition he placed on the book
was that he check the manuscript for factual errors. The form and
content and interpretation were mine. Stamler sought no glory
for himself to the point that he was reluctant to paint himself in a
positive light even when circumstances warranted it. To him the
real story was what has happened to Canada, not the role of Rod
Stamler, supercop. If I failed to tell that story, he told me more
than once, he would write it himself one day.

I spent my research funds many times over travelling to seven
provinces and making several trips to Ottawa and Montreal to
gather the individual strands of this story. Early in the project, I
did something unusual: Stamler arranged for me to become a private investigator so that I might have first-hand knowledge of the
difficulties the police face during fraud investigations. It was a
useful exercise. I worked on two cases, one that took me all over
North America on quite an adventure and one involving a multi-
million-dollar arson fire in North Battleford, Saskatchewan.

Having Stamler's imprimatur on my work opened doors I
might otherwise not have breached. More than twenty current

and former members of the RCMP co-operated with me, but most of them did so on the understanding they would remain anonymous. Some were afraid of retribution, and others did not want to be seen as the agents of dishonour to the force and to their current or former colleagues. I was also helped immeasurably by many current and former civil servants, politicians, and journalists.

To my disappointment some people who were important to the telling of this story refused to be interviewed. I made numerous requests for interviews with RCMP Commissioner Norman Inkster and about a dozen other senior officers and investigators, but the RCMP refused in writing to co-operate officially. Former RCMP commissioner Robert Simmonds, former prime minister Pierre Trudeau, and former Liberal cabinet minister John Munro declined to be interviewed, as did various members and former members of the Mulroney cabinet and Quebec judges Gérard Girouard, Réjean Paul, and Louis-Philippe Landry.

In portraying those who were not interviewed, I have attempted to be absolutely fair. I triple-checked all my information, including direct quotes from Stamler's contemporaneous notes, against the public record or against the recollections of others who knew about that particular matter. Readers should note that I have used three pseudonyms in order to protect the reputations of these individuals.

From the outset, my intent was to publish neither a scholarly nor a sensationalist account, but to make this complex story as accurate, entertaining, thought-provoking, and engaging as possible for Canadians, the real and unwitting victims of those who have placed themselves Above The Law.

Toronto
February 1994

Acknowledgements

This book might never have happened without the help I received from a great number of people. First I should thank Geoffrey Stevens, one of the country's best journalists, who listened to my initial idea for the book, helped me draft an outline, and introduced me to his literary agent, Jan Whitford of the Lucinda Vardey Agency.

As this was my first book, I had little idea of what an agent's job is. Now I am sure that it is normally less than what Jan Whitford did for me. She took my outline and made me rewrite it until it met her standard and then promoted it enthusiastically to her contacts in the book publishing world. Later, after I had completed my first, meandering draft, she helped me shape the story and keep it on course. I can't thank her enough.

My thanks also go to Avie Bennett, chairman and president of McClelland & Stewart, to publisher Doug Gibson, and especially to senior editor Dinah Forbes for taking a chance on me and the story, which might have been mistaken for a biography of a largely unknown former Mountie. I knew they had grasped the story's possible implications when, at our first meeting, Doug Gibson said, "I suspect there is more to this than first meets the eye." I hope I've given him the more he suspected was there. Dinah Forbes edited and polished the final draft of the manuscript and Peter Buck, my copy editor, also made many helpful suggestions.

A number of journalists and former journalists, many of whom were eager to see Rod Stamler's story told, deserve recognition. In particular I want to thank Ottawa *Citizen* editor James Travers, who let me interview him and gave me access to the paper's library; Southam News reporter Stephen Bindman and librarian Kirsten Smith, who "deputized" me for three months to facilitate my research in Ottawa; Robert Fife of the *Ottawa Sun* and Eric Reguly of the *Financial Post*, who gave me their time and their files; Norman Webster, who gave me *carte blanche* to research at the Montreal *Gazette*, and *Gazette* reporters William Marsden and Rod MacDonell; *Hamilton Spectator* editor Rob Austin and librarian John Lawrence; *Toronto Star* editor John Honderich and librarian Carol Lindsay; Peter Rehak and Eric Malling of CTV's "W5"; and last, but by no means least, my friend Stephen Jarrett, editor of *eye Weekly*, who read and criticized my manuscript and helped keep me and my family alive during the whole process. In that regard, I must also thank my understanding bank manager, Effie Lazegas, and the others who gave me paid work when I needed it the most.

I owe a special debt to Paula Jarrett and Deborah Percy, who accurately transcribed most of the taped interviews, sometimes in difficult circumstances. One of the people whose voice was on many of those tapes was the always pleasant Kathryn Giacomello, the official waitress of the book, who fed Stamler and me during our early morning sessions at Shopsy's delicatessen in downtown Toronto.

I must also thank David Savel and Vic Jereb of Options Software and Consulting, who never kept me waiting when my computer and software let me down; Katia Pawlak-Omnes and Seija Virtanen in Toronto; Donald Mitchell, Cliff Kennedy, and Ann Stamler in Ottawa; Michael Harris in Nova Soctia; Harry Fleming and the Canadian Coast Guard in Halifax; the Blixt family in Sprague, Manitoba; Dennis Valdron in Winnipeg; George Wool in Vancouver; the friendly townspeople of Pointe-du-lac,

Quebec; and the helpful librarians in Toronto's, Ottawa's, Winnipeg's, and Saskatoon's public libraries.

Of course, this book would have been nothing without Rod Stamler. I can't thank him enough for agreeing with me that his story and his perspective on Canadian politics had to be told.

Finally, my family. While this project grew and grew and stretched on and on, they were unfailingly patient, loving, and supportive. A million thanks to Cheryl and Lindsay for staying on top of things and for your astute and timely criticisms, and to Virginia for keeping me entertained. I love you all.

1

Parliament Hill, Spring 1989

In April 1989 Rodney Thomas Stamler was on the eve of retiring from the Royal Canadian Mounted Police. He was an assistant commissioner, and the top commercial-crime investigator in the country, based at RCMP headquarters in Ottawa. Head of the Economic Crime Directorate, he commanded a nation-wide squad of more than four hundred investigators. A tiny but noisy corner of his empire – the Special Federal Inquiries Unit – gave him responsibility for investigating suspected crimes against the government of Canada by businessmen and by its own politicians and bureaucrats.

On that cool, breezy day, as Stamler strode out of the Centre Block of the House of Commons, thinking this was his last official visit to the seat of the Canadian government, his spirit was torn. After his superiors had heard he was planning to retire after thirty-three years on the force, plans were made to nominate him for the Order of Canada for his service to his country. He was excited about the prospect of public honours, but he was in despair about the integrity of the force he was leaving. About fifty feet from the west doors of the House of Commons a protester stood rooted to his usual spot. The cryptic message on his placard struck a chord with the Mountie: RCMP (1987) INCORPORATED / MULRONEY JUSTICE (JUST-US) / "PROTECTING POLITICAL CROOKS" / HONEST CANADIANS NEED NOT APPLY.

Stamler was not much for politics. His German-Hungarian immigrant parents had always voted Liberal in gratitude to the party that had let them into the country in the 1920s, but he had voted for all three major parties over the years, even the New Democrats once. But, more and more, politics had crept into his job, and his current investigation was politically loaded. Global TV reporter Doug Small had been leaked details of the federal budget, which he had broadcast on the eve of its scheduled release to Parliament. The breach had forced Finance Minister Michael Wilson to deliver the budget immediately, then the Mounties had been called in. Mulroney publicly called the budget leak "a criminal act," seeming to blame Small, the messenger.

Stamler had trouble seeing it Mulroney's way. True, there had been a breach of security, and a minor criminal act may have been committed by whoever took the document, but Stamler thought it was the media's duty to report that breach. That Small had obtained one of the documents was part of Small's job, Stamler believed, but his involvement did not constitute a criminal act.

Stamler knew well that law enforcement ultimately comes down to a matter of belief because criminal charges are not the stuff of assembly lines. A police officer has to *believe* that a crime has been committed, and once he believes it, a charge must be laid; that's what the police officer's oath is all about. Politics isn't supposed to enter into it.

The Liberals were swept out of office in 1984. Tired, weak, bereft of ideas, yet still power-hungry, the Liberals had been an easy electoral target. Now, with Brian Mulroney, the business-man, at the helm, there was hope for prosperity, change, and respect for the rule of law. That's what Mulroney had promised, but almost from the moment he and his huge majority government first took control in 1984, Canadians had been treated to a constant stream of sleaze and misbehaviour by people connected to the prime minister in one way or another.

There was so little known about the government's activities that even the police were finding it nearly impossible to discern the good guys from the bad and the serious incidents from the insignificant. That was always the way it seemed to be when the police came up against the political process. In his day Rod Stamler had dealt with politicians enough times to develop a connoisseur's appreciation for them. Masters of murk, they seemed to him to be ever willing and able to use their political powers and offices to confuse and misdirect investigations and the interested public; "Honourable" men who were nothing less than scoundrels and crooks.

Stamler could have walked past the lone protestor standing outside the House of Commons with his placard, but his retirement was close and he had little to lose; he decided to ditch decorum. The protester was Glen Kealey. Since November 21, 1988, when Brian Mulroney had been returned to power with a second, smaller, majority government, Kealey had been occupying this spot on Parliament Hill as part of his one-man campaign to expose corruption in the federal government.

Kealey's story was that, four years earlier, he had refused to pay a bribe to a prominent cabinet minister in order to win a lucrative government contract. Now, personally bankrupt, Kealey was getting his revenge on Mulroney and his colleagues. He soaked up every negative story or whisper about the Tory government, shouting out his findings like a town crier to anyone within earshot. Kealey's theories were wild, but rivetting. He figured that the entire Canadian deficit could be attributed to bid-rigging, fraud, and illegal kickbacks involving leases in more than five thousand government buildings. He suspected that somehow the politicians not only had their fingers in the till but also had insulated themselves from the Mounties and, perhaps, had even co-opted them. He was certain that the Mounties, right up to the current commissioner, Norman Inkster, had been compromised. Kealey called it Briangate, and some of the more industrious members of the media had paid attention to his allegations. Feature stories had been written about him, but in April 1989, it looked as if his moment of glory had passed. He had nothing new to say. The Kealey story appeared to be a non-starter, even to Stamler. He had already reviewed Kealey's allegations and had come to the conclusion that it was impossible to prove the truth of what Kealey had to say. It was Kealey's word against another's; there was no independent corroboration.

Kealey had no idea who Stamler was. He looked like just another bureaucrat in a trenchcoat walking by. He offered Stamler one of his latest creations, which Stamler took. It was a freshly minted three-dollar Baloney Buck featuring a cartoon portraying Stamler's boss, RCMP Commissioner Norman Inkster, in a hot-air balloon coming to the rescue of Brian Mulroney, depicted going over the falls of "Leech Lake" in a canoe.

Stamler studied the Baloney Buck, let out a chuckle, and, when Kealey offered his hand, Stamler shook it.

"How's it going?" Stamler asked.

"It's going well, real well," Kealey replied.

"That's good. I like what you're doing. Keep up the good work."

They chatted for a few minutes, and Stamler told Kealey that he admired his courage for standing up, right or wrong, for what he believed, but kept quiet his opinion that Kealey hadn't a leg to stand on in his criminal allegations.

Today, neither Kealey nor Stamler remembers exactly how it happened, but at some point Stamler introduced himself as an RCMP assistant commissioner – the person ultimately responsible, through the Special Federal Inquiries Unit, for the investigation of Kealey's own complaints. A few moments later, Stamler went on his way.

Kealey was dumbstruck by what had just happened. He had met many police officers, but never one who would stick out his neck like that. He had checked out Stamler in 1988 when it had been announced that he was moving over to head the Economic Crime Directorate. Kealey had learned that Stamler was a straight arrow, "maybe even the straightest of arrows in the RCMP." He certainly didn't appear to be a typical Mountie. "Hell," Kealey says, "There's a guy with courage, coming up to me on the Hill when he knows there are twelve cameras on him."

During the next couple of days Kealey turned the seemingly casual occurrence over and over in his mind looking for some hidden meaning. Was Stamler mocking him or just being friendly? Or was there a deeper message? Kealey didn't have the answer. Nor could he have known what had motivated Stamler.

Stamler thought it possible that at least some of Kealey's allegations, however unprovable, could be true. After all, Stamler had investigated wrongdoing on the part of government and politicians many times and had long since shed any illusion that they were paragons. In fact, his first encounter with a politician prepared to break the law for his own gain had taken place long ago, when Stamler had had the job of collecting on an unpaid speeding ticket.

That had been in 1965. A remarkable year, in retrospect, when an unlikely series of events had wrought a fundamental change in the relationship between those who hold political and economic power in Canada and those who were charged with enforcing the country's laws.

2

One Politician, Two Ships, and the Lime-Pit Murders

In the grand scheme of things a thirty-dollar unpaid speeding ticket didn't amount to much. But the fact that the ticket had been run up by an influential politician could complicate life for RCMP Constable Rodney Thomas Stamler. The politician was Gilles Grégoire, deputy leader of the Créditiste Party, a tiny rump of Quebec politicians who had split off from the once-mighty Social Credit party after the 1963 federal election.

In late 1964, the paltry size of the Créditistes was in inverse proportion to the party's strategic importance to the ruling Liberal government of Lester B. Pearson. Six Créditistes had pledged to support the minority government, giving Pearson enough strength in Parliament to stay in power. The Créditistes appeared to be all that prevented John Diefenbaker's and the Progressive Conservatives' return to power.

After nine years with the Mounted Police, five of them in the traffic division in Ottawa, there was very little that could surprise

Stamler and he didn't think it was a big deal that Grégoire was reluctant to pay a traffic fine. In all, Grégoire had run up more than two hundred dollars in outstanding tickets. Perhaps, Stamler thought, he was just another careless administrator who had overlooked traffic tickets; perhaps he was just trying to cause the police some minor grief. Grégoire would probably pay up as soon as a little heat was applied. That's the way it usually went.

Stamler had been acting as a prosecutor in the traffic division for almost a year. In those days, Mounties, dressed in plain clothes, prosecuted minor cases before magistrates. From the outset of his career in Saskatoon, Stamler had shown skill in the role of prosecutor. He liked the feel of the courtroom. It was a glorious way to learn about the law. Making his cases bulletproof, no matter how routine they might be, was a point of pride for Stamler.

There seemed nothing unusual about the unpaid thirty-dollar speeding ticket other than the fact that Grégoire was a member of Parliament. The ticket had been forwarded to Stamler for prosecution and Stamler had instituted proceedings by filing an information – a charge – in the Carleton County Court. The law is quite clear about who can lay a charge – anyone can. Everyone – an ordinary citizen and a peace officer alike – has access to the justice system.

Stamler's information was typical of him, the kind he got a kick out of writing. He was a stickler for detail, and usually had two copies of everything – one for the justice of the peace and another for his own records.

Every document the RCMP put out was in English and French, but the summons issued the next day by the Carleton County Court was in English only. Stamler, like most RCMP members of the time, took the trouble to have summonses translated into French for people he suspected spoke the language. In this case, the translation was done by his assistant, Constable René Délisle, who also served the summons on Grégoire on Parliament Hill.

The next day Stamler received another of Grégoire's overdue tickets – this one a measly five-dollar fine levied at Ottawa Airport. The same procedure was followed and a court date for both summonses was set for January 15, 1965. Grégoire failed to appear in court that day and a week later the case was heard in his absence. Grégoire was convicted and seven dollars in court costs were added to the original tickets, making the total owed to the Crown forty-two dollars. Nothing unusual, so far.

On the morning of February 12, Stamler received warrants of commitment for Grégoire for each of the two convictions, which meant the police could arrest Grégoire at any time. But Stamler didn't want to arrest him. All he wanted Grégoire to do was to pay his outstanding traffic tickets. Later that morning, Stamler called Grégoire at his Parliament Hill office to warn him that he risked a total of seven days in jail should he refuse to pay the fines.

"I'm not paying them," Grégoire said in a matter-of-fact tone that caught Stamler by surprise.

"But there's no problem paying them," Stamler continued. "It's not a large amount. Just make payment to the Carleton County Court so that we don't have to come down there and arrest you."

"I told you I am not paying them," Grégoire said. "I'll take the time in jail."

"Well, if that's the case, sir, I'll have no other choice but to arrest you and convey you to the Carleton County jail," Stamler said sternly, hoping a little officialese would jar Grégoire.

Grégoire was unfazed. "I prefer to go to jail," he said.

"Are you serious?" an incredulous Stamler asked.

"I certainly am, Constable," Grégoire said. "Why don't you come to get me on Monday on Parliament Hill?"

As they chatted, Stamler started to get a funny feeling about Grégoire. He was being too polite, and he was insisting on being arrested on Monday on Parliament Hill. A tiny alarm bell rang inside Stamler's head. Monday? Why Monday? What was happening Monday on Parliament Hill?

Just as he hung up the telephone, he remembered: Monday, February 15, 1965, was the day Canada's new flag would be raised on Parliament Hill. Grégoire was planning his own sideshow, featuring Rod Stamler as the stooge.

Stamler reported the conversation to his superior, a crusty staff-sergeant named Bill Rachel, who ordered him to execute the warrants and arrest Grégoire. Stamler and Délisle immediately drove to Parliament Hill, where they met with Sergeant-at-Arms David Currie. Arresting a member of Parliament on the Hill is a tricky business. Members have the privilege of not being arrested within Parliament, and all police activity on Parliament Hill must be cleared through the office of the Speaker, who acts as custodian of the rules of the House. The Speaker's agent in such matters is the sergeant-at-arms. Soon after the meeting with Currie began, they were joined by Leon Raymond, Clerk of the House. Raymond told the policemen that he had just spoken with Grégoire, who had asked him to use the powers of his office to get him a reprieve until Monday, February 15.

"Would Mr. Grégoire be willing to pay the tickets, today?" Stamler asked.

"I have done everything I can," Raymond replied. "Mr. Grégoire's final words were to return on Monday."

"My instructions are to arrest him if he failed to pay."

"I will not see the arrest take place inside the House of Commons," Raymond replied.

"Then I will arrest him if he leaves the Centre Block."

"Whatever you do outside is your business," the Clerk replied.

Stamler called his superiors and told them the latest development, then he and Délisle waited in their car outside the Centre Block. The uniformed duty officer standing on guard was let in on the plan. At 1:35 p.m. Grégoire strode out of the Centre Block as if he owned the place. The constable on duty fingered him for Stamler and Délisle, who got out of their car and introduced themselves. Stamler advised Grégoire of the warrants for

commitment and told him he was under arrest. Grégoire pro-
tested and demanded the right to call Liberal Justice Minister
Guy Favreau, shouting at the deputy sergeant-at-arms, who was
standing at the door, to phone Favreau for him. Again Grégoire
was read the warrants by Délisle, who orally translated them into
French. "If the summonses were in French, I would have paid
them," Grégoire said, in English. It was the first time Stamler had
heard Grégoire object to the English-only summonses. So that's
what it is all about, he thought, feeling thick as a brick.

For about fifteen awkward minutes they all stood there waiting for a representative of the Justice Department to show up. But
Guy Favreau knew better than to get lured into a public scene
mediating a squabble between a wacky Créditiste and two determined Mounties on the doorstep of the House of Commons. The
Créditiste support wasn't worth that much.

Stamler asked Grégoire once again to get into the police car.
"You are going to have to use force. I'm not getting in," Grégoire
insisted.

Finally, Stamler called Staff-Sergeant Rachel for instructions.
"Use as much force as necessary to effect the arrest, but not
excessive force," Rachel barked over the radio.

Stamler took Grégoire by the right arm and, along with
Délisle and the uniformed officer, led him to the car. Once there,
Grégoire offered mild resistance by placing his hands on top of
the police car. Stamler removed his right hand, Délisle his left,
Stamler pushed his head down and they shoved him as gently as
possible into the back seat. On the way to jail, nobody said a
word.

Within minutes of entering the jail, Grégoire was in the governor's office on the telephone to the Justice minister. Not long
afterward, an official from the Justice Ministry showed up,
having somewhere obtained a French-language version of the
warrant.

The problem now was that Grégoire didn't have any money
on him, only a personal cheque, but the jail couldn't accept

cheques. The kindhearted jail governor put up the forty-two dollars for Grégoire in return for a personal cheque. Grégoire was set free and went directly to the media with his story, calling the RCMP "a bunch of bandits" and their treatment of him "brutal." "What kind of bilingualism do we have in this country when you can't even get a warrant in French?" Grégoire asked.

The story blew up right across the country, but Grégoire received little public support for his self-righteous stand. That didn't bother him, because the concocted confrontation had given him all he wanted – a soapbox. He blamed unilingual RCMP Commissioner George B. McClellan for the incident, calling him the "Public Enemy Number One of bilingualism in Canada," and demanding his resignation.

Grégoire didn't stop there. He wanted to know why the RCMP had what he called the arrogance and temerity to arrest him on Parliament Hill. He called for the matter to be referred to the Standing Committee on Privileges and Elections, of which he was a sitting member. The committee convened on February 25, 1965, to hear his complaint.

That afternoon, the preliminary report of the Royal Commission on Bilingualism and Biculturalism was tabled in the House of Commons, as if to provide an exclamation point to Grégoire's outrage.

Commissioner McClellan insisted that the Mountie brass appear *en masse*, dressed in officer's blue serge, in a show of moral support. McClellan wore the uniform a lot that week. The following day he would be testifying at the Dorion Inquiry into allegations that prominent Liberals close to Justice Minister Favreau and Prime Minister Pearson had tried to help Lucien Rivard, a Mafia-connected drug smuggler, escape from Montreal's Bordeaux jail.

That was tomorrow's problem. Today, the constables in traffic needed McClellan. It was a serious matter. As they moved into the committee room to take up their positions in the front row, McClellan, a hulking six-footer, passed by Grégoire. "There's the little bastard that wants my head," the commissioner said in a loud voice, holding his finger under his nose as if to ward off a foul scent.

Grégoire's hooded eyes opened wide with alarm, then the tiny man nimbly stepped out of McClellan's range.

As it turned out, the Committee had little sympathy for Grégoire. Jean Chrétien, a young Liberal MP, said he believed the police had acted fully within the law and that the affair seemed to be about getting publicity for Grégoire, not about French language rights.

The force had provided Stamler with a lawyer, another young Quebec Liberal, Marc Lalonde, who was sporting an injured arm and black eye from a weekend skiing accident. Clever and urbane, Lalonde lampooned Grégoire's injuries at the hands of the Mounties: "I'm their lawyer. Look what they did to me."

Detail by puny detail, Grégoire led Stamler through his version of their story. He tried to use the fact that because they had a combined weight of 600 pounds and he only weighed 126 pounds, they were using excessive force. Grégoire, with visions of martyrdom in his head, attacked Stamler again and again, to the point of his own humiliation and beyond. In the end, two fellow Quebec committee members turned on him and deftly carved him into pieces. The committee eventually found that Grégoire's privileges as a member of Parliament had not been violated, and that the Mounties had acted within the law and not in a brutal fashion, as Grégoire had charged.

For Stamler, the Grégoire case was an ugly interlude that could easily have killed his dreams. But the opposite happened. He had entered the hearings an obscure traffic prosecutor and left as an up-and-comer in the Mounties. It was made clear to him afterward that he had earned the green light for advancement. His greatest fortune probably was not having Commissioner McClellan promote him on the spot in the committee room, as McClellan was apt to do.

Grégoire had taught Stamler more than he immediately realized about politics, the legal process, the nature of the criminal mind, and about himself. "I can't say that I liked it or I enjoyed what happened, but what it did, in all fairness, was give me strength to know that everybody is subject to the law."

Grégoire's forty-two-dollar cheque to the jail governor bounced.

As significant as the Grégoire incident was for Stamler personally, there were other events in 1965 – in which Stamler was not personally involved – that played a larger role in setting the course of his career.

The first was the last of a string of deadly shipping accidents on the St. Lawrence River in the early 1960s. It occurred on the bright, sunny Saturday morning of April 10. The Dutch-registered cargo-carrier *Hermes* was fifty miles downriver from Montreal, headed toward the Atlantic Ocean, and passing through Lac Saint-Pierre, a fifteen-mile-long bulge in the river between Sorel and Trois-Rivières. Ships navigating the lake had to keep to a 550-foot-wide trench cut into the riverbed. When Jacques Cartier came to Canada in 1534, looking for a route to the Orient through North America, Lac Saint-Pierre, which Cartier called Angoulême, stopped his ship, *L'Émérillon*, dead in the water, ending that avenue of exploration. At its deepest point the lake was seven feet, at best, not enough draft for even the comparatively tiny ships of the sixteenth century.

In the mid 1800s, the Board of Trade of Montreal had begun a dredging project to deepen the river so that ocean-going vessels could make it to Montreal. By 1854, the channel had been cut to a width of 250 feet and to a depth of 16 feet; by 1865, it was 300 feet wide by 20 feet; and by 1907 the channel had grown to 450 feet wide and 30 feet deep. It had become Quebec's largest public-works project.

The dredging business was lucrative, indeed. At the turn of the century the lure of fast and easy money had resulted in a huge scandal and the dredging industry was subsequently nationalized in the early 1900s. After the Second World War the industry was privatized, and the government sold off most of its fleet to Marine Industries of Sorel, Quebec. With the beginning of construction in 1952 of the St. Lawrence Seaway to Lake Ontario, the industry's tugs, dredges, and scows were turned into floating gold mines once again. Over the next two decades the channel was widened to between 550 feet and 800 feet and cut to a constant minimum depth of 35 feet.

On that April 1965 morning the pilot was guiding the 5,500-ton *Hermes*, travelling at its top speed of seventeen knots, through Lac Saint-Pierre in a north-northeast direction to pick up the narrow mouth of the river around Yamachiche Bend, about two miles away. The pilot could see another ship coming out of the bend ahead. It was the German-registered *Transatlantic*, a 7,000-ton freighter fully loaded with a mixed cargo, including a German trotting horse being imported by an Ontario breeder to race in Montreal.

To fix his position in the channel the pilot of the *Hermes* had to line his ship up with the Pointe-du-lac leading lights (known in daylight as marks). The first powerful beacon was mounted on a pier toward the eastern end of the lake, while the second was back on the land behind the hamlet of Pointe-du-lac. The pilot of each ship knew that the front mark had been shifted by ice over the years and was off position by about forty feet. The *Hermes'* pilot lined up the leading marks, then, making the appropriate compensation, found his lane and set a course to steer clear of the *Transatlantic*.

As the two ships approached each other to pass port to port, three ship-lengths apart, something went terribly wrong. The *Hermes* swung sharply to port, shot across the channel and crashed, bow first, into the side of the *Transatlantic*, causing an explosion and fire on board. The alarms were sounded and rescue efforts began. The authorities had two options: they could try to tow the *Transatlantic* toward shore or downriver to Trois-Rivières, or they could fight the fire then and there. They chose to fight the fire, but it raged out of control. After the *Hermes*, which was not badly damaged, backed out, the *Transatlantic* filled with water, rolled over on its port side and died in Lac Saint-Pierre. Two crewmen and the horse-breeder lost their lives, but the horse was rescued. As an emergency measure, the masts were cut off the *Transatlantic* so that ships could squeeze by one at a time, and the call promptly went out for salvagers.

The next day a taxi brought two men to the north shore of Lac Saint-Pierre, Donald Kerr and Walter Partridge. The Vancouver-born Kerr had studied law at Dalhousie University, then stayed on in Halifax where he built a marine law practice. Since 1957, he had been lecturing at Dalhousie on admiralty law. In 1963, he, Walter Partridge, and Partridge's son, Harold, set up Atlantic Salvage. There was a lot of money to be made in the business, but the big incentive to start Atlantic Salvage came from the Protection and Indemnity associations, the London insurance underwriters known as the P&I clubs. Over the years the clubs had indicated to Kerr that they would be happy to see some legitimate competition in the business, particularly in Canada. The underwriters felt that the "Canadian Gang," as they called the country's established ship salvage industry, was too closely knit for their liking. They had even gone as far as raising the delicate matter with the Department of Transport in 1962, but nobody had paid any attention to the griping foreigners.

When Kerr and Partridge arrived at Lac Saint-Pierre, there was a carnival-like atmosphere. The townsfolk were using grapnels to recover cargo from the *Transatlantic* and, eventually, almost everyone in the area got a new German-made bicycle. Kerr and Partridge were also excited by what they found. It was clear that the *Transatlantic* had to be removed as soon as possible because it was a hazard. On the spot they prepared what they were certain was an unbeatable tender. A couple of days later, they learned that, even though they had put in the lowest bid to the federal Department of Transport, the job had gone to Marine Industries of Sorel, run by the politically powerful Simard family in concert with the Quebec government. Kerr and Partridge received a quick lesson in local politics and government tendering. Back in Halifax they chalked up the loss to experience. Their day would come.

Meanwhile, an investigation into the crash by the federal Transport Department was started. The department's investigation centred on the position of the leading light mounted on the pier in Lac Saint-Pierre. Cliff Kennedy, then forty-two, was assigned as legal counsel to the chief investigating officer.

Kennedy came from Hampton, New Brunswick, and had studied law at Dalhousie in the same class as Donald Kerr. After graduation he went into the civil service, and he later tried working on Bay Street in Toronto before returning to the civil service for good. Kennedy was a tough and demanding public servant, but exceedingly fair-minded. He was the kind of person he believes was more common in Ottawa then, someone who finds true joy in serving the public interest well.

The Transport investigators were intrigued by the *Hermes–Transatlantic* crash. It was true that, since it had been constructed in 1937, winter ice had caused the pier to shift about forty feet in a southerly direction. It didn't take a mathematician to figure out that if the front light was off by forty feet, any ship trying to line up with the second light was going to be off course. The press was in a frenzy when news of the displaced beacon got out. Here, they charged, was a case of irresponsible and incompetent civil servants allowing conditions in Lac Saint-Pierre to deteriorate to the point where a tragedy was bound to happen. Now, three men were dead and a $5-million civil suit had been launched against the federal government by the owners of the *Transatlantic*.

None of the experts' explanations for the crash – from the morning sun blinding the pilot of the *Hermes* to earthquake activity – felt right to Kennedy and the Transport investigators. It was no secret that the leading light had gradually been shifting out of place. Every pilot on the river knew about it, and they all made appropriate compensations when moving across the east end of Lac Saint-Pierre. There had to be a better explanation. The investigators learned that, in the week prior to the crash, two other ship pilots had reported that something strange had happened to them in Lac Saint-Pierre. The *Manchester Commerce* had been travelling downriver toward the south edge of the channel when it had inexplicably changed direction and sped across the channel, hitting its north edge. The day before the *Hermes–Transatlantic* crash, the pilot of the *Carinthia* had reported the same problem, with his ship narrowly missing the upbound *London Splendour*.

In their attempt to understand the collision, the investigators decided to construct a model of the channel for the purposes of a federal trial that was to take place after a departmental inquiry. The normal venue for this type of work, the National Research Council in Ottawa, was fully booked. The next best place was in the Rhine River port of Wageningen, The Netherlands, world-famous for such work, and where there already was a forty-two-inch scale model of the *Hermes*. The department sent Captain John Mahoney, son of a schooner captain from Lunenburg County, Nova Scotia, along with a consultant, Dr. Ewan Covlett, of London, England, to monitor the model's construction and the tests upon the *Hermes* in a channel constructed to sounding specifications prepared from data taken at the accident scene.

While work on the scale model progressed in a huge Dutch warehouse, the trial proceedings in the Supreme Court of Canada commenced. Bank effect or bank suction were suggested a number of times as a reason for the collision. This effect occurs when a moving ship gets too close to the bank of a river. The power of the water rushing into the narrow gap between the ship and the bank can push the front of the ship dramatically and uncontrollably away from the bank. The usual way to overcome bank effect is, oddly enough, to increase speed. A similar problem is bottom effect, which occurs when a ship gets too close to the river bed and tends to skid and squirm.

The possibility of bank effect in this crash was never officially investigated because an unknown official in the department blocked the release of the soundings of the lake bottom, which were needed to make the case before the official inquiry. Something as arcane as bank effect, it was argued, would be difficult to prove and would only muddy the legal waters. As a result, the focus of the inquiry rested on the "irresponsibility" of the department and its employees.

There was also a political problem. Two weeks after the collision, Transport Minister Jack Pickersgill was asked during Question Period what his ministry was doing to address the proliferation of shipping accidents in the St. Lawrence River. In his reply on April 27, 1965, Pickersgill said, regarding the *Hermes–Transatlantic* collision, "The preliminary report I had was that it was the kind of accident which would really have nothing whatever to do with the condition of the waterway, but was an accident that might well have happened on the high seas." Pickersgill had placed himself on the hook, if the crash were proven to be anything but an accident. NDP leader Tommy Douglas once referred to Pickersgill as the "the sewage plumber of the Liberals," adding, "Mr. Pickersgill has been the Mr. Fix-it in every Liberal deal that has taken place over the last thirty years."

During the Supreme Court trial Kennedy was sitting at his desk in his office at Transport when a phone call came from John Mahoney in Wageningen.

"Cliff," Mahoney said, "I want you to turn around and look at that chart of Lake St. Peter on your wall." Kennedy had no idea what Mahoney had in mind but did as he was directed. Mahoney told him to find a point on the chart well within the limits of the ship channel, where a minimum depth of thirty-five feet would normally be found. Then he asked Kennedy what depth he found at the given point. Kennedy studied the chart, located the right spot, and said, "Thirty-five feet?"

"Did I hear you say thirty-five feet?"

"Yeah, thirty-five feet."

"Cliff, I was just standing in twenty-seven feet of water," said Mahoney – a depth that came up to his knees in the model lake.

Kennedy was confused. What the hell was Mahoney talking about, standing in twenty-seven feet of water? And then it hit him. Over the past three years, there had been an extensive dredging program in Lac Saint-Pierre, which had been completed the previous fall. The specifications for the project were that the channel be widened to 550 feet and dredged to a minimum depth of 35 feet, with banks sloping at an approved angle toward the shore. The model constructed in the Netherlands based on soundings showed otherwise. The channel was not only significantly narrower, it was also not thirty-five feet deep in the area where those conning the *Hermes* had lost control.

The water had been at a 105-year low in Montreal the previous month, but by April 12 the spring freshet had fixed that problem. The depth of the water hadn't been the hazard in Lac Saint-Pierre, rather it was the lack of clearance in the channel, and the ship's pilots had no idea how shallow the water really was. It was apparent to Kennedy and Mahoney that the real cause of the collision was severe bank effect. Considering that the way to counteract bank effect was to speed up, which the *Hermes* couldn't do since it already was going full speed, the ship had shot out across the river and collided with the *Transatlantic*.

Kennedy, and others, realized there had been a possible fraud by the dredging company, which had not done the job specified. Three people had died because of it, and the taxpayers were liable for millions of dollars in damages. The investigators called in executives from the Toronto-based dredging company, who pored over the findings and pronounced that the problem had not been caused by fraud, but by siltation. If eight feet of silt could build up under frozen Lac Saint-Pierre in six months of winter, a mountain could rise up in a lifetime. Not likely. But the investigators were not hydraulic engineers and therefore accepted the professional advice provided and stored their doubts for future reference. Even if they had suspected criminal fraud, there was no way to investigate it, never mind prove it. The concept of criminal fraud was a foreign idea to police departments everywhere.

The political sensitivity of the issue was enough to convince Kennedy's superiors to ignore the evidence. Government lawyers opted to argue that both pilots had been careless in navigating the channel.

In 1971, the Supreme Court of Canada finally awarded a $2.6-million judgment against the department, which was happy to pay and thereby extricate itself from the sticky problem. Mr. Justice Roland Ritchie of the Supreme Court found the government fifty per cent responsible for the crash, stating that, "there was a breach of duty on the part of servants of the Crown responsible for the care and maintenance of the range lights . . . upon which lights mariners were entitled to place reliance."

Those responsible for navigating the *Hermes* were found to be thirty per cent liable, for not reducing speed and carelessly coming too close to the south side of the channel. The navigators of the *Transatlantic* were found to be twenty per cent responsible for the crash.

From 1965 until 1971, the year Clifford Kennedy and ship-salvager Donald Kerr met Rod Stamler, Kennedy, all the smarter for his experience, was on the alert for the taxpayers of Canada. He was an uncharted and hidden reef on which the pirates of the business world were destined to crash.

By 1965, stock fraud and other business crimes were rampant across North America. Newspapers were regularly filled with stories of one scandal or another; it was a good news year for journalists. It began with a series of three killing landslides in British Columbia and ended with the Great Blackout of much of the eastern United States and southern Ontario. The worst man-made atrocity was the bombing of a Canadian Pacific DC-6B, which crashed near Gustafsen Lake, about twenty miles from 100 Mile House in northern British Columbia, killing all fifty-two people aboard. It was the largest single mass murder to occur on Canadian soil and remains unsolved.

Social tension was high on both sides of the border. In the United States blacks were becoming more militant. One of their leaders, Malcolm X, narrowly escaped assassination, then was murdered four days later in New York City. In Canada the FLQ terrorist campaign was just starting. In May, the Front internationalized their campaign by bombing the U.S. Consulate in Montreal. A month later, four sticks of dynamite equipped with a timer were found on the front porch of the RCMP building in Quebec City.

The most enduring scandal of the year involved Lucien Rivard, the Quebec resort owner and drug smuggler, who escaped from Montreal's Bordeaux prison on March 2, 1965, and was captured only 136 days later.* But another story in 1965, which at the time seemed like a flash in the pan, had the greatest effect on the administration of law in Canada. It was a series of killings in Quebec dubbed the Lime-Pit Murders.

The scandal began innocuously enough in the fall with a small story tucked away on the inside pages of Montreal newspapers. It was little more than a note about a woman's body having been

---

* The capture was made after the extraordinary use of the RCMP's Watcher Service, a unit of the Security Service. Prime Minister Lester Pearson requested Commissioner George B. McClellan to use the Security Service, apparently the first time it had been used for a domestic criminal investigation. It took the Watchers two days to find Rivard, who was hiding less than twenty miles away from the Bordeaux prison.

found on Friday, September 24, in a shallow grave near Sainte-Agathe, twenty-five miles southwest of Quebec City. An autopsy the next week proved it wasn't a woman, but Rédempteur Faucher, a small-time hoodlum. And he hadn't been buried; ugly decomposition just made it look that way.

The major story over the intervening weekend was about an eclectic trio who were about to enter federal politics for the Liberal Party, seeking seats in the upcoming November 8 general election: Pierre Elliott Trudeau, Gérard Pelletier, and Jean Marchand. In the recently released report of the Royal Commission on the Organization of Government, commission chairman J. Grant Glassco had urged that more room be made in Ottawa for a Quebec voice, and the three wise men, as they were known, appeared to be heeding his call.

The following Tuesday, employees of the Quebec provincial roads department came upon the head of Aldéric Bilodeau poking out of a shallow grave beside the road between Sainte-Agathe and Saint-Gilles, about three miles from where Faucher's body had been found four days earlier. The brief newspaper report remarked that the man's body was less decomposed than the woman's. Again, the story didn't trigger any reaction.

On Saturday, October 2, a third body was found in a shallow grave at South Ham, in the same general area. The victim was Paul Brie, who was, as they say, known to police. Few readers missed this story for, even in such sensational times, it stood out. The headline that roared across the top of the Montreal *Gazette*'s front page the next day read: MASS MURDER IN THE UNDER-WORLD / WAGNER SEES GANGLAND PANIC.

Quebec Justice Minister Claude Wagner was reported as saying that five people had been murdered in the past few days and that more bodies were expected to be found. Wagner said four people were already behind bars in connection with the murders, but refused to identify the victims or the suspects because their next of kin had not been notified. Wagner claimed that members of the underworld had become "trigger-happy" as a result of his department's breakthrough in an almost year-long investigation of fraudulent bankruptcies and arsons. Quebec had moved because, as the complaints from insurance companies mounted, it couldn't wait any longer for the federal authorities to act. He said Quebec was losing $5 million a year in revenue and creditors in the province were being taken for at least $30 million a year.

The victims were witnesses who were being eliminated one by one, Wagner said, including an unnamed man who had been interviewed just two weeks before by the police and Justice Department officials. "That person, who must remain anonymous for the time being, went missing September 18. His body was discovered, saturated with caustic lime, a few days ago." Wagner was talking about Aldéric Bilodeau.

The body of the next victim, Paul Chandonnet, an associate of Moise Darabaner, the chief suspect in the bankruptcy scheme, was found on October 7. The next day a ghastly story unfolded in a Quebec City courtroom, where Darabaner faced a preliminary hearing into charges of arson and conspiracy to defraud an insurance company. One of the suspects in the murders, Oliva Boulet, a fifty-two-year-old labourer from Cap Rouge, Quebec, testified about the murder of four of the dead men. Boulet's evidence was so matter-of-fact, it seemed he had watched too many late-night movies.

"Whatever happened to this man you call Rédempteur Faucher?" the prosecutor asked.

"He was rubbed out," Boulet replied.

The hearing heard Bilodeau had been arrested for burning down his own hotel. His co-conspirators somehow learned Bilodeau had talked to the police about the fires. He was lured to a meeting by one of Boulet's co-conspirators, who showed up "secretly armed with a shovel, a bucket of water, and a bag of lime."

The story became more shocking with each day. Wagner

called it the crime of the decade. Twelve prospective witnesses in the Darabaner case were feared dead, killed, as the police put it, "by interested parties." Death threats were made against two bankruptcy prosecutors in charge of the Darabaner case, leading to more heavy black headlines. White-collar crime had never been so bloody.

On the election hustings, Diefenbaker slyly used the murders as an example of the incompetence and possible crookedness of the Pearson government, extracting a promise from the Liberal government that bankruptcy laws would be tightened. Unfortunately for Diefenbaker, no amount of scandal-mongering could make the electorate overcome their distrust of the Tories or forget the incompetence of the party's last majority government, and the Liberals were returned to power on November 8, missing a majority by just two seats. Trudeau, a law professor, would soon become the minister of Justice.

Wagner blamed much of the scandal on crooked and corrupt lawyers, saying the Quebec Bar frequently served as a wall behind which "a good deal of hypocrisy has sometimes been going on." Too many Quebec lawyers, Wagner charged, allowed themselves to work on annual retainer for mobsters and crooks setting up bankruptcy frauds. The *Gazette* reported, "Mr. Wagner also attacked lawyers who 'with a knowing smile' advise and prepare phony alibis for killers or armed robbers and those who hire, to support such alibis – 'directly or indirectly' – cheap bandits, prostitutes and $50 or $100-a-shot perjurers."

But as quickly as the gruesome saga of the Lime-Pit Murders had exploded onto the front pages, it dissipated. The crime of the decade seemed to have become just another overnight sensation. Darabaner drew seventy-four years in separate prison terms for fraud and arson, but was back on the streets by 1972. First-degree murder charges were laid in the deaths of only four of the Lime-Pit Murder victims, although police insisted that between seven and twelve people had been executed. The convictions were easy to get, and by the time of sentencing, the story was no longer front-page news, even when one of the assassins, Oliva Boulet, received the death sentence, which was never carried out.

The Lime-Pit Murders weren't so quickly forgotten by the RCMP. The murders set in motion the final step in the sequence of events in 1965 that would help to make Rod Stamler one of the most successful and respected policemen in recent Canadian history. At their Ottawa headquarters the Mounties were embarking on a modernization program. It was part of Commissioner McClellan's plan to make the Mounties "more than a display police force," as he put it, good at riding horses, parading, guarding public buildings, and acting as photo props for tourists.

Two officers working in the RCMP's legal branch were constables Henry Jensen and Bill Neill, each of whom had benefited from RCMP-paid university educations. They were assigned the task of studying new policies and creating new programs to help the RCMP meet its modern responsibilities.

The Lime-Pit Murders had been a rude, but not entirely unwelcome, awakening for the Mounties. Until then, politicians had treated phony bankruptcies as more a nuisance than a serious crime. But no one had foreseen murder. Now there was a sense of urgency.

Jensen and Neill were both interested in the general area of white-collar crime. The term bore no legal significance, but was first popularized by American criminologist Edwin H. Sutherland in a 1939 speech to the American Sociological Society in Philadelphia. His dissertation was entitled "White Collar Criminality," and in it Sutherland argued, among other things, that such crimes were real crimes, a concept challenged by some of his fellow sociologists. Sutherland said there was an important sociological difference between conventional crimes such as burglary and murder, which are defined without reference to the social status or occupation of the perpetrator, and white-collar

crime such as fraud, embezzlement, price fixing, anti-trust violations, income-tax evasion, misuse of public funds, and abuse of
political and legal powers. Sutherland found that, in general,
white-collar crimes are committed by people of relatively high
social status, who are treated by the police and courts more
leniently and inconsistently than conventional criminals.

Although Sutherland put a name to white-collar crime in
1939, as a crime it was nothing new. As Henry Jensen says, "If
you go right back to the origins of this country, you will find evidence of fraud in the railway debates. Visit Laurier House in
downtown Ottawa. You could convict a former prime minister
based on what you read in the historical documents on the walls
relative to the dealings with contractors. There is clear evidence
of kickbacks."

But Canadian legislators had been slow to recognize and
address the problem. In 1965, the Canadian legal system largely
ignored criminal fraud, taking action only on crimes against
banks and government-financed social programs.

Fraud is a criminal act or omission, committed without
physical force or its threat, that leads the perpetrator to obtain
money, property, information, or other forms of business or personal advantage through dishonesty. The key to any successful
fraud is deception – the construction of a believable and apparently legitimate façade. The various manifestations of fraud are a
tribute to the larcenous instincts of the human race: phony bankruptcies, bribery, bid-rigging, kickbacks and payoffs, computer
crime, counterfeiting, copyright infringement, illegal competition, sweetheart union contracts, credit-card and cheque fraud,
embezzlement and pilferage, insurance scams, insider trading,
and so on, and so on.

Henry Jensen and Rod Stamler each remember how disconcerted he was by the RCMP's unwillingness to investigate criminal
fraud. In a typical case a businessman would make a complaint to
the RCMP only to be told by an officer to hire a lawyer – that fraud
was a civil matter.

"We had to tell them fraud wasn't police business," Stamler says. "I always felt badly doing that because you always knew that the complainant was usually a victim of criminals. We just didn't know what to do." The fraud cases police liked to tackle were the black-and-white ones that wouldn't confuse a child and could be wrapped up in a shift or two. Bounced or NSF cheques were their forte.

In Jensen's opinion the police were reluctant to handle tougher cases because of convention, lack of knowledge, and a pervasive attitude that "if you don't understand something, you're better off shoving it into another realm and hoping it will go away."

In 1965, two factors militated against successful fraud investigations. First, the law gave no clear jurisdiction for the prosecution of various forms of fraud. Second, the concept of a commercial-crime investigation was entirely alien to most police officers.

Solving a robbery or murder case is a relatively simple legal notion – a crime has been committed and the police gather evidence that leads them to a suspect. The chase is from the crime to the suspect. In fraud cases, the suspect is usually known to the police. The hurdle is proving what the suspect did and that it was a crime. The chase is from the suspect to the crime.

Every fraud poses the same basic question for investigators: What was the intention of the suspect? Did the suspect's cheque bounce because he or she didn't receive an expected inheritance or did the suspect have no chance of having any money in the bank in the first place? The answer is in the mind of the suspect. The fraud investigator must find out what the suspect was thinking when the crime was committed.

Henry Jensen and Bill Neill knew it would not be easy to prosecute commercial fraud in Canada. Nowhere in the Western world did police investigate shoddy business practices as a matter of routine. To the list of possible new projects the RCMP could undertake in its modernization campaign, Jensen and Neill added another: a commercial-crime branch – a centralized investigative unit based on function rather than territory.

When the unit was set up in 1965, Jensen and Neill flipped a coin to determine who would run the unit. The "winner" would get to move to Vancouver where he would work as the underling to the "loser" who would remain at headquarters and run the entire operation. Jensen lost the toss and in so doing was destined to become known as the godfather of commercial-crime investigation in Canada.

Rod Stamler was one of Jensen's first recruits to the new unit.

3

To Be a Lawman or a Spook?

When Rod Stamler joined the RCMP in 1956, it wasn't because he wanted to be a policeman. Stamler had quite another agenda, which had as much to with wanderlust and a sense of adventure as anything else. The youngest of Thomas and Anna Stamler's three children, Rod Stamler grew up on the family homestead near Sprague, Manitoba, in the extreme southeast corner of the province.

In 1949, after a quarter-century of trying to beat back the Manitoba bush and the annual hordes of mosquitoes, Thomas Stamler, a shoemaker by trade, moved his family to Ottawa. There he opened a dry-cleaning and shoe-repair business in Lower Town, just east of Parliament Hill. It was a propitious and profitable move; the Stamlers abandoned poverty almost the day Thomas set up shop.

In the summer of 1950, at the age of fifteen, the scrawny, soft-spoken Stamler returned to the West for the summer. He lied about his age and experience and landed a job paying $1.04 an hour on a Canadian National Railways bridge-repair gang, fixing the 1905 bridge across the Assiniboine River, eight miles east of Portage la Prairie, Manitoba. The next summer he was on the road again, but this time he was hungry for more than a labourer's job. He bluffed his way into a clerk's job for a logging company. It was easy. He said he had experience as a clerk (a bookkeeping course taken in high school) and that he could accurately add, subtract, multiply, and divide. Rudimentary as his credentials were, they were enough to give Stamler a leg up on his competitors.

He worked two river drives that summer, one on the White River in Northwestern Ontario, the other at Pine Falls, Manitoba. It was like living in a Canadian storybook, being an explorer or voyageur, camping in the bug-infested bush, riding thirty-foot pointer boats loaded with the camp's equipment, and shooting the rapids all the way downriver. Stamler's job was to keep track of everything.

Back at school that fall, Stamler continued to study bookkeeping to better familiarize himself with his professed skills. By the time he graduated from Ottawa Tech, he knew how to work his way, at least in an elementary fashion, to the bottom line. After high school, he took a six-month course in the principles of accounting at a local business college. There he was drilled in the value of accuracy and the keeping of proper paper records.

His first permanent job was as a payroll clerk for the E. B. Eddy Company, whose famous mill straddled the Ottawa River, just above Parliament Hill. Stamler didn't work there, though. He was sent into the bush to a camp near Des Joachims, a remote chunk of Quebec accessible by road only from Ontario. Later, he moved to a camp near Fort Coulonge, Quebec, about a hundred miles northwest of Ottawa. He worked there for two and a half years.

In his spare time he took flying lessons, an idea inspired by the appalling condition of the so-called highway between Fort Coulonge and Ottawa. He fell in love with the thrill of flight. He purchased an airplane, an Aeronca Champion, for $750. It was a two-seater cloth and tube type, equivalent to a Piper Cub. Stamler equipped it with skis and was soon working on his commercial pilot's licence. As a clerk and a pilot he had a future awaiting him in the far-flung realm of E. B. Eddy. But his airplane took him elsewhere.

One spring day in 1956, Stamler landed his plane at Carp airport, west of Ottawa. The tail wheel stuck and the tiny plane veered to the right off the runway. The next day he had a mechanic repair the damage, and afterward made a test landing. The wheel jammed once more, and he veered right, again, off the runway and toward an unexpected career change. As Stamler studied his predicament, another airplane glided in for landing. It was a Beaver, painted in the blue and yellow colours of the RCMP. Stamler had never seen an RCMP plane before, and had no idea what the RCMP might be doing with airplanes, so he struck up a conversation with the young pilot who told him all about the police force's air directorate. Across Canada the RCMP had a fleet of airplanes ready for the use of investigators and for the transportation of prisoners and goods to and from remote areas. "I immediately thought to myself, now there's an interesting career," Stamler says.

Two days later, Stamler went to the RCMP's "A" Division, then located on Wellington Street in Ottawa, where he picked up an application form. By summer he was training at the force's Rockcliffe barracks, near his home. After riding a horse to school and racing bareback on the dirt roads around Sprague, Stamler thought he knew a lot about horse-riding. "Everyone had to take equitation. The Mountie trainers quickly disabused me of the notion that I was an expert horseman."

Stamler's first posting was in Saskatoon. Before he could become a pilot in the Mountie air force, he first had to pay his dues patrolling the flat highways and dusty lanes of the prairies. The Saskatoon detachment's patrol area was a rough triangle comprising almost twenty thousand square miles, from the Alberta border in the west to sixty miles east of Saskatoon and from just north of the city to just shy of Regina. Almost every day Stamler racked up more than two hundred miles on the car while out on patrol. "It was exciting and interesting work. One day I'd be tracking down a thief who had crawled through a heating system of a building and stolen the cashbox from the concession run by the Canadian National Institute for the Blind, the next it would be a lost child, a minor traffic accident, a drunken domestic dispute, or the most morbid death scenes. It seemed that somebody was always being found dead in a car crash, under a combine tire, floating in a river, or hanging in a back shed. The first time I had to witness an autopsy, the victim was an eighteen-year-old girl who had been a passenger in an automobile accident. As the pathologist sliced up the body, I had to take samples of this or that. It was a hell of a change of lifestyle for someone who had been a clerk in a logging camp not a year before."

All the time Stamler was pining for the air division. Every opportunity he had in his free time he was up in a plane. One of his pastimes was hunting out illegal stills for the Customs and Excise squads. He thought his flying abilities and enthusiasm would get him in the door of the air directorate, but every time he got close to getting in, a more senior officer would bump him for the next opening.

In 1959, he received permission from the force to marry. The catch was that any Mountie who married before putting in five years in the force had to serve a minimum of three years in Ottawa, either guarding federal buildings, or doing airport duty or traffic patrol. Stamler and his new bride, Anne Kowalyk, moved to Ottawa.

Stamler chose traffic patrol. In a high-profile police force such as the Mounties, being in the traffic division in Ottawa was the baseball equivalent of being a utility player for the San Diego Padres; you might be in the big leagues, but who knew? To Stamler it didn't matter. He was still hoping to get into the air directorate, but over the years of waiting his priorities began to change. His growing love of law enforcement and of his family – Karen, born in 1961, Patty in 1963, and Michael in 1965 (a second son, Chris, was born in 1976) – provided the sparks of ambition. The glamour of being a pilot in the RCMP had been tarnished by the reality that all he would really be was an air chauffeur.

Stamler never had envisioned himself as a police officer, but now that he had been one for a while, he rather enjoyed the job's challenges. He had become fascinated by the subtleties of law and hungered for a more important role than that of traffic cop. By 1965, when he became entangled in the Grégoire affair, Stamler was already scouting the horizon for a place where he could play a role in the Mounties of the future.

He knew he would have to improve his education and so applied to the RCMP to study law. At the time, paid government employees were not allowed to attend a law school in the province. Most Mounties, therefore, ended up studying at law school in New Brunswick or Alberta. But Stamler couldn't make that move. His father had died, and he thought his mother and young family needed him at home. He was disappointed at not being able to study at an Ontario school, but he was determined to learn the law.

In 1964, along with several others Mounties, he had been accepted into an extension program at Lasalle University in Chicago. It was an almost impossible way to learn a difficult subject. Stamler spent every spare moment over the next six years studying at a homemade desk in his bedroom of his house in the Ottawa suburb of Aylmer, Quebec. Anne never bothered him and never let the young children do so, either. A self-proclaimed old-fashioned wife, she was determined to give him all the time he needed to improve himself, and their lot as well.

The law course taught Stamler how to read and better appreciate fine print. Nothing about the law was too picayune for him. Being a traffic cop in Ottawa, with its overlapping jurisdictions and the resulting difficulty in describing charges, proved to be conducive to his studies.

Stamler's career had been on anything but the fast track until his run-in with Gilles Grégoire. A month after the committee hearing, he finally received the overdue corporal's stripe, and it wasn't long before another promotion was offered him. He was asked to join the municipal policing division at headquarters. While technically a federal force, the RCMP has been involved, since the Great Depression, in contract policing. The RCMP provides provincial governments and many municipalities with a police force for less than the cost of hiring their own force. The contract work gives the RCMP a national presence that they would not otherwise have, except in Ontario and Quebec, where the Mounties enforce only federal laws.

The offer of a job in headquarters dismayed Stamler. For some Mounties, headquarters represented the glitter of Broadway, the bright lights and the stars. For Stamler, the Alta Vista compound in Ottawa was more like a sleepy hamlet filled with dead-eyed people on some kind of unknown but probably horrible mission.

But there was a down side to eschewing such an opportunity. Just about everyone who was anyone in the upper echelons of the Mounties had spent some time as an administrator in contract policing. That would mean spending up to six years in provincial policing. It may well have been the road to success, but it held no appeal for Stamler. Contract policing in Saskatchewan had been an excellent training ground, Stamler thought, but he wanted to expand his horizons beyond municipal policing. Refusing the job offer would be a career-limiting decision, but he never intended to become commissioner anyway.

There was an alternative – the RCMP Security Service. Getting out of uniform and into plain clothes was considered to be attractive and intriguing work. The Security Service promised all that and more. At one point earlier in his career Stamler had wondered about joining the ss, and probably would have been gladly accepted, with his highly desirable Eastern European heritage. But he concluded that ss work, while high on style, presented little challenge or substance. Dogging commies, spying on dissidents, and checking out job applicants for the civil service were not the reasons he gave up his dream of being a commercial pilot. Stamler thought the role of the ss officer was a contradictory one. While ss officers were technically peace officers, they were not permitted to use their powers of arrest. They were no longer police. What it came down to for Stamler was that ss work had little, if anything, to do with the enforcement of the law.

Stamler believed the law was an expression of both the common good and the fundamental values of society. He thought it was meant to be the same for everyone and protected everyone's interests. The law was not above or outside of society, but was the reflection of society at a given moment in its evolution, the result of the balance of power between social groups. Enforcing the law did not so much give Stamler power as give him huge responsibilities. He believed good law-enforcement officers were important and necessary so that society could function in a just and effective manner. To Stamler the rule of law meant that police must obey the law and the actions of government officers must be authorized by statute. That is, no one is above the law.

The aspect Stamler liked most about being a Mountie was that the responsibility for enforcing the law rested with those who patrolled the streets, that the police were wholly in charge of their own investigations. Authority ran from the bottom of the force to the top. The investigating officers had the discretion to launch investigations and to prosecute and the discretion not to do so, depending on whether they believed a crime had been committed.

In the Security Service the flow of authority ran in the opposite direction: from the top down. The director of the Security Service conceived and approved operations and investigations, which he passed to the investigators. They were merely agents of the director, with no authority to launch their own investigations and no discretionary powers – pawns being pushed around by supervisors, who were being pushed around by bosses, who were being pushed around by someone else. As Stamler would later caution, "Everything is top-down, on a need-to-know basis. What this means in the field is that when agents are assigned to a case, they know nothing about the big picture. Their job is that one tiny aspect, perhaps following one person for two years or more, the dirtiest, cruddiest surveillance work you can ever imagine. Then the assignment suddenly ends and the agent never knows why, or if he or she has done a good job or whatever. Furthermore, there is no real communication between fellow members. They can't talk shop with each other and they can't talk shop at home. The result is that they never learn from either their successes or mistakes because they can't talk about them. There is no building of institutional experience. And because the bureaucracy is in control of everything, it is slow and brutally inefficient."

Although the ss operated under the umbrella of the RCMP, its operating philosophy, forged during the height of the Cold War, made it anything but a police force. The ss was created to hunt communists and saw the world through that ideological prism. Theirs was a shadowy, dingy world where half their responsibilities were related to gathering intelligence and the other half to disseminating disinformation.

"The ss operated in the shadows, out of public view, without the internal and external checks and balances which governed the operations of the Mountie criminal investigators. The ss was there to defend and preserve the government, the country, and the democratic process, if you will, but not the laws of the country or the people." All of this made ss agents doubly dangerous. The Security Service couldn't be trusted to do the right thing when the time came.

After some thought, he decided to stick to law enforcement. At the time there were few opportunities for a Mountie to work in the Criminal Investigation Branch as a detective in plain clothes, mainly because there were relatively few federal laws to enforce. There was the drug squad, but its narrow mandate made it an unattractive assignment: officers were assigned either to a marijuana squad, which looked for smokers of the demon weed, or to a heroin squad, which focussed on operations in the Far East. Neither was considered to be a hot-shot investigative area.

A lingering effect of the Lime-Pit Murders was much talk in the newspapers about the need for improved bankruptcy laws and better enforcement. Being a criminal investigator looking into phony bankruptcies sounded like an interesting job to Stamler. "It seemed like a natural fit for me. I had always had an interest in bookkeeping and accounting and I sensed that commercial crime was going to be a growth area within the force." It was a role that hadn't been invented yet, but rumours within the force were that it soon would be. When that day came, Stamler wanted to be ready. He hit the law books every night.

He earned his Bachelor of Law degree from Lasalle University in 1967, and for the next three years took courses at Carleton University in tax, constitutional, and corporation and business law. In early 1967 Stamler heard of a job in bankruptcy investigations. It was a sergeant's job at "A" Division in downtown Ottawa. The successful applicant would be required to analyze, review, and supervise bankruptcy investigations across the country. Stamler jumped at the opportunity and won the position.

While the politicians struggled to reform and improve the bankruptcy laws, Stamler spent his days poring over investigation files. He found he was an invisible bystander at the crossroads of criminality. The dossiers painted a portrait of Canada that few believed existed: a country with more than its fair share of chisellers, swindlers, and deceivers of all kinds.

Stamler was deeply disturbed by the size of the files and the calibre of work in them. The investigators weren't building cases, they were building files. Reports were followed by more reports and by still more, piling into stacks that were bound to choke any prosecution. The investigators lacked ingenuity and commitment and had little if any knowledge of what kind of evidence was needed to prosecute a white-collar crime. The files were filled with intelligence about criminals but not with evidence of their activities. There was nothing on which a prosecutor could hang a conviction.

Two cases, in particular, stood out. At the centre of each was the Cotroni mob family of Montreal.

The first involved a businessman who was teetering on the verge of bankruptcy. Just before he pulled the plug on his business his credit card was used to purchase fifty airline tickets. These were subsequently used by a Who's Who of the Montreal mob. The businessman claimed he was forced into bankruptcy as a result of the airline-ticket purchases which, in part, was true. The other side of the story was that the businessman was in hock to these mobsters for six-for-five loans that had run into the tens of thousands of dollars. Stamler thought that fraud would be easy to prove, especially since the used airline tickets neatly linked all the co-conspirators. He wrote the investigators and told them so, but they replied that in their opinion they had jurisdiction only to mount a bankruptcy investigation, and since those who used the airline tickets were not bankrupt, they couldn't do anything. In addition, the investigators argued, fraud was the responsibility of the Montreal city police, who were not interested in pursuing the matter.

The second case involved the investigation of the people running a certain food business. The file was filled with reports of other food businesses being bombed and extortion. "The owner of the business just raped and stole property and businesses from his competitors. It was a terrible situation." Stamler recommended an investigation. The reply from Montreal, once again, was that since there were no bankruptcies involved, the Montreal

RCMP office was not interested in pursuing the case. When Stamler insisted that organized crime was involved and, therefore, that the case fell under RCMP jurisdiction, his fellow Mounties still resisted. It wasn't their territory, they said. In their opinion it was up to the local police who, unfortunately, and for whatever reason, were not about to do anything.

If the RCMP was ever going to succeed in investigating commercial crime, there would have to be a sea change in its investigators' attitude, Stamler mused.

The catalyst for that change began with a job advertisement: the Department of Consumer Affairs was looking for investigators for its new bankruptcy branch. The apparently innocuous announcement was a bomb blast in Ottawa's bureaucratic world.

The new Bankruptcy Act was specifically designed to plug the loopholes being exploited by sophisticated and organized criminals. No longer would creditors be required to launch an investigation. Now the Superintendent of Bankruptcy would be given the power to investigate suspected fraud.

The new Act gave the RCMP responsibility for investigations, for the scrutiny of bankruptcy trustees, and the power to make spot checks in doubtful cases, but the government seemed determined to set up its own investigative branch. This new wing of Consumer Affairs would employ special business sleuths and a squad of accountants "to carry out these specialized inspections more effectively than the police."

Justice Minister Lucien Cardin said that the investigation of bankruptcy frauds "is most difficult, because it requires a great deal of knowledge of bookkeeping, corporation and commercial law, and a special knowledge in the transaction of business," characteristics he didn't associate with the police. The government was determined to create a parallel investigative force. After all, since the Glassco Commission had eliminated the role of the tightfisted Comptroller-General, who had controlled federal spending, a looser spending policy had been adopted. The department believed it was free to do as it pleased.

In November 1968, a fresh position for a sergeant was created in Henry Jensen's fledgling Commercial Crime Branch at Alta Vista, and Rod Stamler joined Ron Wolsey, Derlyn Dillabaugh, and Sid Yelle on the team. They saw that the bureaucrats' long-range plan was to phase the RCMP out of bankruptcy investigations, which they thought was a bad idea – and not for reasons of territorial turf. The heart of Jensen's new Commercial Crime Branch was bankruptcy investigation.

Stamler drew up a four-page position paper, the thesis of which was that investigators working for the Superintendent of Bankruptcy could not succeed because they would not have the powers of a peace officer. Another of his arguments was more subtle. He thought the department wanted to set up another security service, a top-down organization in which investigators would be effectively controlled by bureaucratic and other unseen hands. There was too much room for inefficiency and corruption in such a proposed system, Stamler thought. His files had told him that there was already more than enough of both to go around.

The rearguard action by the RCMP caused a political fight that went right up to the cabinet. Prime Minister Pierre Trudeau listened to the various arguments, then sided with the Mounties. He ordered that there would be no duplication of services; only the Mounties would be given jurisdiction to enforce federal bankruptcy laws and to conduct investigations.

The decision gave Jensen's plans for a nation-wide Commercial Crime Branch the final lift it needed. Jensen soon had his handpicked staff in place across the country: Bill Neill in Vancouver, Don Armstrong in Edmonton, John Bentham in Calgary, Bill Sherman in Regina, Don Docker in Winnipeg, Bud Howe in Toronto, Rod Stamler in Ottawa, Bob Roy in Montreal, David Harrison in Halifax, and, later, Sandy McGibbon in St. John's. They were the cream of the Mountie crop.

Stamler received his officer's commission in December 1971. He was made a detective inspector, which meant automatic promotion in two years' time to full inspector. The next move for Stamler was to Toronto, where complaints about stock manipulation had turned the venerable Toronto Stock Exchange into little more than a casino. He took up the post in early 1972.

All the pieces were now in place; circumstance and serendipity had brought together a team whose work and concerns would set it on a collision course with Canada's political and business élite.

4

Rescuing the Irving Whale

The longer Donald Kerr listened to Arnold Gordon, the more angry he became. Gordon had come to see Kerr at his Halifax law office and had just offered him $50,000 for nothing. Well, not exactly nothing. All Kerr had to do was quietly increase the amount of his company's bid on an upcoming federal government ship-salvage tender.

Thirteen months earlier, on September 7, 1970, the tug *Irving Maple* was towing the oil barge *Irving Whale* in the Gulf of St. Lawrence, across the top of Prince Edward Island, when the *Maple*'s master, Captain John Anstey, noticed something was wrong. He could feel a strange vibration. The winds had picked up to about thirty miles per hour and the seas had reached ten feet in short, sharp waves. He had towed the *Whale* through worse weather and had a rule of slowing down, a rule he'd observed a while earlier, when waves were breaking over the bow of the awkward barge. Its deck was almost the size of a football field – 270 feet long – with a continuous U-shaped wall – or bulwarks – of steel plate running down both sides of the deck and around the stern. At deck level the plating was punctured by small doors – freeing ports – which used to be kept open all the time. That practice changed in 1970, immediately after the Liberian-registered tanker *Arrow* ran aground in Chedabucto Bay, spilling 15,000 tons of oil onto the water and the beaches. The Department of Transport branch in Halifax wanted no more *Arrow* incidents, so it had ordered the freeing ports sealed and caulked while a ship was in harbour. The crew handling the *Whale* was used to leaving the doors sealed shut while at sea.

Anstey could also feel the *Maple*'s powerful engines straining. He turned to look over the stern at the *Whale*, and was terrified by what he saw. The bow of the oil barge was pointed almost straight up in the air. The vibration was caused by the stern being dragged across the floor of the gulf, 240 feet below. The bow of the *Irving Whale* joined the stern three and a half hours later, coming to rest thirty-five miles northeast of North Point, P.E.I., some sixty miles north of the rich oyster beds of Malpeque Bay.

Investigators later speculated that water had been accumulating on the barge's deck for at least five hours after leaving Canso Strait. It was trapped by the bulwarks and sealed freeing ports. Watertight doors to the engine and pump rooms below had been left open, investigators believed, aggravating the problem. The water ran down from the deck to the pump room causing the boat to settle astern, thereby trapping even more water within the U-shaped walls. Eventually, the back half of the boat filled to the gunnels and headed for the bottom.

The *Irving Whale* was loaded with 4,200 tons – 1.1 million gallons – of Bunker "C" heavy fuel oil.

Over the next year all eyes were on the Irving family, whose companies owned the *Whale*, and most of the Maritimes, for that matter – it was one of the wealthiest families in the world. Neither the Irvings nor their insurance company were interested in salvaging the *Irving Whale*. There were no requirements for them to do so because the *Irving Whale*'s grave lay in international waters. Furthermore, K. C. Irving, the family patriarch, did not believe the *Whale* posed a pollution threat.

It all had to do with viscosity. The pouring point of Bunker "C" oil is 10 degrees Celsius. The water temperature on the floor of the Gulf of St. Lawrence is almost 0 degrees Celsius – freezing point. It was expected that should the oil leak into the icy sea water it would solidify. Environmentalists, nervous oyster farmers, and many other residents of Prince Edward Island were not so confident.

K. C. Irving's intransigence over the next year in the face of growing public concern about the potential environmental threat pressured the provincial government into acting. Premier Alexander B. Campbell called on the federal minister of Transport, Don Jamieson. He expected Jamieson, who hailed from Newfoundland, to be sympathetic to his demand that the federal government pay for the cleanup of the wreck. At the federal level, P.E.I. Tory MP David MacDonald kept the heat up in the Commons with the occasional question and in the bureaucracy with a series of memos and inquiries.

Since the Irvings refused to do anything about it, and even though the *Whale* was not in Canadian waters, Jamieson told Campbell that the Transport Department would take on the job and foot the entire bill. The call went out for tenders to raise the *Irving Whale*.

Donald Kerr and his partner in Atlantic Salvage and Dredging, Walter Partridge, thought that raising the *Whale* without spilling the oil inside was the greatest challenge ever. But now Kerr was being asked to abandon the project by putting in a false bid and to accept $50,000 in return. In other words, to commit a crime.

The Canadian Gang of ship-salvagers hadn't done their homework. It was precisely their scheming that had brought Kerr into the salvage business in the first place. In 1962, Kerr was representing a Protection and Indemnity club when he put out tenders for the salvage of the freighter *Suerte*, which had gone down at Three Fathom Harbour, Nova Scotia. The lowest bid he received was $375,000, from the partnership of two companies, Marine Industries and the Foundation Company, which had an agreement to undertake such jobs on a joint basis and not to compete against each other. The insurance underwriters believed the bid was typically Canadian – too high.

Kerr thought that he could put together a team and do the job for a lot less than $375,000. He sought out Walter Partridge, whom he knew only by reputation, and pitched him the idea. They took the job on a "no cure, no pay" basis and completed it for $110,000, which included a $20,000 legal fee for Kerr and a $20,000 bonus for Partridge. Both they and the insurers were left smiling.

In the intervening years, the company Kerr and Partridge formed in 1963, Atlantic Salvage and Dredging, had salvaged the wrecks of the circus ship *Fleurus*, the *Fury*, which was leaking oil, and the *Vagabond Prince*.

Kerr and Partridge's anger over losing out to Marine Industries on the salvage of the *Transatlantic* wreck near Trois-Rivières in April 1965 had been forgotten neither by them nor by their competitors. As the relationship between Atsal, as Atlantic Salvage was known, and the London insurers grew stronger, the Canadian Gang moved behind the scenes to head off the upstarts. A prime example of their scheming happened in 1965 over the salvage of the sunken ore-carrier *Leecliffe Hall*, which was resting in two pieces on the bottom of the St. Lawrence, three miles east of Goose Cape, after it collided with the Greek ship *Apollonia* on September 5, 1964. A year later the stern section was declared a hazard to shipping because it lay just eight feet under water.

In November 1965, four companies bid on the salvage operation: Risdon Beazley Ltd. of Southampton, England ($258,000); Dominion Underwater Contractors Ltd. of

Cornwall, Ontario ($463,000); M.I.L.–Foundation of Montreal and Toronto ($495,000); and Harry Gamble Shipyard of Port Dover, Ontario ($635,000).

The Foundation Company, like its partner Marine Industries, was unusually influential and powerful. The two French companies that owned Toronto-based Foundation were controlled by the French government. After the death of patriarch Ludger Simard and financial problems caused by poor management, the Quebec government had moved in to become the major shareholder of Marine Industries. The company continued to be run by the Simard family.

As soon as the *Leecliffe Hall* tenders were in, the two lowest bidders were under attack. On June 1, 1966, Gordon W. Stead, assistant deputy minister in the Transport Department's Marine Division, wrote to the minister, saying that the department had concluded that Dominion Underwater Contractors was not a substantial firm, in the polite parlance of the bureaucracy, and its bid would not be considered. This made the Marine–Foundation bid the lowest Canadian bid.

Meanwhile, the Canadian salvagers, represented by Arnold Gordon, were quietly working the corridors of power to exclude Risdon Beazley. They successfully persuaded the government to enact amendments to the Canada Shipping Act restricting coasting – the carrying of goods or passengers between Canadian ports – to Canadian vessels. But the P&I clubs fought back, arguing that salvaging was not coasting, and the dispute grew uglier. The *Leecliffe Hall*'s owner and its London underwriters insisted on hiring the lowest bidder, Risdon Beazley.

To end the impasse, the government agreed to make an exemption for a Risdon Beazley tug, the *Droxford*, to enter Canadian waters and undertake the *Leecliffe Hall* job. The Canadian Gang appealed the decision. The government, caught between the demands of Canadian politicians and business and labour leaders to protect Canadian jobs and taxes and the determination of the P&I club to hire the lowest bidder, passed an Order in Council. Risdon Beazley could use the *Droxford*, but could not substitute another ship. All other ships in the salvage operation had to be Canadian.

Eventually, Risdon Beazley, frustrated by the growing tangle of red tape, abandoned its bid.

The P&I club absolutely refused to deal with Gordon and his masters, however. They went to Donald Kerr, and Atsal responded with a quote of $300,000, $163,000 under the bid from the Marine Industries group.

The Canadian Gang then turned its guns on Atsal and its proprietors, Kerr and Partridge, complaining to Gordon Stead about a derelict ship owned by Partridge that was moored in Lunenburg Harbour. In the end, despite the pressure, the government did nothing to stop the P&I club from hiring Atsal.

The company took three weeks, as planned, to clear the stern section of the *Leecliffe Hall* from the river. The project went without a hitch.

Kerr and Partridge knew they weren't big enough to take on the *Irving Whale* job on their own. They brought in a partner, Smit-Tak International Salvage Co. Ltd. of Rotterdam, one of the largest and most reputable salvage companies in the world.

Stewart Nellis, a marine consultant, had devised a unique method for raising wrecks. He had considered and rejected two possible methods for raising the *Irving Whale*: external flotation and internal flotation.

Using external floating devices was not possible as the *Whale* was far too heavy. Internal flotation, which meant displacing water from inside the sunken hull with buoyancy material, could result in oil spillage.

Nellis's scheme was to raise the *Whale* mechanically via clamps locked onto its sides. The clamps would be attached by cable to jacking devices placed on two surface ships. This would permit a quick continuous lift of the sunken vessel to the surface.

Nellis thought his system would cut time and costs and generally revolutionize deep-sea salvage operations. On December 8, 1970, he submitted a report to K. C. Irving estimating the cost of salvage at $674,000, excluding insurance, a number that would loom later.

When tenders were first called, Nellis expressed interest, but he backed out after a pre-tender meeting in Montreal. He then offered to act as the representative of the Department of Transport. As the department did not have someone with the right technical qualifications, it hired Nellis to help draft the specifications for the tender and to supervise the raising of the *Irving Whale*. Nellis was given virtually complete control over the entire project.

In their brief time in the business, Kerr and Partridge knew that just being in ship-salvaging was enough to be labelled a thief or bandit. They were determined to play everything above board. But Kerr was not at all surprised when Nils Jorgensen, a Foundation Company vice-president, telephoned to tell him that one of the companies at the Montreal pre-tender meeting, Murphy Pacific of New York City, would be bidding on the *Irving Whale*, but wasn't serious. The American company owed Foundation a favour, Jorgensen said, and now Foundation wanted to work something out with Atsal.

Kerr set a meeting date for the following week, but that afternoon, when he ran into Arnold Gordon at lunch at the Halifax Club, Kerr decided to get the meeting over with and invited Gordon back to his office. Kerr suspected Foundation was interested in a joint venture on the *Irving Whale* project, which didn't make sense, but he was prepared to listen.

Gordon had remarkable information for Kerr. He knew from his "sources" the probable maximum bid that Stewart Nellis had advised the government to accept – $2.35 million – invaluable information for a tender proposal. But Gordon said nothing about a joint venture, so Kerr raised the matter. He said there didn't appear to be much room for profit for Foundation and its partners if they all went in on a joint venture. And to this day he remembers clearly how the conversation then went:

"The Dutchmen are out," Gordon said.

"You mean you want us to drop the Dutchmen?" Kerr asked in astonishment.

"Yes."

"What part will Atsal play in such a venture?" Kerr asked.

"You will bid with the Dutchmen, but you will make sure your bid is high. You will make yourself a nice piece of change. I am sure that you are in a position to say just how much your group bid is going to be, so you can persuade them to go high."

Everyone who had attended the Montreal pre-tender meeting knew that Atsal would come in with the lowest bid, but that was not the way the Canadian Gang wanted it. Gordon told Kerr that he wanted him to raise Atsal's bid to somewhere in the middle of the pack, thereby making the one from Marine Industries lowest and most acceptable.

"How much are you talking about?" Kerr asked, aware that he was being offered a bribe.

"If I were you, I would ask for $50,000 – but of course, you would not get paid unless we get the job," Gordon said, adding, "You're not going to get it, anyway. We have things sewed up."

Gordon told Kerr that he had influential friends in high places – the "right people" in Ottawa, New Brunswick, and Prince Edward Island – even listing P.E.I. Premier Alexander Campbell as one of his close personal friends. He reiterated the prediction that Murphy Pacific would bid high on the *Irving Whale* job because it owed Foundation a favour over something that had happened on the Mississippi River. He also talked about his being involved in a project he called Sugartoppen, of which he was extremely proud.

Before he was ushered out the door, Gordon warned Kerr that if his company didn't co-operate and insisted on putting in a low bid, it would be disqualified for some reason. Take the $50,000 and run, Gordon told him, it would be all profit. The Dutchmen would never have to know about it. Kerr said he'd think about it and get back to him.

Kerr was shocked by what had happened. He immediately went to one of his law partners and reported the incident, then he called Walter Partridge and telexed Smit-Tak in Rotterdam. They agreed not to go along with Gordon.

On October 29, 1971, the Foundation Company vice-president called Kerr and asked him whether he had reached a decision on Gordon's offer. Kerr turned it down.

The final submission date for tenders was to be November 5, 1971. Three groups bid on the job: Atsal–Smit-Tak at $1.7 million; Marine Industries, the Foundation Company of Canada, and Mil-Tug and Salvage at $2.35 million; and Murphy Pacific Marine at $4.4 million.

The tender opening was not public. Stewart Nellis and John Ballinger, the marine-services director, simply looked over the bids. Ballinger later remarked that Nellis seemed intrigued by the Marine Industries–Foundation Company's proposed salvage method. Nellis took all the tender documents home with him. Five days later, he submitted his bid analysis. He disqualified the submission by Atsal–Smit-Tak on the grounds that there was insufficient detail submitted with the tender documents to allow him to make a proper assessment of the scheme.

Gordon, indeed, had predicted the outcome. The Marine Industries consortium won the tender with a bid that was almost four times higher than what Nellis had told the Irvings it would cost.

Kerr was furious. Nellis's reasons didn't hold water. He called Ballinger, but Ballinger told him that there was nothing Kerr could do to alter the decision. Raising the *Irving Whale* would require much planning and co-ordination and there was such a narrow window of opportunity, he said. Time was of the essence. The *Whale* must be raised the next summer.

A week later Kerr flew to Ottawa and met with the government officials. They gave Atsal an extension to improve its bid, but they made it clear that while they would evaluate the new bid, there was no chance it would make the grade. Nellis would stick to his original opinion. Kerr didn't know what to do, but he knew he had to do something. The legal counsel for the government at the meeting had been Cliff Kennedy, Kerr's law-school buddy, so Kerr decided to pay Kennedy a private visit and tell him what really was going on.

Kerr still holds Kennedy in high regard. "He was the Abraham Lincoln type. He didn't make any snap judgments. Cliff did everything slow and methodically, with a sense of absolute fairness. For Cliff it never came down to how much money he made. The law for him was always a matter of basic ethics. If you wanted to be advised in government about what was right and wrong, Cliff Kennedy was the perfect civil servant."

They sat in Kennedy's modest office and Kerr led Kennedy through the twists and turns of his tale. At first Kerr had the impression that Kennedy didn't believe him. "It took me about two hours to get through to him that this bribe had been offered and that we were going to be booted out just as Gordon had predicted." Kerr was not sure what Kennedy would do as he never tipped his hand.

Kennedy wanted Kerr to put his allegations in writing, but Kerr refused to do so. "I was offended that I should be asked to put it in writing," Kerr told Partridge on his return to Halifax. "Putting it in writing was not going to make any difference. The truth is the truth whether it's spoken or on paper. Having it on paper wasn't going to make any difference on whether they were going to pick up the ball."

Kerr was thinking like a man whose word is his bond. But the fuel that propels the bureaucracy into action is paper – nothing matters more in the public service than words on paper. Still, Kennedy did act on Kerr's complaint, and the letting of the tender was postponed almost two months to February 7,

1972. Kennedy was also concerned about two other aspects of raising the *Irving Whale*. The first was money: how was the government going to pay for the bill? There was no money in the budget, and the department feared criticism by the auditor general. Kennedy worried about the cost, especially in light of the second unanswered question: was it necessary to salvage the *Irving Whale*?

The barge had landed intact on the floor of the Gulf. About twenty-five per cent of the oil escaped during sinking and before divers could cap the leaks. Prince Edward Island had demanded that the federal government remove the barge because of the potential pollution, but, as one bureaucrat put it, the *Irving Whale* was an emotional threat, not a real one. It had been in the deep brine for more than a year and the only indications that any oil was being forced out of the hold were a few hard strands of Bunker "C" that washed up on shore every so often.

As the February 7 date approached, Kennedy continued to stall the awarding of the contract to the Marine Industries group by reminding everyone about the possible bribe attempt, but he couldn't get anyone interested in opening an investigation without a written complaint from Kerr.

On February 3, Transport Minister Don Jamieson announced to the press that the *Irving Whale* salvage operation would begin in the summer. Then something strange happened that no one could immediately explain. The tender wasn't let. Another force had been set loose.

Kerr wouldn't put his complaint in writing, but he did tell many of his business acquaintances about his experience, including Phil Neuttyn, president of a Vancouver company called Can-Dive International Ltd. Shortly after that conversation, Neuttyn had a chance meeting in Dallas, Texas, with Dr. Joe MacInnis of Toronto, a scientist and diving expert – and close friend of Prime Minister Trudeau. Neuttyn told MacInnis about Kerr's experience, assured him of Kerr's integrity, and asked him to bring the case to Trudeau's attention. He did, and Trudeau acted swiftly. Don Jamieson was informed of the bribe offer and the attempted bid-fixing and was told not to let the contract until the matter had been cleared up.

Now that the story had new life, Kennedy tried once more to persuade Kerr to complain in writing. He wrote to Kerr, saying, "Information now circulating in Ottawa would indicate that perhaps you do not now regard the confidentiality of the discussions you held with me as being paramount to your current considerations and that you might be prepared to furnish an affidavit with supporting documentation outlining the nature of your allegations. . . . On the other hand, if you are not prepared at this time to provide your affidavit with supporting documentation. . . the Crown. . . will have no alternative but to treat your allegations as mere rumour."

Kerr responded quickly. He telephoned Kennedy and said that since his credibility had become involved, Kennedy should consider the letter to be in the mail.

Kerr's written complaint went to the top of the Justice Department, crossed over to the top of the RCMP, and was passed to Superintendent Henry Jensen in the Commercial Crime Branch with the request that the RCMP provide an investigator to help the Transport Department determine if a crime had indeed been committed. Jensen figured the exercise might interest Rod Stamler. It might well turn into a full-scale commercial-crime investigation.

When he met with Stamler, Kennedy was impressed that the Mounties had sent him an inspector. Until then, he thought inspectors were managers who never lowered themselves to field work. From the moment Stamler walked through the door of his office, Kennedy liked him. He felt there was a meeting of minds. He immediately sensed the integrity of the man.

Popping open his briefcase, Stamler pulled out a notebook and began his interview, the notebook more a prop than a tool, since the conversation was being recorded by a hidden tape recorder activated when the briefcase lid was opened.

Kennedy told Stamler about his concerns about the *Transatlantic* case in 1965 in Lac Saint-Pierre and his belief that Canadian salvage and dredging companies, which often proved to be one and the same, were openly defrauding the government. It was an area of criminality Stamler had not contemplated, but he quickly determined that there were four areas of investigation: bribery, violation of the Combines Act, fraud on the government of Canada, and impropriety within the Ministry of Transport.

Proving bribery would be tricky because it was Kerr's word against Jorgensen's and Gordon's. Stamler visited Kerr in Halifax and interviewed him a number of times over the course of a few weeks. Stamler judged Kerr's allegations to be clear, accurate, and unwavering. Kerr went over the same material many times and did everything within his power to assist in furthering the investigation.

Kerr remembers Stamler picking up on some of the phrases Kerr attributed to Gordon and Jorgensen: "joint venture," "the Dutchmen," "Sugartoppen," "the right people." It was easy to confirm Kerr's outrage about the bribe offer by interviewing all those he talked with about it immediately afterward, including the Dutchmen.

When Stamler met with him, Jorgensen admitted to calling Kerr about a joint venture and sending Gordon to meet him. "Nothing came of it," Jorgensen said. "We really did not offer Kerr a joint-venture agreement. Mr. Gordon did not have the authority to offer a joint venture beyond discussing whether this was a possibility." Stamler had corroborated two parts of Kerr's story: that Jorgensen had called and Gordon had been sent by him to meet with Kerr.

Gordon denied everything. He even denied being in the Halifax Club, which Stamler found amusing since one of Kerr's partners, who had been at another table, remembered seeing him there. Gordon later told Stamler about being involved in the design of a catamaran at Sugartoppen, as he pronounced it and just the way Kerr said he had. The actual name of the town in Greenland is Sukkertoppen. Among those Gordon said he considered the "right people" was his personal friend the premier of Prince Edward Island, the man who had been pushing the federal government to recover the *Irving Whale*. All the denials and obfuscations aside, Gordon's statements were like a replay of Kerr's version of the story. In light of this and other information he gathered, Stamler was convinced a bribe attempt had been made.

Next was the issue of a violation of the Combines Act. It didn't take long for Stamler to find out the nature of the agreement between Marine Industries and the Foundation Company precluded Foundation from engaging in any marine salvage work in the North Atlantic and North Pacific, the St. Lawrence River, and the Great Lakes. Stamler also found that, as the result of a similar agreement imposed on Marine Industries by Mil-Tug, Mil-Tug was the only Canadian salvage company with the capability of undertaking major marine salvage work in the waters of Eastern Canada. The three companies had to work together or not at all. "This monopolistic situation will no doubt have a bearing in respect of future salvage contracts on the East Coast," Stamler remarked in his report. But there was no Combines Act violation because salvagers were considered a service industry and so were excluded from the provisions of the Act.

The third issue was fraud perpetrated on the government of Canada. To many people, bid-rigging and price-fixing are almost synonymous terms, which is not the case. Over the years a number of Canadian industries, sugar and gasoline, to name just two, have been investigated for setting a common price for their products. While undesirable in an open market, fixed prices do not always mean higher prices. In some cases fixed prices have even resulted in savings for consumers. Bid-rigging never has.

Bid-rigging is when one party agrees to refrain from bidding or where there is collusion in the submission of bids. The intention of the bid-rigger is to increase the cost of a tender. It is theft by deception.

As Stamler ventured into the salvagers' world, he discovered that bid-rigging appeared to be the norm in North America. Stamler checked into the controversy over the salvaging of the *Leecliffe Hall*, and found a familiar story. Gordon had told Kerr that Murphy Pacific Marine would not compete. Its extraordinarily high bid on the *Irving Whale* tender call served two purposes: it created the appearance that the range of bids was a fair reflection of the marketplace, and it guaranteed the lower bidders that Murphy Pacific would not be offered the contract.

In New York City, Stamler investigated a 1970 tender call to salvage the *Union Faith*, which sank on the Mississippi River. Stamler found a number of weird financial transactions, some of them leading to other Canadian deals. One involved the Foundation Company. Foundation had paid $65,000 to Murphy Pacific Marine for "chains and anchors." Stamler sent out his staff to find the equipment, but they couldn't locate it. He was convinced that the $65,000 was a payoff to get Murphy Pacific's co-operation in the tender call. The tender had been pulled when the U.S. Army Corps of Engineers found the bids were too high. But even though Foundation didn't get the job, Murphy Pacific hadn't returned the money. It owed a favour to Foundation, which Stamler surmised it had paid by standing aside on the *Irving Whale* tender.

There was also the matter of impropriety within the Transport Department. Stamler's focus was on Stewart Nellis. John Ballinger, the marine services director and the only other man in the room when Nellis had opened the tenders the previous fall, had remarked that Nellis seemed intrigued by the Marine Industries–Foundation proposal. Intrigued? The Marine Industries proposal was using the unique salvaging scheme developed by

Nellis, which featured a jacking system and clamps. He stood to make $32,590 if the Montreal consortium was successful, on top of the money paid to him by the government. Stamler found that Nellis had quoted a salvage price of $674,000 to the Irvings before going to work for the department and advising them that $2.35 million was a reasonable price.

Finally, Stamler wanted to find out who was leaking inside information to Gordon from within the department. During an interview at Nellis's office, Nellis went to great lengths to show Stamler a new method he had developed for raising the *Irving Whale*. It involved the use of pressurized balls approximately six inches in diameter made by a Denver, Colorado, company. He said he was going to recommend to the government that in the new tenders for the *Irving Whale* salvage it change its specifications to the P.S.I. balls, as he called them. Stamler was very interested in the balls, mainly because the day before he had seen a similar ball in Arnold Gordon's office. Later, Gordon told Stamler that he was looking into the possibility of using the product in future salvage operations.

Stamler was sure that Nellis was passing information on to Gordon, especially after he found out that a number of active salvage personnel in Canada, including Nellis and Gordon, had worked at one time for the Foundation Company, but it was impossible to prove.

The most interesting aspect of the case for Stamler was the opinion of the experts who thought the *Irving Whale* posed no danger to the P.E.I. coast and was best left on the bottom. "To the politicians with easy access to the public purse, that never seemed to be an option," Stamler says.

What had started out as a simple bribe investigation for Stamler had evolved into an odyssey through a murky netherworld, where shady businessmen and eager-to-please politicians made a disturbing partnership. Until the *Irving Whale* investigation, Stamler's notion of organized crime was the traditional

Mafia-centric one. He now knew that the Italian Mafia was in many ways a piker compared to the organization and political power of the legitimate business world.

Stamler completed his report. Since he was working as an agent of the government rather than as a law-enforcement officer, he could only recommend what action be taken. It was impossible to prove the bribe offer to Kerr, especially as no money had changed hands and there was no independent corroboration. Stamler considered recommending a charge of conflict of interest against Nellis, but in the end no conflict had happened because the tender had been cancelled. What remained was a strong case of conspiracy to commit a false pretence. There was evidence that Gordon and Jorgensen had conspired to eliminate all competition on the *Irving Whale* tender call. There was evidence that the Foundation Company had conspired with Murphy Pacific to ensure that Murphy Pacific's bid tendered would be substantially higher than Foundation's. The result, if carried to its conclusion, would have been the presentation of three bids, each purportedly representing a price arrived at through a free competitive process, but which was arranged by the bidders.

Since the offence had occurred in Nova Scotia, Stamler submitted his recommendations to the federal Justice Department, which passed them to the Crown attorney for Halifax. He then packed up and moved Anne and the three children to Toronto to take up his next assignment. He fully expected the Nova Scotia Attorney-General's Office to prosecute the case, but it never did. It was already embroiled in another controversy. Donald Marshall had been convicted the year before for the murder of Sandy Seale and the Attorney-General's Office was adamantly refusing to listen to his protestations of innocence.

The attorney-general's staff was displeased with Stamler's recommendation, but at first didn't say why. In discussions with federal Justice officials about the case, a senior representative said the province was not interested in pursuing the matter. When pressed, he indicated that if the Justice Department persisted with its demand, Nova Scotia might consider setting up its own provincial police force the next time the contract with the RCMP came up for renegotiation. But the Justice Department would not back down.

Finally, the Nova Scotia representative conceded that the province would not prosecute the case because it might prove to be embarrassing to members of the Halifax Club. The Justice Department threw in the towel.

In 1989 and 1990, the Canadian Coast Guard conducted two surveys of the *Irving Whale* using robot cameras. It found that there was virtually no deterioration in the ship's hull and that after twenty years more than 3,100 tons – at least seventy-five per cent of the oil – remained in the barge's holds. K. C. Irving had been right: the leaked oil had solidified. Six of the sixteen vents on the barge had small leaks out of which the oil leached in long, thin ribbons. Every so often these would break off and find their way to shore, where they were easily collected. The Coast Guard concluded, "The *Irving Whale* does not pose a significant risk to the marine environment at its present location and condition."

Despite the Justice Department's failure to prosecute anyone, Stamler and Cliff Kennedy were pleased that they had stopped a fraud from being perpetrated. It had been a sophisticated and complex investigation for both of them, almost like going to school to study bid-rigging in North America. The lesson would serve them and the Canadian taxpayers well.

5

Minting First Impressions

Norton Cooper appeared to have acquired all the trappings of success. His opulent office was on the forty-seventh floor of one tower of the prestigious Toronto-Dominion Centre in Toronto. One October afternoon in 1972, Stamler was sitting in this office conducting another interview with Cooper in his latest investigation when Cooper's secretary buzzed her employer.

"The judge is here," she said over the intercom.

"Tell him I'll be with him, shortly," Cooper told her.

Forty-five minutes later, the secretary reminded Cooper that the judge was still waiting in the outer office.

"Don't bother me. I'll see him later," Cooper barked back, as if to impress Stamler with his disrespect for a judge.

Since first meeting Stamler when the Mountie had executed a search warrant on his office the previous month, Cooper had been on the phone almost every day to Stamler asking how things were going. He had come to like the policeman so much that now he readily told Stamler, "The judge and I are working out a business deal."

Stamler didn't blink an eye. Cooper was a stock promoter suspected of manipulating the Bay Street market for the financial benefit of insiders, a decidedly illegal activity. On a previous occasion Stamler had seen a District Court judge visiting with Cooper. Were the judges insiders, too? Finally, Cooper called in his corporate lawyer. "Take the judge into the boardroom and get him happy with his favourite beverage."

The lawyer reached into the cupboard for a bottle of Canadian Club.

"Better take two," Cooper admonished him. "He likes that stuff. And order him a steak."

Cooper's contempt for the judge implied disdain for all law officers, but Stamler wasn't insulted. He had learned it was to his advantage to let Cooper say whatever he wanted to say. When Stamler and Sergeant Jim McIlvenna had executed their search warrant, Stamler let Cooper think he was in charge the entire time. He couldn't help but be amused by Cooper's bravado. At one point Cooper had indicated he might call his lawyer, but had decided against it. His ego wouldn't allow him. When they had come through the door, the two Mounties had mentioned something about an investigation into possible stock market manipulation, not an uncommon complaint on Bay Street.

Stock manipulations have a long and ignoble history. In England in 1814, eight men were convicted of conspiracy to raise the price of government bonds by spreading a rumour during wartime that French leader, Napoleon Bonaparte, had been killed and that peace soon would soon be at hand. An infamous Canadian case involved a brokerage firm, Solloway and Mills, which operated on the Calgary Stock Exchange at the time of the stock market crash of 1929. The brokerage firm owned its own oil company, a fact it didn't disclose. However, it placed advertisements in newspapers and published a magazine extolling the virtues of certain oil stocks, including its own. The Alberta Supreme Court later declared, "The plan was to educate the public mind to buy, thereby creating a market for the stock which the broker had bought or optioned from the oil companies or from their directors. Having created a demand for this stock the broker then supplied it from its own purchases, at an advanced price, of course, and this to its own clients as well as the public generally, at the same time charging the clients brokerage. When the public mind was ripe it was to be 'given plenty' and so enable it to 'sink' its money." As the court observed, to sink meant to invest, and monies sunk would stay sunk.

Despite the scandal, there was little concern in government about regulating stock markets. The purpose of the markets, it was argued, was to help provide foreigners with a place to make money in a growing and ever prosperous Canada. The great hope was that the foreigners, having made money, would stay to invest even more money in the economy.

By the 1960s, markets across the country were in a mess. In 1963, the Toronto Exchange was rocked by a huge scandal involving the manipulation of the stock of Consolidated Golden Arrow Mines and a number of associated companies run by Viola MacMillan. The scandal resulted in a royal commission, which led the Ontario government to enact securities legislation in 1968.

Even with such legislation in place, Bay Street was an odd and frustrating bird to the Mounties. It was considered Canada's most respectable stock market, but that wasn't saying much. On the Toronto Exchange at any one time almost eighty per cent of the companies listed were controlled by a handful of families. The result was that Bay Street behaved largely as an insiders' market, which the police felt was to a great extent unregulated, in spite of, and perhaps because of, the Ontario Securities Commission.

To Norton Cooper, the Mounties who came to visit him

seemed about as harmless as Ontario Securities Commission investigators. Probably because he was used to dealing with the OSC, Cooper showed no anxiety. In a typical OSC investigation he would be summoned to the commission's headquarters and ordered to bring appropriate records along with him. Cooper would show up with only those documents that supported his version of the story. It was usually all that was required. That the Mounties had decided to pay a visit for themselves was an inconvenience, but Cooper was convinced they were not going to find anything anyway. After all, policemen were more comfortable with guns and billies, not sharp pencils and bottom lines. He assumed they were looking for evidence that he had illegally given stock in two of his companies to two federal public servants suspected of being compromised by him. Cooper knew he was clean, at least in that area.

When Cooper eschewed the opportunity to call his lawyer, Stamler and McIlvenna discreetly exchanged a knowing look. Deception and misdirection on the part of the cops were often at the heart of successful police investigations. From the police point of view, it was ideal for the executive officer, the president, or the person in charge of the office to be present during a search because that person had a natural tendency to want to explain everything. Anyone who thought himself smarter than his lawyer, or who underestimated the intelligence and determination of the police, usually proved to be the best kind of suspect with whom to deal. As Cooper took the two men on a tour of his filing cabinets he never stopped talking.

"How many kids you got?" he asked Stamler.

"Three."

"I've got five and still counting," he boasted.

Cooper liked to talk about gold. The price of gold was going up, he said, and silver tracked gold. That's why he was getting into silver in a big way. He was always promoting something, especially himself. He would describe himself as, among other

things, flamboyant, energetic, and a maverick. All the public relations in the world couldn't hide the fact that he was the principal
behind numerous questionable companies, as *Financial Post*
reporter Douglas Marshall put it at the time, "lost in the mists of
Bay Street."

Stamler kept up the disarming banter with Cooper while
McIlvenna flicked through the files, occasionally stopping to
peruse an interesting find. Over the years, McIlvenna had honed
his skills in document searches; he knew exactly what to look for,
and he began taking one possibly incriminating file after another
out of Cooper's cabinets. Cooper, McIlvenna could see, ran with
an interesting crowd – top politicians, lawyers, businessmen,
judges, and the Mafia.

Michele Sindona. Now there was a name that rang a bell for
both police officers. Sindona had been involved in Canadian mining projects since the early 1960s and liked to call himself a financier – "the only merchant banker in Italy in the American or
English sense" – but police intelligence files had him pegged as
Mafia. He was thought to be a money-launderer and swindler.
Stamler and McIlvenna couldn't figure out from Cooper's files,
though, what exactly he was doing with Sindona other than that
Sindona, through his shaky U.S. company, Argus Inc., had been
involved in the takeover of Cooper's former business, Seaway
Multi-Corp Ltd., both of which companies had an eccentric
financial history.

Cooper's files told other interesting stories. While Cooper was
slow to pay some lawyers for their services, stringing out payments for more than two years, the bills from others were
honoured promptly. The Mounties were intrigued by one from a
prominent Toronto lawyer and political fundraiser. Cooper had
paid the lawyer $15,000 for helping him get a $25,000 exploration grant from the Ontario government. The lawyer's worksheet
showed that he had done very little actual work. It smelled like a
hidden contribution to the ruling Progressive Conservative Party,

one masked by the lawyer. They didn't pursue it because it was not their mandate and was probably impossible to prove.

Another file contained correspondence that painted a neat picture of Cooper's style and Bay Street attitudes.

A Toronto lawyer had written on January 14, 1972, "Receipt is acknowledged of a basket of fruit and a bottle of Vermouth. On behalf of my wife and myself we really wish to thank you for your generosity and contribution to our sustenance. If you would be so kind as to keep [us] in mind we would appreciate your thoughts in the future in so far as meat products, mortgage payments, furniture payments and broadloom payments. We do not wish to exclude from your thoughts wallpaper and paint payments."

Then there was a short letter from Ontario Premier Bill Davis, thanking Cooper for his "loyal support," and one from Senator Paul Martin, thanking Cooper on behalf of former prime minister Lester Pearson for a silver medallion. The venerable Senator Martin was among the most powerful of federal Liberals. Ten days later, Pearson had sent Cooper his own letter of thanks.

Cooper appeared to feel sorry that the Mounties were wasting so much of their time. But the Mounties were far from bored.

In the three years since the Department of Regional Economic Expansion had been started in 1969, the federal government had given away $250 million in industrial incentive grants. DREE, as the department was known, was intended by the Liberals to be a public engine driving the economy in the less fortunate reaches of the country. The stated aim was to alleviate regional disparities by creating new jobs, although critics saw it as a blatant attempt to purchase loyal voters – after all, considering the distribution of seats in Parliament, one vote in the hinterland was worth about ten in each of the country's urban areas. A decade or so earlier, with a Comptroller-General keeping the federal treasury in shape like a tough-minded military quartermaster, DREE's free spending would have been checked. By 1972, however, departments were in charge of their own spending. Under Jean

Marchand and his successors, DREE was one of the great all-time sinkholes for Canadian tax dollars.

Norton Cooper's three-step plan looked great on paper. It presented a natural appeal to nationalist sentiments and DREE bureaucrats. Through one of his companies Cooper had taken over the old Silver Shield mine at Cobalt in northeastern Ontario. Step one was to get the mine working again. The second step was to process silver from his and other area mines in a new refinery to be built next to the mine. The silver bullion – 99.9 per cent pure – would be used in the manufacture of new, limited-edition commemorative medallions, plaques, and other fine metal pieces at Cooper's new private mint. Cooper brought some historical lustre to his proposal by naming it the Jacques Cartier Mint, after the first French explorer to Canada. The mint was to be located in Toronto but, Cooper conceded, he might consider building it in Cobalt if the government insisted – that is, paid him a larger incentive. The entire project brought with it the promise of a hundred jobs, and in Cobalt, a town desperate for investment, it didn't take much to get the local politicians firmly on his side.

Private mints were becoming an extremely profitable business in North America. In its first seven years, ending in 1971, Franklin Mint sales had grown to $60 million annually. Two similar mints had opened in the United States, the Kennedy and the Liberty. A Canadian mint, the Wellings, had been purchased by the Franklin Mint soon after it opened in suburban Toronto and was being run as a subsidiary. Wellings' volume had reached $10 million in Canada by 1971.

Cooper's proposal to set up a silver refinery made his plan very attractive, as there were none in Canada. All Canadian silver was being shipped to Helena, Montana, for processing. Stories in the press about his negotiating a deal with Buckingham Palace to strike a commemorative coin marking the Queen's twentieth anniversary as monarch set the bait for investors. All that was needed was an ounce of faith from the federal government and financial backing from DREE. Lost in the hyperbole was one big question: was there any silver left in the old Silver Shield mine? No one ever answered that question for it was soon lost in the storm that followed Stamler's October visit to Cooper.

Cooper figured that the best way through the door of the government treasury was with a political fixer on his arm. Cooper told the Mounties later that he was told by "someone" to contact Senator Paul Martin, which he did in January 1972. The senator responded by setting up a meeting in his office on February 29. Cooper brought with him to that meeting people whose very presence gave him credibility. Days before the meeting, Cooper dropped the senator another note describing those who would be accompanying him: consultant James E. Armstrong; the company's lawyer, Jack A. Gilbert, Q.C.; Cale B. Jarvis, "a director of the Cartier Mint Inc., a fellow of the Royal Numismatic Society and . . . a columnist with the *Globe and Mail* since 1961"; and Jerome Forman, a financial consultant and a former senior officer of the Bank of Nova Scotia in charge of gold and silver trading.

Martin arranged to have Gerald McKendry, the director of DREE's Incentives Branch, attend the meeting. McKendry had been in the bakery business in Ottawa for eighteen years before drifting into a government job in 1967. He was brought into DREE because the government believed it needed more people with a business background in the department. McKendry was being paid $22,522 a year in 1972.

After introductions were made, Senator Martin scooted from the meeting.

Immediately after the meeting, Cooper submitted an informal application for a DREE grant. One month later, before DREE had announced its decision, Cooper transformed his privately held Jacques Cartier Mint into a public company that could be traded on the stock market. During April, speculators began to take interest in Cooper's mining companies' stock. On April 27 Cooper held a press conference at the Park Plaza Hotel in

Toronto to announce the awarding of the DREE grant and his plans for Cobalt and the Jacques Cartier Mint. McKendry, the DREE official, gave a speech strongly supporting the concept.

The *Globe and Mail* reported the next day that Cooper had received two DREE grants – $619,000 for the Jacques Cartier Mint and $119,970 for setting up Canadian Smelting and Refining. Cooper had cut through the red tape as if it were gossamer. The first time many key DREE bureaucrats involved in the proposal had heard about the awarding of the grant was when they read about it in the *Globe*, and questions began to be asked inside the department.

Soon the word was out that McKendry had given a subordinate just one hour to study and approve a recommendation to issue the grant. The subordinate had not been involved in the project up until this point. He had given qualified support to the grant, saying he would like to see a report from another ministry regarding Cooper's plan to use an acid-wash cyanide process in the refinery. McKendry had assured the subordinate that he had seen that report and that it had given its approval to the process. He foresaw no problems. But McKendry had lied about the assessment of the acid-wash cyanide process. The report, in fact, was highly critical of Cooper's plan and recommended that further studies be carried out.

The news of federal money being ploughed into the project naturally helped Cooper's companies on the stock market, and Cooper and other insiders helped themselves by manipulating the price of the stock upward by buying heavily in a closed circle. The scheme worked for four months until a newspaper reporter got wind that two public servants involved in the awarding of the grant had purchased shares in Silver Shield mine before the announcement. Assistant Deputy Minister J. Douglas Love announced the suspension of two unnamed officials, McKendry and one of his associates, and called in the Mounties.

Henry Jensen assigned the case to a team led by Stamler at the

Toronto Commercial Fraud Section. It looked like a case of stock market manipulation.

During their original search of his office, it never occurred to Cooper what Stamler and Jim McIlvenna were really after. He knew it had to do with McKendry. He also knew that McKendry and one of his staff had been suspended for using insider knowledge to buy stocks in the Silver Shield mine. McKendry had used Cooper's broker to buy $22,699 worth of stock during the month of April, an expenditure that equalled his yearly salary. Cooper also knew that this was not proof of a crime.

The Ontario Securities Commission had temporarily suspended trading in Silver Shield mine and International Mariner Resources, but Cooper didn't see that as much of a threat, either. He saw the Securities Commission as a minor nuisance, and believed it had no interest in getting to the bottom of things. Cooper was prepared to take the slap on the wrist and move on.

Cooper had, in writing, offered McKendry the job of president of the Jacques Cartier Mint after the $739,000 DREE grant was approved, but this was not evidence of a crime either. Copies of the letter had been sent to two of McKendry's superiors. Cooper had offered McKendry $60,000 a year, almost three times as much as he was making in the government, plus stock options and other benefits.

Stamler surmised that Cooper's actions were disingenuous, an attempt to deflect attention away from the fact that McKendry may have been offered the job much earlier. Still, it was unlikely that the Mounties could prove McKendry had been hired verbally by Cooper before the DREE grant approval. Neither McKendry nor Cooper was going to admit to that. The entire question was clouded further by the fact that McKendry had rejected Cooper's written offer weeks after receiving it, after considerable internal pressure from concerned government officials.

Cooper was certain there was nothing else the police knew or could prove. He never suspected they might have another agenda. Days before the visit to Cooper's office, Stamler had gone through McKendry's Ottawa office, which hadn't been touched since the day he was suspended. While flipping through the calendar on McKendry's desk, his curiosity had been piqued. One day in February, McKendry had made a note to himself: "Call Senator Martin." Stamler realized that McKendry probably hadn't known Cooper before the meeting arranged by the senator.

Also marked on the calendar for the end of February was a note about a trip to Ocala, Florida. In March, there had been another trip. To understand if a fraud had been committed, Stamler had to get into the minds of Cooper and McKendry. What were they thinking? Why did they do what they did when they did it?

He interviewed McKendry's former secretary, who remembered that he had gone to Florida two or three times. But every time he had gone, he had wanted tickets booked only to Toronto. He had said he was meeting someone there.

The paper chase was on. Stamler seized McKendry's expense accounts and then headed back to Toronto. At the Air Canada office he sorted through manifests and found that McKendry had gone to Florida on March 3, March 17, April 7, and May 5. Each time he had travelled first class with Norton Cooper from Toronto to Tampa. On two of the trips Cooper and McKendry were accompanied by their wives. But how did they get to Ocala?

This was definitely smoke, but it wasn't fire. Stamler delved deeper into the relationship between Cooper and McKendry. He found someone who had met with McKendry at the end of March, before the DREE grant was approved, quietly, on April 5 (three weeks before the formal announcement). The man said McKendry had told him that he had been offered a job in the private sector, calling it the best opportunity he had ever seen in his life. McKendry had boasted that he would be president, making $60,000 a year. More evidence of a relationship, but the job-offer line of inquiry probably led to a dead end.

A public servant who was acting manager of the loan guarantee section of DREE remembered receiving a call from McKendry prior to the DREE grant being approved. McKendry had outlined to him the projected capital costs of two related projects – a silver refinery and a private commercial mint – and asked the man if he knew anyone in the private sector who would be interested in lending to such projects. McKendry was in Toronto at the time. When the civil servant called the number McKendry had left, Norton Cooper answered the phone. Circumstantial evidence, but still not proof.

Then Stamler thought of the reporter from *Fortune* magazine. The reporter, Paul Nowak, was a freelancer who had sold *Fortune* on the idea of a story about Cooper and DREE. The story was scheduled for the May issue of the magazine. Nowak had shown up one March day in Ottawa and interviewed a number of DREE officials. Everyone at DREE had been excited about the prospect of an article on their program in such a prestigious magazine as *Fortune*. But when the story came out, there was no mention of DREE. It was just a short profile of Norton Cooper.

Stamler sought out Nowak and found that he had enjoyed an all-expenses-paid week-long visit to Cooper's Florida estate. In early February 1972, Nowak had been asked to do some publicity work for Cooper and his companies. Nowak had subsequently contacted *Fortune* about the Cooper story. On April 14, after the grant was approved but before news of it or the *Fortune* story were published, Nowak purchased $11,000 worth of shares in Silver Shield mine. After Nowak completed his story on Cooper and had submitted it to *Fortune*, Cooper offered Nowak the job of vice-president of the Jacques Cartier Mint. He took up the position on May 1, just as the story on Cooper hit the stands. It was a masterful public relations stunt by Cooper, but it was not evidence of a crime.

Finally, Stamler found the key. On the first day they had met, Cooper and McKendry had lunched at the Chateau Laurier in Ottawa. It hadn't taken Cooper long to find out that McKendry had a small farm just south of Ottawa. He loved horses, so did Cooper. About a month later, McKendry had attended a dinner meeting at the Chateau Laurier with DREE officials. In the course of conversation he told them that he had purchased two quarter horses at a very good price through a friend. Stamler was sure the horses were the currency of the bribe, and if there was one thing the Mounties knew more than anything else, it was the value of horseflesh – they weren't nicknamed Horsemen for nothing.

The case had started out as a suspected stock manipulation; now Stamler was in the quandary where the police often find themselves. There were many possible charges: stock manipulation, insider trading, influence peddling, bribery, and various frauds, including McKendry's claim of false expenses from the government. Stamler could combine them into one huge case, but decided not to as too much of the evidence was soft. So he opted to focus on the bribery.

When Stamler and McIlvenna conducted the search at Cooper's office, they were more interested in the free trips to Florida and the quarter horses than in any stock McKendry might have purchased in Cooper's companies. The entire time the police were in his office, Cooper was defending an area that wasn't under attack. The major hurdle for Stamler was to prove McKendry had actually taken the trips to Florida. As they chatted about McKendry, Cooper loosened up. "Everything is above board on this one," Cooper said, pulling some pictures out of a file. They showed McKendry and other ministry officials in the Silver Shield mine and they were dated. Good, Stamler thought, evidence of who was where and when.

Cooper, thinking he was distracting the Mounties, went into detail about his contact with Senator Martin, the first meetings in Ottawa, and how he had come to meet Gerald McKendry.

"I see McKendry travelled to Florida with you a couple of times," Stamler said nonchalantly, hoping not to set off any warning bells.

Yes, Cooper said, McKendry had met him in Toronto and they had flown to his ranch.

"So what time did you meet in Toronto?"

Cooper answered the question.

"I fly my own plane," Stamler said. "When I go commercial, I like window seats. Where did you sit on the way to Florida?"

"We went first class," Cooper bragged. "Gerry got the window seat."

Stamler now had evidence of them on the plane together, with McIlvenna as a witness to the conversation.

"Is your farm near Tampa?" the Mountie asked.

"No, no. Ocala. I had Gerry's luggage tagged specially so that his luggage would come off with mine and would be transferred to the private jet I had standing by to take us to Ocala." Now Stamler knew how they got from Tampa to Ocala.

Cooper told Stamler about McKendry's interest in the horses and about how he had previously told McKendry he had a matched pair of dun mares – Muncho Ann and Miss Salty Leo – at the ranch in Ocala.

"Did you sell him the horses?"

"Well, the price never came up," Cooper said. "We never talked about price."

Stamler checked out the history of the mares. At the time he had met McKendry, Cooper didn't own the horses. After learning that McKendry was interested in them, he had them shipped to his farm in time for McKendry's first visit, and pretended that they were his. Later, he bought the mares for McKendry. Stamler was not surprised by the former owner's complaint that Cooper had been slow to pay.

No money had changed hands between McKendry and Cooper, but Stamler thought he had them both cold. The breakneck speed at which McKendry had pushed the DREE grant through the bureaucracy was no accident, and Stamler knew exactly what each man had been thinking at the time.

In November, Cooper was charged with unlawfully confer-
ring an advantage or benefit on a civil servant. McKendry was
charged with accepting an advantage or benefit. The charges, of
course, didn't tell the whole story, but the case was rock solid.
Although it had approved the grant, DREE had not yet forwarded
the money to Cooper. When DREE pulled the grant after the
charges were laid, the Silver Shield mine went bankrupt. Cooper
sued DREE for $45 million in damages, as he fought to stay out of
the courtroom.

But Cooper was eventually convicted by a jury and jailed. The
civil suit disappeared. After he was released in the late 1970s,
Cooper hung around Toronto for a couple of years, then moved
to California. McKendry was also convicted and served time in
prison. After his release he became chairman of a Kingston,
Ontario, company, Plastic Engine Technology Corp. A laudatory
story on McKendry appeared in the *Globe and Mail*'s "Report on
Business" on November 24, 1986. The plastic car engine business melted into bankruptcy in 1989.

As they had done in the *Irving Whale* case, the Mounties had
managed to stop a fraud from being perpetrated against the taxpayers of Canada. The thrill of success for Stamler was muted,
however, by what he'd seen again of the close relationship
between criminals, reputable politicians, and the public service.
It disturbed him.

6

Buffalo Oil & Gas

Federal civil servant Cliff Kennedy wasn't the only one impressed by Stamler; his fellow Mounties, such as George Wool, were, too.

After five years of patrolling the Northwest Territories and the high Arctic, mostly on a dogsled, Wool's curiosity about an advertisement placed in a Yellowknife newspaper led him on a circuitous route to becoming a commercial-crime investigator. The advertisement led Wool to uncover a sophisticated financial swindle which took him to Europe and back and had resulted in a number of arrests. Wool had ended up working with Stamler in Toronto.

What impressed Wool the most was that Stamler was unlike the other senior Mounties with whom he had served. Stamler seemed so modern in his thinking. "There was a lot of animosity when Rod was assigned to Toronto," Wool says. "He was the first commissioned officer to actually go out on the street and work. We had all worked with senior officers and didn't have a lot of faith in them. Stamler was a curiosity to most of us. But once he was in there for a while and we saw how good he was, the animosity just melted away.

"There is a rule in the RCMP that officers aren't spoken to unless they speak first," adds Wool, now a Vancouver-area lawyer. "Rod spoke to everyone. He was one of the first to do so. He didn't buy all the regimental rules like so many of the military types on the force. Rod didn't care if the flag was positioned at the proper place on the mast, how much oil was in the car, if the whitewalls were showing, or your shoes were shined just right. All Rod wanted was for you to be a good investigator."

Another characteristic about Stamler that Wool liked was that his refreshing attitude about the small stuff extended to his approach to criminal investigations.

"Across the country," Wool recalls, "the force spent all its time on low-level criminals, building them up to be more than they were to make it look as if the police were doing a great job. They were more intent on chasing and arresting lowlifes and Natives than tackling people on the social register. Rod and Bud Howe [the head of the Toronto commercial-crime squad] were equal-opportunity cops. It didn't matter who you were, if you did wrong, they would be after you. It was a real morale booster for everyone."

Wool first worked with Stamler on a massive case, which began with an investigation into a dubious public company, Buffalo Oil & Gas, whose shares were traded on the Canadian Stock Exchange in Montreal. The other investigators were Jim McIlvenna and John Beer.

Seven years had passed since the crash of Atlantic Acceptance Corp. in 1965, and the near-universal cries for stronger securities laws and better enforcement of them. Federal and provincial politicians had tinkered with the laws, but had implemented few substantive improvements.

There was reluctance even within the RCMP to treat stock

manipulation as a crime. While stationed at Fort Smith, N.W.T., Wool, for example, had noticed how active the telex machine was. The Mounties were so busy sending material back and forth to stockbrokers in Edmonton that the police work was often put on hold.

It was a familiar pattern throughout the force. The police were inveterate players of the stock market. Mountie investment clubs had natural advantages over ordinary mortals. When club members had a tip about something, they could have it checked out easily. Mounties working in the hinterlands had a lot of time on their hands. It was a regular practice for members on patrol to investigate news about mines by interviewing prospectors and employees and then relaying the information back to their particular club, which could be anywhere in the country. Furthermore, mining promoters made it their business to get close to the police, providing individual members with hot tips and helping them to make fast money with dubious stock promotions.

There was, therefore, not an inconsiderable body within the force wondering what in the world Henry Jensen was trying to do when he was pushing ahead with the development of the Commercial Crime Branch. "Mining promoters were seen by many members as good guys," Wool says. "Why would anyone want to put them in jail? They're not criminals."

Stock fraud was so rampant in the 1960s and '70s that it should have surprised no one when the Mounties' investigation into Buffalo Oil & Gas touched off a nation-wide scandal.

Buffalo Oil & Gas (also known as Buffalo Gas & Oil in the U.S.A.) was formed in July 1970. Its founder, a shady Atlanta mining promoter, said he named the company after the American border city where he was required to land on his way to Canada. However, the Mounties, familiar with the tongue-in-cheek nomenclature often preferred by fraud artists, suspected it came from the slang verb "to buffalo," which means to intimidate or hoodwink.

For Stamler, investigating Buffalo Oil was like earning another university degree, a major in stock market manipulation, with a minor in witness protection programs.

The investigation began as a seemingly routine matter with complaints about the possible criminal behaviour in Toronto of two Americans, James Danielson and Steve Dinneen.

Danielson and Dinneen liked to call themselves financiers or stock market specialists, depending on the circumstances. They were nothing but confidence men. Danielson was blessed with superior intelligence, a photographic memory, and a self-proclaimed encyclopedic knowledge of evil ways and means. What made him most dangerous was his winning personality and charm, which made him so believable that he could con a con. Stamler had never before met anyone like Danielson.

Dinneen was terse, business-like, and looked respectable – and was considered to be one of the biggest and most successful fraud artists of his generation by those in the "industry." Both men were fugitives from justice in the United States after fraud convictions.

A typical Dinneen fraud was one he pulled in the late 1960s in Atlanta. Legend has it that he arrived in the city with one dollar in his pocket, but managed to rent the top floor of the best hotel in the city. He then hired the biggest limousine he could find and invited the controlling shareholders of a large insurance company to a meeting. The company had a solid cash flow and a huge treasury. Dinneen offered to buy the company. The shareholders knew that he was probably going to use the company's own money to buy it out, but they couldn't touch that money and he was offering more than they might get on the open market. The deal was done in no time and soon afterward, Dinneen left the city with the company's treasury parked in his offshore bank accounts.

The first step the Mounties took in the Buffalo Oil investigation was to set up a simple sting operation on Danielson and Dinneen. A French-Canadian policeman, Norm Doucette, now an assistant commissioner, was brought in from Montreal. Posing as a crooked lawyer, he arranged a meeting with Danielson to make a payoff. Danielson took the bait. The Mounties didn't have much on Danielson, but he didn't know that. Fearing the police knew everything, Danielson, worried about the future of his wife and young son, decided to roll over on his cronies. The police had conned the man who could con the cons.

Dinneen soon followed in Danielson's footsteps, going to work for the Mounties. In exchange for their information, they were both given immunity from prosecution in Canada and the promise of remuneration, which they later received.

When Danielson decided to talk to the Mounties, entire criminal empires were immediately placed in jeopardy. He painted a breathtaking portrait of criminality, giving the police a list of the names of stock manipulators and fraud artists that even today is used across the continent as a reference guide.

The Buffalo Oil manipulation had included dozens of other companies and perhaps hundreds of co-conspirators operating on four of the country's stock exchanges: the Canadian, the Montreal, the Toronto, and the Vancouver. The scam extended into the United States, and the stock was even being sold through the European "boiler rooms," phone banks operated by high-pressure sales representatives. Investors in North America and Europe were being bilked out of millions of dollars.

One centre of stock market manipulation was the L. J. Forget brokerage firm in Montreal, which was run by Montreal financier Irving Kott. Until then, Kott had enjoyed a relatively clean reputation, but the Mounties now knew from Danielson and Dinneen that Kott was in fact a front for those who had become involved in the Buffalo Oil and other manipulations. These included Montreal Mafia boss Vincent Cotroni and his heir apparent, Paolo Violi, along with Sheldon "Sonny" Schwartz and Stanley Bader from Toronto, John "Johnny Pops" Papalia from Hamilton, and a gang from Vancouver.

Danielson and Dinneen had been hired to look after the

financial interests of the Cotroni family; that is, manipulate the stock upward for the benefit of the Montreal mobsters.

When the stock price began to fall, the Mounties learned through wiretaps that the Cotronis wanted Kott killed because they blamed him for the price collapse. Further, the police found that gang members were even victimizing each other. Papalia was using the Cotroni name to extort $300,000 from Bader and another man. When Cotroni learned about this, he wanted Papalia to pay him some of the take.

The wiretaps of a conversation between Papalia and Cotroni about how Schwartz had shorted Papalia in a payment showed just how brutal and unsophisticated these men were:

Papalia: "He's got two-sixty [$260,000], believe me, if he took three hundred, he's got two-sixty.

Cotroni: "Yeah?"

Papalia: "I got forty. Take the two-sixty off him."

Cotroni: "Yeah! But you see the guy, he gonna say, 'I gave this money to Johnny.'"

Papalia: "He can say he gave it to Jesus Christ! I don't care what he says. He didn't give it to me, Vic."

Cotroni: "Let's hope because, eh, we'll kill you."

Papalia: "I know you'll kill me, Vic. I believe you'll kill me."

Cotroni: "Because the guy said, he give, he give it to Johnny. He say. The guy say that."

Papalia: "What, what do you want me to do? Just tell him he's a fucking liar."

During the investigation of Buffalo Oil, the police learned that at least one public official had been corrupted, that a go-between had been murdered, and that dozens of floor traders and brokers had accepted bribes and secret commissions. The police estimated that, under the less than watchful eyes of the provincial securities commissions, at least half of all stock traders and brokers were on the take. There was little, if any, room in the stock market for the honest businessman or investor.

As a courtesy, Howe and Stamler informed the Ontario Securities Commission of their plans to investigate the Buffalo Oil leads and invited the OSC to assign an investigator to assist them. The OSC usually refused to co-operate with the police because it believed it had the sole responsibility to enforce securities law, even though it didn't have qualified investigators to mount investigations.

On those rare occasions when police investigating a Criminal Code offence came snooping around, the OSC would start its own investigation and cut the ground out from under the police. Almost always, the police would back off and the OSC would treat the case as a securities violation, paying no heed to possible Criminal Code offences.

Stamler was determined that the Mounties would conduct the Buffalo Oil case on their own. During the Norton Cooper case he had struck up good relations with Clay Powell, assistant deputy minister and head of prosecutions and appeals in the Ontario Ministry of the Attorney-General. Stamler now contacted Powell, telling him that the Mounties wanted to investigate without interference from the OSC. Powell promised his support in any dispute between the two organizations, as long as the Mounties were enforcing the Criminal Code.

Stamler and Howe then met with an OSC official who was adamant that the OSC would do its own investigation. They had hoped to convince him to go along with them without using the stick represented by Clay Powell, but such was not to be. They argued about jurisdiction, but neither side would back down. The Mounties finally suggested that they would be happy to let the Attorney-General's Office arbitrate. The OSC official must have figured them for dolts for suggesting an appeal to that quarter, and the Mounties didn't bother to disabuse him of the notion.

Two days later, an OSC investigator phoned Stamler and said he'd been assigned to work with the Mounties. It was a small but significant victory for Stamler and the force.

It didn't take long for the police to make arrests, and as the various cases wended their way through the legal system, the criminals were on the defensive. In many ways Danielson was all that stood between the crime bosses and freedom so, naturally, as go the rules of the Mafia, a contract was put out on the turncoat Danielson's life. As the lead investigator, it was Stamler's job to keep him alive.

In 1973, there was no witness protection program, so the Mounties had to improvise to protect Danielson. They tried to keep him close to them in Toronto, but neighbours of one safe house became concerned about the amount of activity as plain-clothes police officers, both investigators and guards, came and went.

Danielson was a difficult man to deal with; a week's worth of expenses was only enough for one night's dinner for Danielson, who couldn't forgo the best French wines.

Dinneen's tastes, on the other hand, were ascetic. He lived with a single Mountie guard for a year. When his clothes wore out, the force had to insist that he buy a new suit. The only unusual demand he ever made came about a year after he was in custody when, after living so long with a male cop, he asked if the police could find him a woman with whom he could spend some time. Dinneen was given $75 to spend on a prostitute. Dinneen returned from a short excursion with a smile on his face and never asked for extra money again.

Danielson made the Mounties agree not to use surveillance equipment in his living quarters. Stamler ignored the deal, made under duress, and brought in the RCMP's best man from Ottawa to install bugs. Before the end of the first day, Danielson com-plained about the surveillance equipment. He had built a radio receiver and just walked around the safe house adjusting its chan-nels until he received feedback. Because of Danielson's inventive-ness, the Mounties changed the way they bugged rooms – one of the many useful things he, inadvertently and otherwise, taught the police over the next couple of years.

At the time Stamler was trying to find more suitable housing for Danielson, Cliff Kennedy, the Justice Department lawyer, was learning of a problem that had arisen in Hamilton over the activities of the city's Harbour Commission. Because of the ongoing *Irving Whale* case, Kennedy and Stamler had stayed in touch. In passing, Stamler mentioned to Kennedy that he needed an isolated place where he could hide a witness. Kennedy remembered that the Department of Transport owned an abandoned airport near Gore Bay on Manitoulin Island, in Lake Huron. There were two derelict wartime houses on the property near the end of the runway. It looked like the perfect setup. Danielson and his family could stay in one house, and his RCMP guards in the other. Stamler planned to make use of the RCMP air force to shuttle Danielson to and from his various court appointments around the country. The cover story for Islanders would be that Danielson was leading a team conducting environmental research in the area.

The cover didn't last long. On Manitoulin Island, anyone doing anything out of the ordinary was news, and Danielson knew better than anyone else how to create news. Danielson played being an environmental researcher to the hilt, so much so that people in Gore Bay, the nearest town, flocked to him every time he came around to listen to his ideas and plans for Manitoulin Island. The Mounties began to joke that Danielson was getting so popular he might run for mayor, but not everyone was joking. Danielson was eventually approached by a prominent politician, who wanted to get him interested in federal politics. When he was asked to speak at a political rally, the Mounties knew it was time to find Danielson more anonymous digs. This episode taught Stamler that the best place to hide a witness is in a highrise apartment in the heart of a city, where nobody knows or cares who lives next door or across the hall.

On a deeper level, Stamler knew that if the Mounties were going to be successful at fighting sophisticated and vicious criminals, they would need a proper witness protection program.

Otherwise, with potential witnesses fearing for their lives, there was no incentive for anyone to step forward and help the police make a case. Stamler put a witness protection program on his list of things to do when he became king. Two decades later, in spite of his concerns and efforts during that time, neither the federal government nor the RCMP had fully implemented such a program.

The Buffalo Oil prosecutions took years to wind through the justice system, resulting in many convictions. One of the most significant outcomes was the demise of the Canadian Stock Exchange. It closed its doors at the end of 1973 and merged with the Montreal exchange. Stamler considered his work in helping to shut down the CSE one of his foremost accomplishments in the service of the public.

7

Hamilton Harbour

Nestled into the Niagara Escarpment at the western end of Lake Ontario and protected by a long, deep sandbar, the shallow waters of Burlington Bay were once one of the most beautiful natural habitats in North America. As late as the 1930s, the bay was a choice fishing ground and recreation area for children and young adults, many of whom dared to swim from the shores of Hamilton to LaSalle park more than a mile away. After the Second World War, however, the people of Hamilton lost the bay as a recreation spot, as commerce enforced its will.

The decline of the bay had begun innocently enough in the early 1800s. A major concern of the Parliament of Upper Canada was the creation of commercial shipping lanes in Southern Ontario. Starting just twenty-five miles east of Burlington Bay, the Welland Canal, connecting Lake Ontario and Lake Erie, was completed in 1829. In 1832, nine years after authorization had been given by Parliament for its construction, the Burlington Bay Canal opened, linking the bay with the lake. The government's intention was for ships to reach Dundas, the planned commercial centre for the region.

The capabilities of the dredgers changed all that. Out of the swamp to the east of Dundas they carved Hamilton Harbour. Propelled by the steel companies and foundries which took up residence around the harbour, Hamilton became the industrial capital of Canada, a chipped-tooth town that also became a centre for organized crime.

In the ensuing years, under the guidance and direction of the federal government, which held absolute jurisdiction, Hamilton Harbour grew to become a dirty, busy, and profitable place to conduct business. It was a honey-pot for shady entrepreneurs looking to make a fast buck and greedy politicians hunting for so-called campaign contributions.

In 1972 the Hamilton Harbour Commission had three members, two federal government appointments and one municipal, each of whom was paid the small sum of $4,000 a year. Chairman Edwin Delbert Hickey, Q.C., and Commissioner Joseph Lanza had been appointed by the federal government, at the suggestion of Liberal MP John Munro. The city's appointee was Kenneth R. Elliott. All three carried a Liberal Party card.

Del Hickey was also an executive officer of Ronark Developments, one of the directors of which was Hamilton businessman Sam Lax. Under Hickey's leadership, the Harbour Commission gave Lax permission to fill in fifty acres of waterlots, upon which housing could be built. This would have instantly doubled the size of Lax's land holdings had enormous public pressure not succeeded in stopping the filling.

Joseph Lanza, a former tailor and city alderman, was vice-president of Munro's Hamilton East riding association, a prominent Liberal fundraiser and Munro's former campaign manager. When he had been appointed to the Harbour Commission, neither Lanza nor anyone else had mentioned that he had been convicted in 1943 and again in 1948 for keeping a common betting house.

Ken Elliott's family had long been in the ship-chandling business. He grew up hanging around the docks in Hamilton's two-fisted North End, and there were rumours that he associated with known criminals. Even Elliott's bankers were a bit leery of him. In a 1971 report, his bank manager wrote, "Mr. Elliott . . . has other sources of income which he chooses not to disclose. As a matter of fact he was last in our office on Thursday of this week and had $29,000 in cash in his possession." In another report that year, the bank manager observed, "Mr. Elliott is very evasive about his sources of income but claims to have $120,000 in cash. . . . Elliott obviously is a rather difficult person to deal with, and we have still not made up our mind about him. His unknown sources of income intrigue us and, obviously, it is in the back of our mind that the federal revenue authorities would be most interested in his present style of living."

On August 4, 1972, a Toronto-area businessman, Kenneth Barfknecht, revealed a sordid little tale about Elliott to a Hamilton city controller, Herman Turkstra. Barfknecht said he had tried to start a ship-breaking business in the harbour, but Elliott had refused to let him lease any land for the enterprise, unless Elliott and a certain Robert A. Henderson were given a piece of the action. A fifteen-page agreement had been drawn up between Barfknecht, Elliott, and Henderson, who owned a company with business in Hamilton Harbour. Under the terms of the agreement, a ship-breaking company would be set up. Barfknecht would run the company and draw a $15,000 salary, and Henderson would supply it with a crane and machinery in return for a third of the profits. Elliott's role would be to negotiate the purchase of ships for scrapping in return for his expenses, a new car, and a third of the profits. Barfknecht balked at the agreement because he realized he would be making comparatively little money, then complained to Herman Turkstra, who ignited the political fireworks.

Turkstra had been hounding the Harbour Commission for more than a year to no avail. He had told the city council that the port director, Earl Perkins, had a conflict of interest because of his involvement with a cargo-handling firm, and that Elliott, among other things, worked for a scrap metal company that had a close relationship with the steel companies. Furthermore, Turkstra pointed out, Elliott, through his partial ownership of a cable television company, stood to benefit from the Harbour Commission's decision to let Sam Lax fill in waterlots in the western harbour and build housing.

Then the Harbour Commission, without advising the city, completed a huge land exchange in the eastern end of the harbour with the city's two major industries, Dominion Foundries and Steel and the Steel Company of Canada. Over the years the steel companies had reduced access to Hamilton's once beautiful bay and were continually expanding their land by filling in waterlots. This latest land exchange allowed the steel companies to fill in almost one third of Burlington Bay without consultation with the city. What was not appreciated at the time was that by extending their lands the steel companies would encroach on the shipping lane in the bay, and taxpayers would have to pay to have the lane relocated. In the book *Their Town*, Turkstra aptly describes the commissioners as "three men, responsible to no one, agreeing with . . . men responsible to two bodies of shareholders, to take an asset that belongs to the citizens of Hamilton and convert it to the use of the companies, without the public's being aware of it." *

Harbour Commission chairman Hickey, with his usual steady-as-she-goes attitude, took the position that the commission was following its federal mandate to plan the harbour as it saw fit, and that there were no problems. Transport Minister Don Jamieson said he wouldn't get involved in the matter because the

---

* Turkstra and Copps are quoted from Bill Freeman and Marsha Hewitt, *Their Town: The Mafia, the Media and the Party Machine*, James Lorimer & Company, 1979.

commission, for which he was responsible, was an "autonomous body." Hamilton's mayor, Vic Copps, another Liberal, also sided with the commissioners. In the same book, he's quoted as saying: "Our greatest problem in this city isn't ecology. It is unemployment. This deal will help ease the problem."

Barfknecht's revelations were not so easy for the politicians to dismiss, and Turkstra finally drew blood. His allegations were debated at city council, to Mayor Copps' dismay. Copps said he was concerned about "all this McCarthyism," and at another council meeting, he exploded in anger, saying, "It's about time you stopped your dirty smearing of people by suggesting we've got something to hide. I've nothing to hide about the harbour and I don't like your smeary suggestions. But I'm not prepared to act irresponsibly by rushing to the federal government demanding an inquiry." Despite the mayor's bluster, the council eventually dismissed Elliott and called for a federal inquiry. But Ottawa denied the request. There were rumours of an RCMP investigation, but the Mountie in charge of the local detachment, unaware that the Toronto squad of the Commercial Crime Branch had been assigned to the case but was too busy just then to begin it, told the media he knew of no such investigation. The public confusion was aggravated when it was reported that the local police were investigating the matter but, later, this was denied by Police Chief Leonard Lawrence, who said he had no record of a complaint being lodged.

Then Elliott took refuge in a convenient port for Canadian scoundrels and criminals – the country's libel laws. Elliott sued Barfknecht and a number of council members who were critical of his activities. Elliott's lawyer called a press conference and said his client was "just thirsting" for court action, and he called the council's decision to sack Elliott a plot "conceived in iniquity and carried out with wickedness." Until late spring 1973, the matter seemed to be in limbo, but then Stamler came free from his other cases. He began his investigation by interviewing Barfknecht and

Turkstra. While he thought their tale was interesting it was, unfortunately, muddied. The deal with Elliott had never been consummated, Barfknecht was still owed money, and the fact that he would benefit financially from the investigation made him a weak witness.

Stamler had to find a better starting point for his investigation. He knew it was a bad idea to go into the city blind and start banging on doors, since the picture of Hamilton that had been painted for him was of a city where everyone was into everything and where everyone knew everyone else or, at the very least, their relatives. He'd learned that Elliott was mindful of his contacts. The police chief's son was his accountant and one of the mayor's daughters worked part-time at Elliott's Dairy Queen. A normal course for Stamler might have been to contact the local police, but the Hamilton Police Department right up to Police Chief Leonard Lawrence was suspect. Stamler had learned that several prominent Hamiltonians had asked Lawrence to launch an investigation into the Harbour Commission's activities. The local police even had the jurisdiction to do so, since Elliott was the city appointee. But Lawrence insisted that he had received no such complaint and said he wasn't about to respond to hearsay and newspaper stories.

Stamler was familiar with the "no complaint" excuse. "In criminal frauds, especially those against governments, formal complaints are rarely brought forward," Stamler says. "A prime reason is that the very people who would normally launch such a complaint – politicians or bureaucrats – are usually reluctant to do so; they risk being embarrassed for being administratively inept or arrested for being the perpetrators. In either case they usually have the power and wherewithal to cover their tracks and to deflect or squelch any investigations."

In his interview with Stamler, Barfknecht had told him about the plight of Warren Barton, the city editor at the *Hamilton Spectator*, the city's only daily newspaper. Barfknecht said Barton had been "run out of town for rocking the boat." This, perhaps, was the place to start. Stamler, hoping to gain insight into who scratched whose back in Hamilton business and politics, decided to give Barton a call. As city editor of the *Spectator*, Barton heard every whisper worth listening to in Hamilton. From Barton, then others, Stamler learned about an illegal drug distribution network working out of the harbour and that there was so little turnover in some of the city's scrapyards the inventory was rusting away, which didn't seem to matter to the operators. The real purpose of the yards, where all transactions were in cash, he was told, was to launder money for organized crime. Stamler also heard stories about a judge said to be on the take, who for a fee would give advice and fix cases.

Stamler learned that the crossroads for all these dirty dealings was the Hamilton Club, the businessmen's association. Barton told Stamler that the *Spectator* began its coverage of the Hamilton Harbour Commission after he first met Ken Barfknecht in 1970, when the issue of the selling of waterlots had come up. Barton had assigned a reporter to the story, but the Harbour Commission refused to release any information, so Barton had threatened to take the commission to court. Someone at the commission phoned the publisher in an attempt to have him call the *Spectator* off the story. But the newspaper's publisher, Tom Nichols, a former reporter, backed Barton. The Harbour Commission caved in and the story was published.

Police officers usually view the media as the enemy and treat them as such, but as Barton outlined for Stamler the layers of Hamilton society, Stamler realized that he and the newspaperman were in much the same line of work, although each professional's code of ethics dictated that they not directly help each other. A police officer is a servant of the law, but a journalist is a servant of a story. Their mutual interests often collide, yet their combined presence on an investigative story can provide a powerful and positive one-two punch. Stamler says, "A policeman should want the media on his side because they have an uncanny ability to track situations. If a good reporter is working on the same case as you are, the reporter creates sparks here and sparks there, some of which might prove to be extremely useful."

Jim Travers, now editor of the Ottawa *Citizen*, came to know Stamler during the Hamilton Harbour investigation. Travers describes their relationship this way: "Stamler was like a psychiatrist for reporters. It was like you would go into his office, lie down on the couch and talk about your story. Every so often he would say, 'I wouldn't spend a lot of time on that,' and you would know right away that's a dead end. He wouldn't tell you anything directly, but somehow he gave you enough insight so that you could find the threads of the story yourself."

At the time Stamler met with Barton the biggest story in the world was the Watergate hearings by the Senate Select Committee on Presidential Activities, which had begun about a month earlier in May 1973. Since the burglary at the Democratic National Committee headquarters at the Watergate hotel almost a year earlier, *Washington Post* reporters Robert Woodward and Carl Bernstein had through their determined and accurate reporting brought enough pressure to bear to force open the issue. Although Watergate was seen to be a journalist's story, Stamler and many of his fellow Mounties were strongly influenced by it. They were instilled with the notion that theirs was a more important job than they had ever imagined. While Henry Jensen's original intention had been to check phony bankruptcies and stock market manipulations, these Mounties could see that there was another line of criminals who, until now, had been largely ignored.

That the U.S. media and investigators could work on parallel tracks and put the attorney-general and almost all the president's closest advisers in jail and force the president himself out of office, was vivid testimony to the strength of the belief in the rule of law in the United States. If there were to be one law for everyone in Canada, Stamler realized, that meant the Mounties might soon find themselves arresting prime ministers, premiers, and all sorts of powerful people.

Later that same year Tom Nichols at the *Spectator* announced that he was retiring, and that his replacement would be John Muir, who had come up through the business side of the paper and thought that investigative reporting had no place in his newspaper. Not long after Muir took over, he fired Barton.

It took Stamler so long to feel comfortable enough to conduct his Hamilton Harbour investigation openly – more than a year – that the suspects had been lulled to sleep. Ostensibly, the investigation was centred on Ken Barfknecht's complaint that Elliott wanted a piece of his proposed ship-breaking business. Stamler wasn't about to disabuse anyone in Hamilton of that notion, even though Barfknecht's allegations were merely Stamler's springboard.

During the *Irving Whale* investigation, Cliff Kennedy had schooled Stamler in the nefarious practices of the dredging companies. Kennedy now wanted to know if the public's interests were being protected in Hamilton, where many of the same companies were working. Stamler's real job was not to verify Barfknecht's complaint, but to catch the dredgers in the act of committing a crime.

When Stamler executed his search warrant for the Hamilton Harbour Commission offices, the obliging manager, long anticipating the day, had set up a procedure. He assigned someone to accompany Stamler and show the Mountie everything he wanted to see, the perfect setup for Stamler. At one point during the search, he walked over to a big map on a wall. On it was marked the work in progress at the east end of the harbour, where a berm was being constructed out of silt and sand dredged from the bottom of the bay. Stamler's immediate suspicion was that the berm construction was just another version of the *Irving Whale* case. "I suspected bureaucratic decisions were being made to create work that didn't need to be done, with the end purpose of defrauding the government," he says.

Stamler's plan was to concentrate on the commission's most recent contracts, an area likely left undefended by anyone who suspected they were under investigation over Barfknecht's allegations. "I wouldn't mind looking over the contracts for that project," Stamler told his eager escort, pointing to the proposed berm on the map. The files were pulled for him. A few days later, while Stamler was examining the files, he came upon a copy of an invoice to J. P. Porter Company Ltd., a Montreal firm which had beaten out McNamara Corp. and Canadian Dredge and Dock for the latest Hamilton Harbour dredging projects. The Harbour Commission had the invoice in its files because the contract was let on a cost-plus basis, and J. P. Porter had to prove its expenses before it could be paid. J. P. Porter had become a huge player in the dredging business since taking over control of Richelieu Dredging, an arm of Marine Industries.

The invoice to J. P. Porter was from Wm. Seymour, Electrical Contractor, 1223 Gerrard Street East, Toronto. It carried an apparently legitimate work-order number: HAM 224A-70. It was for expected services: overhaul of diesel engine, etc., $3,250; rewinding of generator, $4,780; replace wiring, $2,640; check and clean generators, pump motor, transformers, and controls, $2,830, for a total of $13,500. The work was said to have been completed August 25, 1970. The engine job was guaranteed for ninety days and the rewound generator for one year. It was even noted that no troubles could be located on the main generators, pump motor, transformers, or controls. Stamler had almost passed the invoice by when he realized something about it bothered him. He studied the invoice carefully, then it hit him: there was no telephone number. How many businesses didn't display telephone numbers on their invoices?

The next morning, a Saturday, he drove to downtown Toronto from his home in the suburban neighbourhood of Bridlewood. Stamler dawdled along behind a Gerrard Street streetcar looking for number 1223, expecting to find a business of some sort there. What he found was a typical Toronto semi-detached brick house. He checked his file once again to make sure 1223 was the address listed on the invoice, got out of his car, went to the door, and knocked. It was answered by Thomas Sheridan, a plumber by trade.

"I'm looking for William Seymour Electrical Contractor," Stamler said.

"You've got the wrong place," Sheridan replied.

Stamler persisted. He showed him the invoice, but Sheridan scratched his head and said he had lived in the house for six years and had never heard of a William Seymour or his business.

"Perhaps he lived next door?" Stamler asked.

"No, he never lived there, either," Sheridan said flatly.

"If you've only lived here for six years, how can you be so sure?"

"I was born in that house. I lived there for thirty-five years until I moved here. My father owned both houses."

"Is that so?" Stamler said quietly.

Other checks would have to be made of telephone books, registries, licensing bodies, professional associations, and other neighbours, but Stamler was sure that the answer from all of them would be the same – William Seymour Electrical Contractor was a dummy company. The bogus invoice was a key to a door that led to a criminal mind or two – but whose?

As it turned out, there was a real William Seymour. He was the late uncle of one of Elliott's friends and business associates, Reginald Leigh Fisher, a former bank manager who had lost his job after getting entwined in a conflict of interest. But the company was definitely bogus.

It wasn't long before Stamler had search warrants and the Mounties began raiding the homes and businesses of suspects. Stamler had just two assistants, Corporal Gerry Grant and Constable John Banks. Banks had recently moved back to policing after a number of years in the RCMP Security Service. Considering the care taken by the suspects to cover their tracks it might have been impossible for the average detective to unravel the strands of the case, especially with so few investigators, but Stamler had an unseen advantage: the *Irving Whale* investigation had taught him about many of the techniques used by the dredging industry to hide its illegal activities. He had seen, for example, how the Foundation Company and Murphy Pacific Marine had tried to disguise a $65,000 bribe as an invoice for chains and anchors.

In Hamilton there appeared to be many invoices of this ilk. Elliott was buying and selling ships, but the prices he paid were significantly less than market value. Elliott would then turn around and resell the ships and their fittings at a higher price. It was a neat sidestep to mask a payoff, Stamler suspected. Steel pipe was supposedly being sold and resold between various parties, but the police could not find the pipe or anyone who had ever seen it. There was even evidence that Elliott had received a $2,000 ship's grapnel for the reduced price of $400, money which the police learned was a down payment on a $15,000 kickback.

The initial set of raids in the Hamilton Harbour investigation showed Stamler that there was a criminal conspiracy operating in and around the city's Harbour Commission, but he still wasn't sure of its scope.

In a raid by the Mounties on Robert A. Henderson's company, Aldershot Contractors, it was discovered that the company had paid $10,800 to Clifford W. Morgan, the former port director of the Harbour Commission, who had died five days before the cheque was cut and cashed by someone who had been sloppy about the timing. That someone, Stamler soon learned, was Ken Elliott, who had boasted to an associate that "dead men can't talk," not appreciating how easy it would be for the Mounties to have Morgan point his finger from his grave.

During a raid on the J. P. Porter Company in Montreal, the Mounties found many strange documents. What caught Stamler's eye was an invoice for $122,884 to J. P. Porter from

International Marine of Zurich, Switzerland. International Marine's letterhead contained every kind of information anyone might want to know about the company and the invoice was complex and passably legitimate. But, once again, there was no phone number. This time there wasn't even an address. Stamler decided on the spot that he would chase down the invoice. When he asked J. P. Porter's chief financial officer if he could see the contract and background file relating to the invoice, he was told that it was a consulting company that had advised Porter on a contract for a dredging along the north channel of the St. Lawrence at Ile d'Orléans.

"Who are the engineers?" Stamler asked.

"I don't know," the J. P. Porter executive replied. "The president would know that. He's dealing with that."

"Where's the report? I would like to see the report and the file that goes with it," Stamler persisted.

The executive pulled out a file, which contained only a copy of the same invoice that had sparked Stamler's original inquiry. The only person who could explain it, president Horace Rindress, wasn't in that day.

Stamler knew that Sergeant George Wool of the Commercial Crime Branch was heading to Switzerland on another case, and asked him to check out International Marine while he was there. But Wool found no record there of International Marine, except that Elliott's friend (and William Seymour's nephew) Reg Fisher had recently been to Switzerland.

At Fisher's house the Mounties found another crucial piece of evidence, a J. P. Porter Company envelope addressed to Ken Elliott at his home. The envelope was postmarked "Montreal, December 20, 1971," and was covered with writing. Someone had scribbled an address in Hollywood, Florida, and a couple of telephone numbers. There were instructions about directing four copies of an invoice to Porter, two to Elliot, and the figures $25,000, $25,000, $15,000, and $12,500, the last one dramatically highlighted. On the back of the envelope the writer had compiled a list of names with rough German translations beside them: Marine Consultants, Marine Engineers, Marine Architects, Marine Surveyors, Marine Studies. There was a note to order letterhead. Finally, there were flight instructions to Miami, apparently from Toronto. *Voilà*, Stamler thought, the creation of International Marine. Reg Fisher was clearly a key person in the conspiracy, as was Horace Rindress of J. P. Porter.

During the raids, the Mounties uncovered another important lead, a cancelled cheque to International Marine, which had been cashed at the First National Bank in Fort Lauderdale. Stamler now knew where the money trail led, but there was no way he could get a search warrant to look at bank records in the United States. There was no agreement between U.S. and Canadian police for criminal investigations, something that Stamler would help enact more than a decade later. What did exist, however, was a tax treaty, and Stamler did have *prima facie* evidence of tax evasion by a number of individuals and companies, so he paid a visit to the Hamilton office of the Department of National Revenue and persuaded the staff to participate in a two-pronged attack – criminal and tax.

Working with Revenue Canada wasn't the best or easiest arrangement for Stamler. Canadian tax laws were so stringent about privacy that once tax investigators got their hands on evidence, the police were blocked out; the law says the rights of the taxpayer must be guarded above all else. Ironically, Stamler had come to know, those who benefited most from the extraordinary privacy were the crooked and the rich. By bringing in tax investigators, Stamler was applying as much pressure as he could on the suspected conspirators. He hoped to pick up crumbs from Revenue's investigation that would help him with his own case. His optimism would be rewarded.

Stamler met with the U.S. Internal Revenue Service and secured their co-operation, then travelled with Canadian tax investigators to Florida to begin the U.S. investigation. Stamler found the IRS agents a refreshing change from the Canadian tax authorities. At least, he thought, the IRS was playing the same tune as the police when it came to the prosecution of criminals.

Later, when Stamler came up with other leads requiring a second trip to Florida, Revenue Canada couldn't send an agent, so Stamler went alone. The proviso was that he must work in concert with IRS agents. The IRS office was busy with other matters on the day he arrived, but instead of sending him home empty-handed, the U.S. tax investigators authorized Stamler to go about his investigation in the United States.

The U.S. banking system was a delight. Unlike the secretive Canadian system at the time, U.S. banks kept microfiche of all cheques cashed, front and back, and cheques could easily be found by account or date.

International Marine's account at the First National Bank in Fort Lauderdale showed a steady flow of tens of thousands of dollars. One day, almost two years earlier, someone had withdrawn $50,000 in cash, ostensibly to pay workers of a company in the Bahamas. Stamler didn't believe there was any company in the Bahamas, he sensed the money was just being moved around. He tried to put himself in the shoes of a man walking out of a bank with $50,000 cash in his briefcase. "What would he do with it?" Stamler wondered after emerging from the First National Bank. "He'd put it into another bank," he answered himself. He surveyed the Fort Lauderdale skyline, such as it was, and noticed one building, higher than the rest, about a block away: the Fort Lauderdale National Bank. It was a good guess. Only a few minutes later he was being shown the records for a safety deposit box that had been opened in June 1972.

The signing authority on the box was shared between Harry Atkins, his wife, Elizabeth, and Daisy June Elliott, Ken Elliott's wife. Stamler had heard stories about Harry Atkins, a former Ontario Provincial Police constable based in the Hamilton area. Now living in Florida, Atkins seemed to be in business with Elliott, and doing well for himself. Until Atkins hooked up with Ken Elliott, the retired constable had had a running balance of about $800 each month in his chequing account. Afterward, his account ballooned to hundreds of thousands of dollars. Stamler thought Atkins was a key to the conspiracy but, being a former policeman, he knew better than to co-operate with Stamler, who was undeterred by Atkins' stance. Stamler thought he had enough evidence to gain convictions and was certain that whatever he missed Revenue Canada and the IRS would catch with their own prosecutions.

In the ensuing weeks, Stamler was able to match up cheques from the various companies with the deposits to Elliott's accounts. Although he didn't understand all the ins and outs of his case, he was sure he had nailed down a straightforward scheme involving almost $350,000 in illegal kickback payments from various companies to Elliott in his public role as a harbour commissioner. The evidence against Elliott was overwhelming, and Stamler was ready to bring forward his charges when he was presented with an unexpected twist. Stamler believed he had been operating deep in the world of business crime, but he'd been standing on a relatively shallow ledge and he was about to be pushed off. He had not appreciated the effect his investigation was having on Horace Rindress, the president of J. P. Porter and of Richelieu Dredging, who was petrified about the prospect of prison.

Stamler wanted to talk to Rindress, but when he tried to arrange a meeting in the weeks after his return from Florida, the call was returned by Morris Fish, Rindress's lawyer. His client wanted to talk to Stamler, Fish said, but he wanted to make a deal. Stamler wasn't in the mood. In addition to the kickbacks, he was sure there had been bid-rigging. He figured that J. P. Porter, McNamara Corp., and Canadian Dredge and Dock had planned their bids on Hamilton Harbour work, and he assumed the two losers were being paid a percentage of the profits for standing aside. He had the paper, he could prove it, end of exercise.

"It's not that simple," Fish told Stamler. "If you agree to talk to my client you'll find that this thing is much more complicated, and there are many more issues. This is just a drop in the bucket."

Stamler now had another decision to make. If the case was more complicated, it might only muddy the waters. On the other hand, "if the evidence is important and significant and it affects the evidence I have, I have to find out whether it's worthwhile, whether it's something bigger." Stamler told Fish he would get back to him.

Clay Powell, Ontario's chief Crown counsel and assistant deputy attorney-general, lived around the corner from Stamler in Bridlewood. Powell and Stamler had become close friends, and their proximity to each other served them well in the next months, especially as the eighty-hour weeks piled up both for them and for Crown prosecutor Rod McLeod.

Powell and Stamler agreed they had nothing to lose by talking with Fish, and although he wouldn't give them details when they met at the University Pub in downtown Toronto, Fish struck Stamler as being a straightforward, honest lawyer. Fish promised that his client would deliver information that might help the police go beyond Elliott, and might show them how the Hamilton Harbour contract illustrated the way the dredging industry dealt with other government contracts. Rindress intended to illustrate bid-rigging for the police, a puzzle Stamler had been prevented from completing in the *Irving Whale* investigation, and one to which he desperately wanted the answer.

Granting Rindress immunity, as a way of giving the police an entry point to investigating an otherwise undetectable crime, proved to be no problem for Ontario Attorney-General Roy McMurtry.* Stamler was not surprised. While the OPP seemed reluctant to muck around in political cases, the Mounties felt unhindered in their efforts to enforce federal statutes in the

---

* The Quebec Justice minister, on the other hand, would not grant Rindress immunity and charged him, Stamler thought, out of vindictiveness for embarrassing the province's élite, including Premier Bourassa's in-laws.

province. Stamler thought the relationship between the federal police and the Attorney-General's Office in Ontario was among the best in the country, one of the few places where the Mounties could do their job unimpeded by nosy politicians.

Rindress gave Stamler details on more than fifty instances of criminal acts in the dredging and salvaging industries. Across Canada and the United States, companies had colluded to rig prices and defraud governments and other clients out of millions of dollars. Rindress had even written this all down, because, as he told a court later, "I wanted to have a clear, legible, understandable scoresheet available in case of some future reconciliation, and, secondly, I was concerned about the possibility of an early death, and should that have happened, I wanted to leave behind some document which would clearly outline the extent of the situation in which I had been involved."

The dredging industry had been given inadvertent encouragement in its shady dealings by the 1965 Glassco Royal Commission on government reorganization. A key but little-appreciated recommendation of the commission was the virtual elimination of the Comptroller General. Under the old system an agent of the Comptroller General monitored all contracts and all spending. Glassco recommended that departments be given responsibility for their own spending, which effectively moved control over spending from the bureaucrats to the politicians. The recommendations were quickly approved and, in an instant, the Comptroller General was transformed to a rubber stamp. Accountability for spending was placed in the hands of the House of Commons, which could "perform its traditional function as custodian of the purse," while the Auditor-General was empowered to keep the politicians honest, as much as was possible after the spending had taken place.

In the Department of Transport, which let the huge dredging contracts, this new political control over spending was aggravated by a dearth of understanding about the dredging business.

Cliff Kennedy had told Stamler that when the private sector had taken over the dredging industry in the 1950s, the government had failed to set a benchmark price for such work. "It was a haphazard system in which government officials would estimate costs by looking at previous bids for comparable work, with no idea if the original prices were accurate reflections of the real cost," Kennedy said. "For example, if the government was contracting for the dredging of so many cubic yards, it would take last year's price and add five per cent for inflation. They had no idea what the real cost might have been."

Freed from the strict hand of the Comptroller General, Transport Department mandarins now found it all but impossible to resist political pressure in the awarding of government contracts, particularly when the pressure came from senators who were appointed to the Senate as a reward for their party fundraising efforts. Once there, the senators could exercise their influence without fear of interference by the police.

When Horace Rindress told Stamler about how, in the old days, cash payoffs had been made to politicians to guarantee contracts, and about how the money was passed through senators and into offshore bank accounts, Stamler knew what he was talking about, thanks to Kennedy. Using offshore banks allowed Canada's élite to avoid paying taxes. And it was the wealthy élite which Stamler now saw had the advantage of being able to block legislative reform and investigations by their control of the political process.

Rindress showed how the dredgers had split Canada along the Saskatchewan–Alberta border. Those on one side of the line would not compete against those on the other. Rindress was even able to explain the notations on the back of a business card belonging to Robert Schneider, president and general manager of Canadian Dredge and Dock, that had been found by the RCMP during one of its raids. It, too, was an impromptu list of "owesies" between various companies.

The owners of dredging and salvaging companies formed a neat, tightly knit club to which many of the country's highest rollers belonged, including Rindress's boss and Premier Robert Bourassa's cousin-in-law, Jean Simard of Laval-sur-le-Lac, Quebec, Harold McNamara and Sydney Cooper of Toronto, and Frank Hamata and Albert Gill of Montreal. Many were men of apparently impeccable character, which prosecutor Rod McLeod later pointed out was the main reason why they had got away with their crimes for so long. The scheme had worked extremely well, until the dredgers encountered Ken Elliott. The fast-talking harbour commissioner was aware of their illegal activities and talked them into a fifteen-per-cent personal kick-back. He had also offered to help them launder their money through his non-existent Swiss-based system. The con men had been conned.

Rindress and Stamler had one common interest above all – to have Ken Elliott corroborate his involvement in the wider scheme. Stamler persuaded Rindress to wear a hidden micro-phone and help the police make their case.

At the beginning of 1974, the people of Hamilton were getting edgy, wondering what had happened to the Hamilton Harbour investigation. Jokes abounded that, once again, another made-in-Hamilton miracle had taken place and the Mounties had been persuaded to lose interest. The investigators were said to have become part of a junior Musical Ride somewhere in northern Saskatchewan. In fact, the Mounties were working overtime on nailing first Elliott and his cohorts, then the dredging companies. The investigations were being conducted in tandem.

Corporal Gerry Grant and Constable John Banks were detailed to watch and record Elliott and Rindress, whom Elliott called by his nickname, Joe. Going from being a business executive to a snitch was an interesting experience for Rindress.

In April 1974, Elliott met with Rindress at Charleston, South Carolina, where Elliott was dismantling a submarine he had

purchased. The recorded conversation paints a wonderful portrait of Elliott's mind and his attitudes toward his pursuer,
Stamler. At one point, Elliott, in his own semi-illiterate and pro-
fane manner, talked to Rindress about those holding public
office:

"How come the whole fucken politicians are all the same?"
Elliott asked. "They've got everything of life and these assholes
think they're gonna nail me for any graft?"

"Well, I think you're right on that, but ah . . ."

Elliott cut Rindress off. "Well, there's no doubt in my mind."

"A very high percentage of these guys are on the take, but to
prove it is something else again, eh?" Rindress said, lobbing a
bomb to Elliott.

"That's right."

"It's funny, when they die, they all, they all end up with big
estates and yet only make $20,000 a year," Rindress continued,
leading Elliott on.

"You know what gets me?" Elliott asked. "Not so much in
Canada, Joe. But you know what gets me in the States? These sly
fuckers run for jobs like, like the Commissioner for Dade County.
It pays $22,000 a year. Now get this – $22,000 a year. I know. I
live in Hollywood."

"Yah?"

"And do you know how much his campaign was to get him
elected?"

"Hundred thousand, I suppose," Rindress guessed.

"Hundred thousand? Shit, a million and a quarter dollars."

"He's the top man, is he?" Rindress asked.

"Yah, he approves all building permits, all highrise permits.
You know, how fucken stupid can, gullible can, the courts and
public be – $22,000 a year – a two-year job for a million and a
quarter? Well, you're not that fucken stupid, are you?

"No," Rindress said.

Elliott went on to talk about laundering money in Las Vegas
by playing *chemin de fer* and appearing to be a big tipper. The

money moved around the table, in and out of the casino bank, and was scrubbed clean.

"Stamler's a prick," Elliott said at one point. "Be very cautious of him, Joe. Be very vague. Don't give too much detail. Make sure your lawyer's with you."

"Oh, you can be sure of that," Rindress said.

"If they ever had anything on me they would have had my ass long ago. Two years he's taken [actually it had been about ten months since Stamler had started]. He's got no more now than he had when he started. He's got odds and ends put together but nothing, he's got nothing but circumstantial. This could have happened, that could have happened. Who's to say you done the million yards dredging in the harbour? Who's to say you done it?"

"Well, he can go out and survey it today and find that, ah, the material is gone," Rindress replied.

"Who's to say the material was there in the first place?"

"DPW [Department of Public Works]. You got DPW surveys."

"Yeah, but they were five years old."

Elliott had taken an interesting gambit, which Rindress picked up the next day, in hinting that the entire dredging contract in Hamilton Harbour wasn't necessary, as Stamler had long suspected.

"We needed that like we needed two assholes, that job," Elliott said.

"The dredging job?" Rindress played on. "It wasn't urgent?"

"Come on, Joe. It wasn't needed."

"Well, I think it's gonna be needed in time, eh?"

"Don't con and play games with me. We had a thousand-foot channel there. [Why] the fuck did we need a five thousand? Don't bullshit with me, please."

"I swallowed, I swallowed your story on that," Rindress said. "I believed it. You mean, you mean it's not right?"

"No, it wasn't fucken needed," Elliott reiterated.

"Well, when the harbour headland went out that cuts into the old channel. Well, I'm stupid, uh, I never twigged to that."

"You're not stupid. You're, you're just trying to justify something you've done, that's all. . . . You believe in your own mind that it was justified. Well, it wasn't."

For the Mounties listening in, Elliott had just confirmed fraud against the government. Rindress kept talking about their mutual predicament, but Elliott was getting suspicious.

"You prick, you got no speakers on have you, eh?

"No, for Christ's sakes," Rindress assured him.

"Huh?"

"No shit, Ken. I'm, I'm upset about this."

In conversations over the next two days, Elliott assured Rindress that they were all safe. He had figured a way out – the income tax department. The revenuers in Hamilton were known to bend to political pressure and ease off the rich and powerful when called upon to do so.

"Six months ago, I went over everything," Elliott said at one point. "The worst it can be is taxes or nothing. The worst. What is there. . . . It's not gonna ruin my life. It's not going to upset me anymore. I nearly ate my ass out. I couldn't sleep. . . . The worst I can do is wind up with a fine and a conflict of interest, so they can criticize me in court and in the newspapers. . . . Joe, you haven't heard of anybody going to jail on income fraud."

Later, he corrected himself. "The only case I know of is Al Capone, and they sure as hell got him. That's why this Stamler's getting pissed off. He realizes now it's just a straight tax case. He's going to walk away from it sooner or later. . . . That's why I say, fuck it. As far as the political payoffs – they can kiss my ass. All he's after is political payoffs."

If he had to go to court, Elliott said, "I'll stuff it right up their fucken ass, Joe, and I don't give a shit if you got fifty lawyers in the fucken court. None of them is gonna tie me up because you know how fucken cool I am in that cage."

Stamler had better stop messing with him, Elliott told Rindress, adding that he was going to call Paul Martin and a few people in cabinet and get them to warn the Mountie: "You'll never get any higher than inspector. I realize you want to solve a case that doesn't exist, I don't blame you for that if you think it does, but you better go a different route."

Elliott dismissed Stamler's potential as a threat, saying, "There's no way he's going to get me. He's only an $8,000-a-year cowboy trying to make a name for himself."

Stamler chuckled about that one. Elliott had not only underestimated him, but also his income. His salary in 1974 was $21,700 a year.

Elliott was convinced that Stamler would soon move on to another case. That's what policing was all about – every officer juggling more than he could possibly handle. He didn't understand that Henry Jensen's Commercial Crime Branch officers had the time to conduct long, deep investigations.

Back in Hamilton a few weeks later, the Mounties fitted Rindress with a microphone inside the heel of his shoe, a move right out of the TV spy-spoof "Get Smart." The Mounties were on the verge of making their arrests, but Stamler wanted a last shot at linking the two other commissioners, Del Hickey and Joe Lanza, to Elliott's fraud. The police believed they were going to meet that night.

Elliott had grown wary of Rindress, so when they met that night at the Royal Connaught Hotel in Hamilton, Elliott told Rindress his plan that they both strip and go into the steam room. "There are some people I want you to meet," Elliott told Rindress. "This is one way we can be sure of having a conversation without being listened to. There can't be any bugs in there."

"I'm not worried about bugs, for heaven's sake. If you're concerned about that, search me," Rindress said opening his coat. "I just don't want to take my clothes off. This is a stupid idea."

Elliott relented, dressed, and the men went to a bar in the hotel where the popular Elliott introduced Rindress to a number of people, talking openly about the RCMP investigation and what a "waste of the taxpayer's money" it was. One of those who joined them was a Provincial Court judge. The judge told Rindress how much he hated the Mounties because they had once searched his house in an income tax case. At the time the judge's daughter was dying of leukemia and the Mounties were so callous they even tossed the little girl's bed while she was in it. Rindress sat with his legs crossed, the heel of his shoe pointed toward the judge's mouth, not two feet away, but the microphone had stopped working. The judge's allegations were quietly checked out by the Mounties, who had no record of any such investigation of the judge or such a search. They assumed that the judge was co-operating with Elliott in an attempt to scare Rindress away from the Mounties.

Two days after the failed "Get Smart" bugging attempt on Elliott, on May 30, 1974, Stamler laid his first of twelve fraud charges against the conspirators. Stamler wasn't present at the arrests. "My arrests aren't exciting," he later told a reporter. "My job is finished when I lay the charge, before the arrest is made." Those in Hamilton were called to the RCMP's offices on Hunter Street and charged there. Robert A. Henderson and Harry Atkins were in Florida at the time but returned to Canada when asked to do so.

The first stage of the Hamilton Harbour case, the charges against Harold Atkins, Robert A. Henderson, and Robert P. Henderson (a consultant and no relation to Robert A.), soon went to a preliminary hearing. Rindress and his prodigious memory were stars. The most stunning revelation was about George Kerr, who had been the Ontario Environment minister. The court was told that Kerr had asked for and received a $10,000 contribution to his 1971 election campaign, which was paid after the election. A witness claimed that Kerr had said "he could get the cash safely through a system." The court was told the reason Kerr wanted the money was to help him get over the annoyance of fending off environmentalists concerned about the filling in of waterlots and other dumping in the bay. At the time Rindress testified at the trial in the spring of 1975, Kerr was serving as solicitor-general – the top policeman in the province – and the Mounties had no problem executing a search warrant for his offices. Kerr denied the allegations but resigned his post immediately to allow for an investigation.

The Mounties weren't surprised when the OPP, which conducted the investigation, couldn't find any evidence of wrongdoing. Knowledgeable observers didn't call the OPP the Ontario Political Police for nothing; the OPP hadn't charged a sitting politician with a major offence in living memory.

Eventually, all the conspirators were convicted, with Elliott receiving the heaviest sentence, ten years in prison, but an unsolved aspect of the Elliott investigation bothered Stamler. It was evident that Elliott had handled almost $350,000 through his Florida account, but Stamler could not account for $137,000 which had been withdrawn in a lump sum. After he was charged, Elliott, wanting to bring everyone down with him, told Stamler that the money had arrived in Hamilton a few weeks prior to the federal election of October 30, 1972. Elliott said he gave the money to Joe Lanza, campaign manager of cabinet minister John Munro.

Stamler had come face to face with Munro twice during the investigation. The first time had been at Munro's constituency office, where Stamler had noticed that one corner of Munro's desktop was chewed and scarred.

"Inspector Stamler," Munro had said, "I demand to know who you are investigating and when your investigation will be completed." As he spoke, Munro pounded his fist on the desk, burying the school ring he wore on his pinky into the soft wood.

Stamler responded to what he took as an attempt at intimidation with a well-placed barb. "I couldn't tell you that, Mr. Munro, because you may well be a suspect in this case."

Munro calmed down and, for the rest of their meeting, appeared to co-operate with Stamler, but the Mountie remained doubtful about the politician, who took what Stamler liked to call the Paul Martin approach to answering questions – he rarely if ever answered the question he was asked. Stamler found that Munro had an unusual memory. "He could immediately recall the most innocuous events, the most obscure personalities, and his own minutest accomplishments, as if they had just happened. At the same time, Munro consistently drew blanks on anything that might potentially link him to controversy."

His second meeting with Munro gave Stamler another insight into the man. Stamler had been invited to meet the politician at a Barton Street East address, the home of a man nicknamed the Senator because of his hope that his friendship and support of the Liberals would someday make him one. The apartment was filled with Munro's hangers-on and go-fers, who created the impression of importance and business. Stamler suspected that Munro wanted them present to avoid being alone with the Mountie. The retinue whirled around Munro constantly: "The minister is in the other room. . . . Mr. Minister, telephone for you. . . . Would you like more ice in that, Mr. Minister?" Stamler left the meeting learning only that Munro was clearly a man of importance to these people.

Although he continued to be suspicious about the missing $137,000, Stamler ran out of leads and couldn't find its final resting place. The money had a two-year head start on him, and he couldn't catch up to it.

8

Pierre Trudeau and the Rule of Law

Through the trial of the dredging conspirators, Stamler's work caught the attention of the public and the politicians. As a result, he found it nearly impossible to conduct a widespread and controversial probe in such secrecy again. Now, the investigators were visiting choice Canadian neighbourhoods, where businessmen, political fundraisers, and other prominent politicians lived.

Everything Stamler and his colleagues did left a trail of headlines: the raid on Labour Minister John Munro's Hamilton office, the testimony about Ontario Solicitor-General George Kerr and his subsequent resignation, even the fact that the Mounties had seized enough documents in the dredging investigation to fill a ten-foot-square room.

In early 1975, rumours began to circulate that the Ontario Attorney-General's Office was about to lay criminal charges resulting from, as the *Toronto Star* said in a front-page story, "a massive fraud against the Canadian people." Fourteen businessmen and thirteen companies faced charges of defrauding public agencies of $4.73 million between 1969 and 1973. Stamler had gathered evidence in fifty cases based largely on the evidence of dredging executive Robert Schneider, who said he had been fraudulently billing for twenty-seven years. After a preliminary hearing, three men and four companies were discharged, and the Crown decided to prosecute only six offences and treat the rest as similar-fact evidence. Even in those six, the evidence would be so complex and difficult that the Crown feared it would lead to the longest jury trial in Canadian history.

Those prosecuted included Jean Simard, the dredging magnate, and Gérard Filion, a Companion of the Order of Canada. John Munro had not been arrested, even though many Canadians, primed by news reports, expected him to be prosecuted. For almost a year, the opposition parties had used Question Period to pound at Munro, who had revealed his patronage system in the pages of the *Globe and Mail* for all to see. Under pressure, Munro tended to break into a sweat and bluster like a cartoon character, which, of course, made him all the more appealing a target for the Opposition's barbs.

Trudeau's government could not be toppled over the issue, but the talk of corruption infecting its inner circles was a serious matter.

One late spring day in 1975, Stamler was called to RCMP headquarters in Ottawa to brief D. R. Ross, the deputy commissioner of operations, ostensibly about the politically sensitive cases he had investigated. It was an unusual procedure, the first time Stamler had been ordered to account for his work. Stamler and his colleagues believed that reporting the details of their findings to their superiors was cause for concern, as the closer the information got to the top of the force, the nearer it came to the force's political masters. Stamler resolved to talk only in generalities and not to let slip any evidence that should be revealed only in a court of law. But the meeting with the deputy commissioner was over almost before it had begun. Ross simply told Stamler to go with him to the parliamentary offices of Warren Allmand, the federal solicitor-general. Stamler assumed the issue would be what the police planned to do with Munro.

Stamler was determined to stand his ground should anyone attempt to apply political pressure at the meeting with Ross and Allmand. Allmand himself had been under attack during the past year, as the Opposition questioned him rigorously over police activities, especially illegal wiretapping.

Introductions taken care of, the diminutive Allmand ushered the two Mounties out of his office in the Centre Block, along the corridors of the second floor, through a series of offices, and then into an oak-panelled and serenely elegant room. There stood Prime Minister Pierre Elliott Trudeau, dressed in an open-collared beige safari suit. Allmand introduced the three men, who shook hands. Stamler took a moment to look around and noticed a small statuette of a Mountie in dress uniform astride a horse. Stamler wondered for a brief moment if the statuette was some vile portent of his future. Then Trudeau moved behind his desk and sat down. Allmand and the two Mounties took the chairs lined up in front of the desk.

Stamler was more on guard than he ever had been. Like most policemen, he thought that Trudeau possessed more style than substance, that he was a master of illusion, too iconoclastic, too liberal, too unbusiness-like, and with too-long hair. Worst of all, his government was probably corrupt.

When Trudeau spoke, he had no questions, nor did he mention any cabinet minister by name. "I am not interested in the details of your investigation, Inspector Stamler, how it is going, how quickly you might be proceeding, or how difficult it might be. If you have any problems within the government because of the involvement of a minister, I would expect that minister to co-operate with you fully, to the extent of their official position in cabinet."

Then Trudeau, a former law professor, described the relationship between police and government as he saw it, touching every base, recognizing every position of power, outlining everyone's responsibilities – the separate roles of the police, the courts, and the political process. "We have a duty and a responsibility to ensure that the criminal justice process is carried out without interference and without any influence being put on any investigator or investigative process," Trudeau said. "That has to be continued above all, and we want to ensure that this is done in terms of everyone in this government, me, the solicitor-general, the deputy commissioner, and all who might be concerned with the legal process."

Stamler was immeasurably relieved to learn that Trudeau was on the same side of the law as the Mounties. "I have the responsibility as the prime minister to appoint cabinet ministers to positions of power and influence, and I am very concerned about the integrity of my cabinet and that someone might have improperly used their power. If I am made aware that such has occurred, I will take immediate action."

The prime minister clearly was looking for assistance as he wrestled with how to deal with the problem of Munro. A cabinet shuffle was due, and Stamler was under the impression that Trudeau wanted to make his decision on Munro's future in a knowledgeable fashion. Trudeau clearly intended not to prevent a prosecution but to prevent a crime.

Stamler responded by outlining the missing links in the Hamilton Harbour case, particularly the $137,000 in cash that he couldn't trace, the allegations about possible illegal political contributions to the Munro campaign, and his concerns about the harbour commissioners. They had been interviewed by Stamler, and each had declared he had never seen the money. Therefore, Stamler told Trudeau, the police could find no evidence of any criminal activity by Munro.

When the meeting broke up forty-five minutes later, Stamler left the prime minister's office with an entirely different impression of Trudeau than he had held less than an hour before. The prime minister truly was a magus, Stamler thought, one who had played his hand brilliantly and entirely within the law. "It was a perfect meeting," Stamler recalls. "Trudeau told us that if we had to lay a charge against anybody, that we should lay the charge, and that he would react accordingly. I felt proud to have a leader of the country who so strongly believed in the importance of preserving the integrity of the Canadian criminal justice system. It was clear to me that he would never interfere with any police investigation, no matter how sensitive it might become."

Stamler also thought that the fact Trudeau felt compelled to define the legal relationship between police and government in the meeting was a shrewd and deliberate comment on his disappointment over the increasing number of calls for greater political intervention in policing. Trudeau was not alone at the time in worrying about the long-term negative effects of such "progress." Ontario Attorney-General Roy McMurtry was also concerned about political interference in the judicial process and the importance of adherence to the rule of law for the well-being of all Canadians. "Fundamental to our system of law enforcement is that the police are independent of any direct political control," McMurtry told a gathering of police chiefs in 1975. "They are not the servants of individual ministers of the Crown or even of the government as a whole. The police are not errand boys for the prosecuting attorney."

McMurtry went on to quote the great English jurist, Lord Denning, who stated with reference to the office of the Commissioner of Police of the Metropolis of London: "I have no hesitation in holding that, like every constable in the land, he should be, and is, independent of the executive. . . . It is the duty of the Commissioner of Police of the Metropolis, as it is of every chief constable, to enforce the law of the land. He must take steps so to post his men that crimes may be detected; and that honest citizens may go about their affairs in peace. He must decide whether or not suspected persons are to be prosecuted; and, if need be, bring the prosecution or see that it is brought. But in all these things he is not the servant of anyone, save of the law, itself."

Stamler would always hold McMurtry, now chief justice of the Ontario Court, General Division, along with Trudeau, in the highest regard.

Stamler's meeting with Trudeau led him to conclude that, while the prime minister possessed integrity and wisdom, he was probably surrounded by dozens of knaves who were decidedly less pure.

In the House of Commons Trudeau continued his staunch defence of Munro, but Transport Minister Jean Marchand moved quickly to fire Hickey and Lanza from their posts on the Harbour Commission, citing suspicions about their ethics and conduct.

Munro, undeterred by the controversy, went on record just before the axe fell on Hickey and Lanza, telling a newspaper reporter that there "has never been any doubt on my part with respect to the competence and integrity of Del Hickey and Joe Lanza on the Hamilton Harbour Commission."

Hickey was replaced by another Liberal who was close to Munro, but there were no more controversies in Hamilton Harbour.

9

Making Political Enemies
Across the Country

Commanded from headquarters by Henry Jensen, now a rising star in the force, commercial-crime investigators across the country in the early 1970s had been just as busy as Rod Stamler.

One case, investigated by Inspector Don Docker and Sergeant Frank Kobie, involved Churchill Forest Industries at The Pas, Manitoba. Successive governments had ordered the Manitoba Development Corporation to begin a major project in the north, as Docker put it, "yesterday." The development corporation had finally proceeded with such reckless abandon it was soon snared by a gang of international fraud artists, led by Alexander Kasser and Oscar Reiser. The Manitoba government advanced $100-million in loans and lost at least $87 million, a considerable embarrassment to the provincial government. The same gang tried to work its magic in a similar scam in Saskatchewan, but Docker and Kobie were able to stop them before taxpayers there lost their shirts, too.

Mountie investigators Sandy McGibbon, Norm Doucette, and Chris Sampson were active in Quebec and Newfoundland. For twenty years, the scent of corruption had clung to Canadian Javelin, a Quebec-based company operated by financier John C. Doyle, who was close to Newfoundland's provincial government headed by Premier Joseph Smallwood. Finally, in 1973, the Mounties arrested Doyle.

The investigation into Doyle had begun almost at the moment Smallwood was humiliated at the polls on March 24, 1972. It took McGibbon and Sampson twenty months to cut through Doyle's misdirections, lies, half-truths, and cooked books, but the Mounties eventually found enough to charge Doyle and a government official with fraud involving the transfer of $540,000 in Canadian Javelin stock.

The official, Oliver Vardy, was the former deputy minister of Economic Development and a Smallwood confidant. Vardy faced three charges of breach of trust, two of fraud, and two of accepting bribes totalling more than $200,000. A Montreal businessman and associate of Doyle's was also charged in the case.

From the beginning of his years in power, Smallwood promised to spend money to make money for Newfoundland through the creation of new industries and factories. He wanted to bring full-time, high-paying jobs to a region that had suffered too long for its dependency on the fishing industry.

Vardy's arrest wasn't the first. In 1954, one of his predecessors in the Economic Development Department, Dr. Alfred Valdmanis, had been in trouble with the law. Valdmanis, another Smallwood confidant, was charged with fraud for extorting large sums of money from various firms he had dealt with on behalf of the provincial government. Although there were strong suspicions about Smallwood's involvement with Valdmanis, there was no further police investigation.

However, the close relationship between Smallwood and John C. Doyle was carefully watched by the police. In 1953,

Smallwood had embarked on a program to privatize the New-foundland and Labrador Corporation, which Smallwood had envisioned might someday become the modern equivalent of the Hudson's Bay Company or the East India Company. More than eighty per cent of the shares in the Newfoundland and Labrador Corp. were purchased by the little-known Canadian Javelin Foundries and Machine Works Ltd. of Joliette, Quebec. Mining promoter Doyle planned to manufacture a new type of coal-burning stove and cooking utensils.

Doyle soon abandoned his rather modest plans for Javelin when he learned that Smallwood had bigger plans for New-foundland. For a down payment of $2,500, Doyle obtained mineral leases on 5,000 square miles of land, paying the remaining $789,000 later. Javelin was turned into a holding company for the leases. Eventually, with Smallwood's blessing, Doyle controlled 30,000 square miles of mineral concessions, which were estimated to contain 2.5 billion tons of iron ore and $170-million worth of timber. In Smallwood's eyes, the fact that Doyle had been handed incredible booty was secondary to the dream that he would make everyone in Newfoundland rich. "I would make a deal with the devil himself, if it were for the good of Newfoundland," Smallwood said, announcing the government's deal with Doyle.

Shortly after that announcement, Javelin shares on the Toronto and Montreal exchanges soared from $2.25 to $10.75 before falling back to $5.75. The immediate suspicion among stock market watchers was that the devil had done his business; that Doyle had pumped up the stock, lured innocent but greedy marks to the scam, let them in at the top price, taken his profits, and then let the price collapse – a classic stock manipulation. Security commission regulators moved in and temporarily delisted the Javelin stock, but long after the victims had been fleeced.

In spite of Javelin's notoriety, Smallwood remained undeterred in his support for Doyle. A year later, Smallwood's government backed Doyle's development plans with a $16.5-billion bond issue, a sum that equalled half the total provincial debt. In the debate over the bond guarantee, Smallwood lauded Doyle and claimed, among other things, that the Société de Banque Suisse had invested $4.8 million in the venture. The Swiss bankers immediately pointed out that it was not they who had put up the money, but an unnamed investor. The bank did not disclose that the investor was Doyle himself.

When U.S. authorities began investigating Doyle, Smallwood defended him, going as far as attempting to lobby U.S. Attorney-General Robert F. Kennedy to halt the court proceedings. Kennedy rebuffed Smallwood. In 1964, Doyle was convicted in the United States of securities fraud and sentenced to three months in jail. He jumped bail and fled to Canada, never to return to the United States. When the heat was turned up in Canada, Doyle slipped out of the country to Panama. In Canada, the Restrictive Trade Practices Commission charged Doyle with five counts of orchestrating a series of deals during the 1960s and 1970s that allegedly defrauded Javelin shareholders of $10 million. Smallwood was named an accomplice. In 1983, the commission upheld four of the five charges against Doyle, charges that were overturned on technicalities in 1985 by the Federal Court.

That year, the most damning insight into the close, hidden relationship between Doyle and Smallwood, which had been suppressed for thirteen years, came to light. On June 12, an unusual court hearing took place. The Quebec Superior Court had sent a special rogatory commission to Panama to gather evidence from Doyle regarding the Canadian Javelin fraud. At the hearing, a federal government lawyer revealed that during the 1972 raid on Doyle's Montreal apartment, the Mounties had found a "payoff list" in a suitcase. Listed were $375,000 each for Smallwood and former Newfoundland attorney-general L. R. Curtis. The Mounties were convinced that the payoffs had been made, but found it impossible to trace the flow of the money through Doyle's many foreign bank accounts.

After Smallwood had been forced out of power in 1972, the political appetite to mount a full-fledged investigation against him, the last living father of Confederation, had subsided, and the investigation had been dropped.

In the fall of 1974, the Mounties became entangled in New Brunswick. The Mounties charged J. C. Van Horne, the former minister of Tourism, with accepting "rewards" for exercising influence on behalf of parties doing business with the government. The government of Premier Richard Hatfield was not happy about the Mounties' work and said as much.

The newspapers were no help. Anywhere else the case might have been a sensation, but in New Brunswick, where the Irving and McCain families dominated the economy and the Irvings controlled all the English-language dailies, the papers were not interested in investigative reporting.

But then along came *Financial Post* reporter Philip Mathias, who had just finished reporting on a scandal involving Ontario Hydro which narrowly missed, by a grey hair or two, ensnaring Premier William Davis. Mathias dug deep beneath the surface of the Van Horne case. Mathias wrote a front-page story, published November 6, 1974, which created three years of headaches for the Mounties and political turmoil for even longer.

Mathias found twenty examples of political improprieties in New Brunswick. Some were conflicts of interest and cases of favouritism, but others were more serious. Mathias wrote that he had found strong indications that members of the government were systematically receiving kickbacks of between two and ten per cent of the value of a contract. The kickbacks were paid in cash to a slush fund held by the ruling Progressive Conservative Party and to the federal Liberal Party, Mathias reported, through a network run by Senator Nelson Rattenbury, who died just before the story was published.

Mathias struck a nerve in his description of the relationship between the Mounties and the provincial government. He wrote that senior New Brunswick-based RCMP officers submitted to political pressure for fear of losing the provincial policing contract. In doing so they had politicized the policing function and had implicitly, by giving up their independence, defeated the rule of law. In short, money talked while ethics walked.

Mathias concluded his stunning story by showing how the Mounties had pursued the Van Horne investigation vigorously, but had let all other cases slip by the wayside.

Henry Jensen knew Mathias was absolutely correct in his observations. It was as if the law that everyone is entitled to unimpeded access to the justice system didn't apply in New Brunswick. "Hatfield did everything he could to impede the investigation," Jensen says. "The Hatfield government set up a procedure whereby justices of the peace could not hear an information unless the charges were approved by one of the Justice Department's prosecutors. The next step they took was that the police could not get a search warrant unless it was initialled by the prosecutor as well." There were and are no provisions in Canadian law for such actions.

Jensen suspected that there was a dual purpose to the rigging of New Brunswick's rules. "First they wanted to impede the investigation but, secondly, and more importantly, I believe the system was designed to find out what the police were doing and to relay the information back to the political people, who ought not to have the information. To me, that was an extremely corrupt process."

On March 3, 1977, three years after Mathias's story, New Brunswick Liberal leader Robert Higgins rose in the Legislature and outlined how the kickback system worked in the province, dating back to a 1972 meeting between Hatfield and other key Conservatives. Higgins added: "The RCMP in the province became aware of these activities. I am informed and believe that as early as 1973, the Department of Justice of New Brunswick attempted to thwart investigation into financing of the Progressive Conservative Party. I am informed that a meeting took place in 1973 between the Department of Justice and senior officials of the RCMP. As a result of this meeting the investigators were instructed by their superior not to pursue investigation into Progressive Conservative financing."

Hatfield responded by kicking up clouds of dust to obscure the sleight-of-hand to come. He set up a judicial inquiry headed by Chief Justice C. J. A. Hughes. From its outset the commission seemed designed to rebut Higgins's allegations rather than to get at the truth. Mr. Justice Hughes was asked to investigate only the charges that the Department of Justice had interfered with certain police and court proceedings as early as 1973. There would be no investigation of the kickback scheme. Hatfield announced the inquiry in a windy, thirty-eight-page speech filled with mock outrage and personal attacks on Higgins, whom he accused, among other things, of "insinuation, implication, and innuendo."

The shameless Hatfield even went so far as to state that Higgins was trying to "short-circuit" current police investigations, "bypass the process of justice, and remove the right of those who might be charged – if any are charged – to a fair trial."

In January 1978, Hughes issued a 140-page report totally exonerating the Hatfield government and forcing Higgins's resignation. The result came as no surprise to the Mounties. Later that year, Higgins was appointed a judge of the County Court of New Brunswick.

Hatfield waged war against the Mounties for the rest of his political career. In 1976, Hatfield hatched a plan to replace the Mounties with his own provincial police force, which would be more compliant. The first step was the creation in 1980 of the New Brunswick Highway Patrol, which began to replace the Mounties on all the province's highways, leaving only criminal investigations to the Horsemen. Hatfield, of course, at the time denied in public that it was all part of a vendetta against the Mounties.

The New Brunswick investigation was a humbling and distressing experience for Henry Jensen and his fellow Mounties. An underlying assumption of their work was that Canadian institutions were sound, but the Mounties were beginning to see that there was disturbing evidence to the contrary. They had never before thought of just how many powerful enemies they would make while in pursuit of their lawful duties.

Meanwhile, in 1975, Stamler was chasing down the dredging-business conspirators and, unknowingly, heading into deeper political controversy. Following the numerous leads from the Hamilton Harbour investigation was like being lost in an underground mine, Stamler thought. It was as if he were feeling his way along the walls trying to find the light, while every so often coming across a smaller, interesting passage that might lead somewhere else. "I had to be disciplined enough to stay the course and stick to the main tunnel," he says. Even so, Stamler spun off many cases to the tax department, which was only too happy to have solid leads land in its lap.

A 1973 diary kept by dredging executive Harold McNamara, seized during a raid, had provided the Mounties with insight into the value of political influence to business, and into how it was secured, particularly in Quebec. (McNamara misspelled Camu's and Filion's names, and like many Quebecers, called the premier "Prime Minister" or "P.M.")

> August 12: Left for Quebec in the morning with JSB attending official opening of North Channel job in afternoon. Marchand, Gerard Levesque (Quebec Minister of Commerce), Pierre Camus and Gerard Fillion handled politics.
> August 13: Spent morning in offices of Highway

Department where learned we are not being recommended on Seven Islands work – 'Not a Quebec company.' Left Forget to find out what stage recommendation rests and returned to Toronto. Called Bourne who spoke to Deputy Minister Rouleau. On his advice called Rouleau myself.

August 16: . . . People contacted in Quebec and Montreal: Peter Daigle (had lunch with him and Forget), Rene Hebert (very high party man), Paul Desrochers (Prime Minister's right hand), Guy Bernier (#1 collector and PM's cousin).

August 23: To Montreal with letter for Bourassa (Quebec P.M.) which delivered through Guy Bernier, president of the Quebec Liberal Party. Received much sympathy and his assurance he would deliver letter to Bourassa and further would argue the merits.

August 26: . . . P.M. Bourassa of Quebec phoned with lengthy apologetic explanation of reasons why we lost Seven Islands job. Result was it has already gone to Simard–Beaudry but he will make sure it doesn't happen again.

August 30: Lunch with Bill Kelly for discussion of (Ontario) Conservative Party needs in forthcoming election. He is No. 1 collector and forecasts early election.

Stamler passed the information about Bourassa's possible involvement on to the Quebec provincial police, whom he also briefed about the case. It was the last he ever heard about it.

McNamara had also written in his diary about Nova Scotia Premier Gerald Regan and the former Liberal Party president, Senator John Connolly. Connolly had served as a cabinet minister under Pearson, and was now one of the Liberal Party's chief fundraisers. McNamara's diary talked about a proposed government contract at Mulgrave, Nova Scotia.

March 23: . . . summing up, it has been suggested to Moore we might help out in drive for new hockey rink in Regan's area. Moore will bring down small donation (5 grand). Called John Connolly and tracked him down in Toronto. He will call Regan Monday and tell him what good Liberals we are & how good to build Mulgrave. Will then call me back. Wouldn't be a bad idea to go & see Regan, I believe.

Stamler passed on the information about Regan to the RCMP in Nova Scotia, but never heard back from them either. Regan was never charged, and when the evidence from the diaries came out during McNamara's trial in 1978, Regan said he had no record of talking with Connolly nor did he think McNamara's company had contributed money to the Mulgrave arena project.

In Ontario, Stamler turned leads over to the OPP. Charges were never instituted.

There was one thread of investigation Stamler kept for himself. In his search of Marine Industries in Montreal, Stamler noticed that the company had sold its headquarters on St. Catherine Street West in March 1971. The listed sale price was $2,066,000 and all the papers seemed in order, but Stamler came across a couple of cancelled cheques that didn't fit with the other evidence. One was for $40,000. His experience taught him that crooks usually took care in handling extraordinary sums of money, but tended to be sloppy in dealing with relatively small amounts, such as $40,000. Huge caches of gold often could be found by following the trail of the occasional nugget or two.

Subsequently, Stamler was told by an informant that the building's sale price had been overstated in the official records by about $540,000. Most of the extra money – $500,000 – had been shipped offshore to an account in Bermuda. Stamler later swore in an affidavit in the Ontario Supreme Court that this half-million dollars was "for the purpose of payments to Government officials for the receipt of confidential information in respect of pending Government contracts." The Bermuda account was an undetectable political slush fund designed to be operated out of the sight of Canadian police and tax officials.

It took three trips to Bermuda by Stamler and Ontario Crown prosecutor Rod McLeod before they gained access to the bank's records. Once they did, they discovered the money had rested temporarily in an account in the name of Carolus International, set up four years earlier in Bermuda. Ownership was distributed among six Simard family groups, each of which held 5,000 shares. According to a reference letter used to open the account, the family members had combined net assets of $50 million.

The investigators soon learned that some of the $500,000 had been shipped through Miami to Switzerland, and the extra $40,000 had been paid as "commission" to a Montreal man. A chunk of the $500,000 had gone to someone operating a Canadian foreign-aid project in Africa, a lead which the Mounties didn't pursue. Once again, the money had moved faster than the police, coming out clean somewhere via an efficient laundry operation. The best Stamler could do was turn the case over to the tax department.

While working on the dredging case, Stamler was handed a lead to another case involving apparent irregularities in a leasing agreement with the federal government for a duty-free shop at Dorval airport in Montreal. The company, Sky Shops Exports, already held the duty-free concession at Montreal's new second airport, Mirabel, and at the Saint John, New Brunswick, airport. At first, it seemed to be a minor matter, almost insignificant when compared to other controversial public works in Montreal – Mirabel itself and the construction of facilities for the 1976 Olympic Games. The newspapers – especially the *Globe and Mail* – were full of horror stories about cost overruns and loose tendering procedures, but the Liberal government remained unconcerned, or so it seemed.

Stamler had no time to think about Mirabel and the Olympic

Stadium, and anyway, the Montreal police had jurisdiction. But he considered Sky Shops his own because it had evolved out of one of his investigations, and Henry Jensen agreed with him. Stamler poked away at the investigation at the same time as he was busy preparing for the trials in the Hamilton Harbour and dredging cases. As he gathered information about those cases, he would casually slip in a reference to Sky Shops, which earned him a few more leads, and his best source, a well-respected Montreal lawyer.

At their key meeting, Stamler popped open his briefcase and pulled out his notebook, but didn't write down much. The Montreal lawyer talked into the hidden tape recorder, laying out his secret life as an agent for the Security Service inside the Liberal Party. Stamler, already concerned about what was happening to the ss under its new civilian leadership, was alarmed that in the name of combating Quebec nationalist aspirations and possible subversive activities, the ss was planting spies everywhere.

Stamler's informant knew intimately the history of political corruption in Quebec. He knew dates, times, people. He told Stamler that the Hamilton Harbour and dredging scams were only fragments of the whole story. He also said that he was disgusted by the rampant corruption and wanted to do something about it. He had even gone to the Mounties in Montreal in 1974, but the officer in charge had just yawned and turned him away. Now that Stamler was making headway and seemed to have the proper mandate, he had decided to meet with him.

Stamler put Sky Shops on his long "must do" list, but hurriedly moved it to the top when, on November 3, 1975, Tory Transport critic Elmer MacKay rose in the House of Commons under a little-used procedure known as a petition. MacKay's previous criticisms of the bloated $600-million Mirabel airport deal had attracted the attention of a former Sky Shops principal who was miffed about the way the company was being operated and had gone to MacKay with his story. When the story checked out, MacKay brought it to the floor of the Commons where he demanded a police investigation and a public inquiry into the tendering of the lease for the duty-free shop at Dorval airport. MacKay revealed what Stamler already knew: Senator Louis de Gonzague Giguère was suspected of having lobbied the government to extend the lease to Sky Shops, which was about to be sold to a larger company. The lease extension had driven the value of Sky Shops stock to $20 a share. The key to the crime, MacKay said, was that the Sky Shops board of directors had quietly voted 5,000 shares of stock to Giguère at a dollar a share. Giguère turned around and sold the shares a short time afterward, realizing a profit of $95,000.

The case was hot for three reasons. First, Senator Giguère was the Liberal Party's key fundraiser in Quebec. His friends called him Bob, but his nickname was *L'Aspirateur* – the vacuum cleaner; legend had it that he could scoop up a buck at fifty yards. He had helped raise money for Trudeau's leadership campaign. Trudeau had dated his daughter, Diane. Five months after becoming prime minister, Trudeau's first appointee to the Senate, the country's most sought-after sinecure, was Giguère. Second, the airport deal was ultimately the responsibility of the minister of Transport, who at the time of the deal had been Jean Marchand, Quebec leader of the Liberal Party, and Marchand's executive assistant was suspected of having been the go-between in the Sky Shops deal. Third, Giguère was known to be a business associate of the Simards.

The shot by MacKay was like the one fired by the German battleship *Bismarck* to sink the British battleship *Hood* – down the smokestack, right into the engine room. Giguère did what many a politician does in a similar situation; he rose in the Senate and set out his version of the truth:

The story is quite different when one knows all the facts. In December 1969 or January 1970, the chairman of the board of the company, Sky Shops, who is a good friend of mine, offered me an option to buy 5,000 shares of the company at one dollar per share, which was the price paid by all other shareholders. About two years later – in December 1971 or January 1972 – the matter was discussed between us again, and when he reiterated his offer I agreed to buy 5,000 shares at one dollar per share ... I then forgot the whole affair until I was told in November 1972 that a company, Lawson Travel Agency, had offered to purchase all 119,000 shares of Sky Shops at twenty dollars per share. All the shareholders decided to accept this offer, as did I. I later reported the transaction in my income tax return and paid the required taxes.

Giguère went on to deny he was in conflict of interest, or that he had lobbied the government. As earnest and forthright as Giguère appeared to be, there was one big problem with his story – it was an outright lie. In December 1969 and January 1970, the shares of Sky Shops had sold at an average price of $12.50 each, not one dollar, and no one in the Sky Shops company could find any record of the offer he claimed had been made to him.

The Opposition could smell a kill, maybe even of the prime minister himself. The Liberals were already reeling from other scandals. One of them was the so-called Judges Affair, in which André Ouellet was forced to resign from cabinet after being found in contempt of court, a political mistake compounded when another minister, Bud Drury, called a judge on Ouellet's behalf. In a second scandal, Air Canada chairman Yves Pratte had resigned after a two-month-long judicial inquiry that had uncovered highly questionable business practices within the publicly owned carrier. The cumulative damage was so great to the Liberals that, in Parliament, Trudeau was reduced to calling Opposition members "hyenas" and "donkeys." The new Transport minister, Otto Lang, said MacKay was not "doing the country a service" by denying him a chance to check out the allegations before making them in the House.

Marchand kicked up his own dust, charging in a *Maclean's* article that the media purposely sought out wrongdoing by French Canadians. "It's partly a prejudice against French Canadians. It might also be political," Marchand said. "If you want to destroy the Liberal Party, if you don't believe in it, and it's your right not to believe in the party, of course – Quebec is where you have to hit. At the same time, the implication is that they hit us because we are French Canadians, not because we are Liberals."

When Stamler learned about MacKay's allegations, he told his superiors, "We've got to move right away and do the searches, otherwise the documents and evidence will be gone." The Senate was talking about conducting its own investigation, so Stamler had to move quickly to beat them to the documents. Within two days he had drawn up meticulous requests for search warrants and had sworn them before a Montreal justice of the peace, Cyrille Morand.

Stamler's team of investigators raided Giguère's Senate office, Jean Marchand's parliamentary office, and the offices of those businessmen and lawyers involved in the Sky Shops deal, all of which was duly noted in the press.

Later, the press named the others caught up in the investigation: National Hockey League president Clarence Campbell; leading Montreal businessman Louis Lapointe; Gordon G. Brown, a wealthy businessman from Freeport, Bahamas; and James Lavery of Toronto. It was another sensational story in an era of sensational stories.

Stamler quickly learned that Louis Giguère was, to borrow baseball player Reggie Jackson's words, "the straw that stirs the drink" in Liberal fundraising circles. He had also worked closely with Marchand in awarding Transport Department contracts. The Transport Department was one of the government's biggest piggy banks, and Giguère had proven he could deliver Transport business to his top-drawer friends, for a price. Stamler learned that Giguère, Marchand, and Sky Shops executive Louis

Lapointe had golfed together a couple of times at the exclusive Indian Creek Country Club near Miami – important evidence for the conspiracy case that Stamler was trying to prove. Stamler also knew that Giguère was a partner in an advertising agency that had won lucrative federal government contracts, and he had been told that Giguère received kickbacks from all federal government consulting contracts awarded in Quebec.

One document that caught Stamler's eye was for consulting work at Mirabel. An untendered contract for $12,167,000 had been increased to $19,414,500 and then to $24 million. The principals of the company were linked closely to Giguère. The senator was also suspected of laundering kickback money by investing it in a $50-million Miami real estate project together with nine other partners who cut a wide swath across Montreal's anglophone business community. The scheme sounded a lot like the one used by Ken Elliott in Hamilton, but Stamler couldn't find a conclusive link between Elliott and Giguère.

In Ottawa, Stamler's informant, the Montreal lawyer, said, Giguère was bribing public servants responsible for selecting consultants and preparing contracts. According to the informant, the senator supplied these public servants with a short list of individuals and companies to be awarded contracts.

Stamler also learned that Giguère had collected $55,000 from some of Montreal's top companies ostensibly to help the Liberal Party fight Quebec separatists. Power Corporation, Distillers Corporation, Canadian Pacific, the Royal Bank, and the Bank of Montreal had each donated $10,000, and Steinberg's had given $5,000 to the cause. Much of the money had somehow been diverted into Giguère's personal bank account.

Almost every search and every interview the Mounties conducted resulted in more leads. In Giguère's office the Mounties found a letter from an architect which explained the accompanying cheques of $2,000 and $1,000 respectively made out to Giguère's and Jean Marchand's campaigns: "We have just received from The Canadian International Development Agency confirmation of our employment for the technical school project in Zinder. . . . It will be in the order of $1.8 million to $2 million. It is our pleasure to co-operate in your electoral campaign. . . . It is well understood that our contribution will be completed as soon as we know the size of this project."

Stamler found that SNC, the huge Quebec-based engineering conglomerate, had spent $2 million for unidentified purposes from a special bank account. All he knew was that the company was working through the Canadian International Development Agency on a project in Turkey. Stamler was told that there was collusion between the CIDA and SNC to jack up the price of the project and, thereby, raise money to pay for the necessary bribes and to meet other hidden costs. Some of the money had gone to Turkey via the bank accounts of a respected and established British company involved in the manufacture of chemicals, drugs, and medicines. The British company had no other apparent involvement in Turkey.

Stamler had tumbled into the case of a lifetime – he had exposed the soft underbelly of political corruption in Quebec.

The Mounties had a search warrant for Marchand's parliamentary office, but Marchand told them there was no need for them to execute it; he agreed to turn all his files over to the force. In them, the Mounties found correspondence showing how the little world of Quebec politics worked. One example was a letter in French dated January 29, 1971, from André Montpetit, a prominent Quebec judge, saying he would appreciate it if Marchand could find work at the new Montreal airport for the engineering firm operated by his brother, Guy, and Guy's son, Jacques. The Montpetit firm had already been awarded business with the government in previous years, but the judge felt the company could handle more. In May 1972, Judge Montpetit dropped another brief note to Marchand politely asking him to find more work for his brother's firm. It was the second letter Marchand received that month lobbying for the Montpetits. The first had come a few weeks earlier from Aurélien Noël, the MP for Outremont.

Marchand had come to Ottawa with Trudeau and Gérard Pelletier in 1965 as one of the so-called three wise men. He was committed to the cause of Quebec and the improvement of the lot of French Canadians, but time and exposure to the public had shown him to be scatterbrained, disorganized, and much too fond of alcohol. Stamler had been warned that Marchand was corrupt, but the charge had been impossible to prove. If Marchand was corrupt, Stamler concluded, it wasn't intentionally so; he really just didn't understand how the political process should be properly financed. "People were always shoving money into his pockets, actual cash, and he wouldn't even notice who did it. He would spend it and go on with life. There was no sense of returning favours. Marchand had grown up with it in Duplessis's Quebec and just figured that was the way politics worked," Stamler says. "He never kept a record of anything. He had no idea how much being a politician cost or how much he spent."

Marchand had co-operated with the Mounties' raid, Stamler believed, because he had no appreciation that they might find evidence of wrongdoing. In fact, Marchand knew few details about anything for which he was responsible. He delegated everything and trusted his underlings implicitly, Stamler found. When someone such as Louis Giguère came to him asking for something, Marchand wouldn't even bother to listen; he would just tell him to see his executive assistant. Giguère would then tell the executive assistant that Marchand had already agreed to meet Giguère's demands.

The raids had gone well from the Mounties' point of view, but then Marchand pulled a fast one. Almost as soon as the Mounties had left his office, he learned about the gravity of the situation. He began complaining far and loud about the Mounties' behaviour, trying to obscure their objectives in a whirlwind of rhetoric. Marchand charged that the Mounties had taken cabinet documents: "I don't think police should believe they are king in the country," he said.

Marchand accused the force of deliberately using publicity – a television crew had filmed the raid on his office – "to gain a strength they wouldn't otherwise have." Stamler laughed it off. Television crews on Parliament Hill were everywhere, and as soon as the Mounties had showed up with their search warrant, a camera crew was on to them in no time.

10

A Sweet Offer and a Cold Shoulder

In the late 1960s and early 1970s, the restaurant atop the Skyline Hotel in downtown Ottawa was the kind of pricey establishment to which a host took guests to impress them with his style and substance. Stamler was invited to lunch there one day by another prominent lawyer, a Queen's Counsel at a mid-sized Quebec law firm, who said he wanted to talk about the Mounties' investigation into Sky Shops. The case was moving ahead nicely. Stamler long ago had nailed down the lucrative share deal by which Senator Giguère had benefited by $95,000, and the scope of the investigation had now expanded well beyond the tiny intrigues around Dorval airport.

The lunch began innocently enough. The lawyer set the tone by ordering the most expensive entrée on the menu and encouraging Stamler to do the same. The lawyer was obviously used to playing in a higher league than was an RCMP officer with three kids, a fourth on the way, and a mortgage.

157

As they ate, the lawyer picked his words carefully, wary of the hidden and forgotten meanings of each utterance. Nevertheless, he made it clear that he was representing the interests of some of those people or corporations caught up in the Sky Shops investigation. This set off the caution bells in Stamler's head.

Stamler knew that the best way to avoid danger was to deflect it. He made a joke and the lawyer shifted the conversation away to other matters, the food, the wine, the pretty girl at the next table. He then observed that societal attitudes were different in Quebec than in the rest of Canada. Quebecers saw themselves as a tiny francophone island in a tumultuous sea of anglophone hostility. Theirs was a garrison mentality, he said, a collectivity, everyone with the same mutual interest – survival. That being the case, the élite were given a wider berth than they might otherwise receive elsewhere. What might be considered a crime in Toronto or New York was dismissed in Quebec as a perk of public office, part of the just reward for holding power in the name of the wider group, the lawyer said, almost solemnly.

Eventually, he returned to the matter of his client. Stamler had to listen in case the client, whoever it might be, was ready to work for the Mounties. Stamler searched for an opening to exploit, but opportunities to do so were ephemeral, there for a moment then gone. Everything said was as innocuous as the lawyer's white-bread looks and deportment. "You've got a great future ahead of you," the lawyer said. "You did such a super job in the Hamilton Harbour case and the dredging case. You know, there are a lot of politics involved in getting ahead in the RCMP. You need support to get to the top level."

This, Stamler realized, was the opening to which he was supposed to respond. The lawyer was an agent for some unknown power, whose duty was to size up the man on the white horse and head him off at the pass. This is how it happens, Stamler thought to himself. It doesn't start with an envelope filled with money or tickets to Tahiti, but with the opportunity for someone to show concern, understanding, vulnerability, and compliance, and then, once he has made the right gesture, the real dealing begins.

Stamler wondered who was standing in the lawyer's shadow and what kind of bargain he might be willing to make, but he knew he was unlikely to be told, and the conversation petered out. The bill for the lunch was at least four times his expense-account rate, but Stamler still reached for his credit card. He couldn't afford the expense, should the force refuse to accept his claim for reimbursement, but he felt he had no choice but to pay half of the bill, the best way he could think of to express his neutral position.

Nothing specific had been offered to him, but there was no doubt in his mind that if he had not defended his position, he would have been seen as a useful friend. He filed a verbal report about the meeting, having concluded that it would be unwise to put anything in writing, because that might serve to weaken his position in the Sky Shops case. Stamler sensed he was on to a major political scandal. He knew he had strong evidence and didn't want it clouded by news of an attempt to bribe a police officer, which would only make him look paranoid and deflect attention away from the real issues. Stamler bore down even harder on his multiple investigations, but there were few within political circles who seemed eager to help him.

Marc Lalonde had been a young lawyer with a black eye in 1965 when he defended Stamler over Gilles Grégoire's complaints that the Mounties were harassing him over forty-two dollars in unpaid parking tickets. A little more than a decade later, Stamler and Lalonde faced each other across Lalonde's desk. There was no hint of recognition between the two men, although neither had forgotten their last meeting.

In the intervening years Lalonde had hitched his wagon to Trudeau's star. When Trudeau was made Justice minister, Lalonde was his adviser on constitutional affairs. When Trudeau became prime minister, Lalonde was his policy adviser and then his principal secretary. In 1972, Lalonde had been elected to Parliament, and before long was in the cabinet. Now he was minister of Health and Welfare and a member of the powerful Priorities and Planning Committee, the inner cabinet comprised of a handful of Trudeau's ministers. As well, he had become Quebec lieutenant of the federal Liberal Party.

Stamler and Inspector Kornel "Curly" Kereluk had been ushered into Lalonde's spacious office in the Confederation Building, next to the House of Commons. Stamler had been shown to the single, antique chair that was dwarfed by the massive desk it faced. Inspector Kereluk sat in the only other chair, almost twenty feet away from Lalonde's desk, near the entrance to the office.

For a few long minutes Lalonde kept busy with papers on his desk, signing his name, scribbling notes, doing everything but acknowledging the presence of the two Mounties. Stamler decided to retaliate. He pulled out a notebook and, perching it awkwardly on his knee, began jotting notes – the place, the time, the purpose of the visit. As Quebec lieutenant, Lalonde would be the official complainant in the theft charges that Stamler planned to lay against Giguère over the money that had been destined for the party's fight against separatism, but had somehow landed in his personal bank account. The cool reception he was getting from Lalonde did not surprise Stamler. He knew that, even though they were the victims of the theft, the Liberals were anything but enthusiastic about complaining that their chief fundraiser in Quebec might also be a thief. Stamler had also heard on the streets that the Mounties' raids of Quebec businessmen was considered to be bad for federal–provincial relations.

The scribbling duel ended with a splendid flourish by Lalonde and a shuffling of papers at the end of which he asked, "So, Inspector Stamler, when will your investigation be completed?"

Stamler quickly finished what he was writing and replied, "It will be completed when it is completed, sir."

The naturally austere Lalonde didn't waste a word on the two Mounties. He said he wasn't aware of any of the circumstances involving the senator, which was probably true. Almost as soon as Lalonde had ascended to the role of Quebec lieutenant in 1975, he had dumped Giguère and taken away his powers, not waiting for the conclusion of the police investigation. He had also read the riot act to his fundraisers, pointing out what was crime and what wasn't. He had even fired a fundraiser who had approached a contractor bidding on a federal contract. Lalonde said he would co-operate with the prosecution and testify at any trial, should there be one.

Stamler had the premonition that Lalonde, the reluctant victim, wouldn't make a very good witness. He was right. When the matter eventually came before a judge, Lalonde's testimony was so close to the line between co-operation and total indifference that it was difficult to tell whose side he was really on.

In preparing the dredging companies' case, prosecutor Rod McLeod devised a complicated coding system which gave every one of the thousands of documents, each defendant, and every scheme a series of numbers and letters easily recognizable by the jury. McLeod took fourteen months to prove that five men and eight firms were guilty of conspiracy to commit fraud of at least $8 million against the federal government. They were all convicted. But in January 1981, the Ontario Court of Appeal ordered new trials for three of the men – Jean Simard, Albert Gill, and Frank Hamata. The new trials never took place. The only individuals convicted, Toronto businessmen Harold McNamara and Sydney Cooper, were sentenced to five and three years in prison, respectively. McNamara served ten months and Cooper five before being released.

Their releases in 1982 sparked a minor uproar, as they were allowed to serve their day parole in their own homes, instead of at a halfway house, and Cooper was allowed to vacation in Florida and the Caribbean while on parole. In the House of Commons, the NDP Justice critic urged the Commons to pass the motion "that this House condemns the National Parole Board and the Solicitor-General for this vivid illustration that there exists one law for the rich, powerful friends of the Liberal Government and another for the poor."

The *Globe and Mail* added in an editorial: "What deterrence will the treatment given Mr. Cooper and Mr. McNamara have for other businessmen tempted to abuse the public's trust? What does it say for the system's view of the seriousness of the offences, or the magnitude of the sums of money involved? How many other people are offered the chance to take a vacation outside the jurisdiction while on parole?"

The motion didn't pass.

11

Sky Shops:
The Quebec Justice System

A full six weeks before Elmer MacKay had called for a police investigation into Sky Shops in 1975, Stamler had already considered the problem of choosing the right location to swear his information about Giguère and his co-accused: Ottawa or Montreal? Ontario authorities suggested that the case be pursued in Quebec where, his experience had taught him, judges, in spite of their vows, might not be entirely neutral. His suspicions were strengthened by explicit warnings to be careful because the Quebec courts would not look favourably on a prosecution, no matter how much evidence he had gathered or how strong it might be.

It was unusual to seek advice before laying an information, but Stamler felt he had no choice given the jurisdictional complications of the case. He called for a meeting with Louis-Philippe Landry, the regional director for the Department of Justice in Montreal. Landry was in the process of moving to a new job in

Ottawa, but was temporarily performing both jobs, commuting between the two cities. Stamler, accompanied by Inspector Kereluk, visited Landry in Ottawa and told him about their investigation of Giguère, without going into crucial details.

Landry told Stamler that, under a special agreement with the attorney-general of Quebec, federal prosecutors handled all matters relating to bribery of federal officials in Quebec. The only difficulty that Landry foresaw was that, once the charges were laid, Quebec might cancel the agreement and prosecute the matter themselves, given Giguère's stature in the community. That, Landry said, might lead to the real danger that the Quebec prosecutor assigned to the case would be so green there could be little hope for a successful conclusion to the case. Also, the RCMP's role in Quebec in criminal investigations was not well defined, and the prosecution of such a high-profile case could raise public concerns about what exactly the federal force was doing in Quebec.

For those reasons, Landry suggested, proceeding with the charges in an Ontario court might be preferable. Landry said he would not do anything further and would keep the information he'd heard confidential. He said he would act only if a search warrant was challenged in the Quebec courts, which Stamler later realized might have been meant as a warning to the Mountie.

A little more than two months later – three weeks after MacKay's call for an investigation – Landry telephoned Stamler and asked him how the case was proceeding. The two men agreed to meet in Montreal, where Landry still had an office. Landry examined the preliminary evidence and gave his opinion that there was a strong case against those who gave the shares to Giguère because it could readily be shown why they did so. However, Landry warned, the case against the senator was weak because the Mounties had not proved what was in Giguère's mind when he accepted the shares. Landry thought that Giguère would have to be tried separately and that much of the evidence against him might be inadmissible.

Stamler wondered if Landry had misread the evidence. He argued that one charge of conspiracy should be laid against all the accused, including the senator. It would be impossible to prove a conspiracy, Stamler said, if the case was split in two. How could any jury find just one person guilty of conspiracy?

Landry said that he agreed and asked to be informed about the cases when all the evidence was ready. He ended by reiterating that, unless there was better evidence showing that a crime had been committed in Ottawa, the matter must proceed in Montreal.

In the first week of February 1976, Stamler learned that the procedure for the prosecution of Criminal Code cases in Quebec had suddenly been changed. Henceforth, the Quebec Justice Department would prosecute all such cases; the federal prosecutors were left to deal only with violations of federal statutes. This meant that Landry would no longer have a role in prosecuting the case. The ground was being shifted under Stamler's feet. It made him nervous.

On February 6, Stamler met with Gérard Girouard, the chief Crown prosecutor for the Montreal district, and got the impression that Girouard didn't have much time for him. Girouard assigned assistant Crown counsel Joseph Tarasofsky to the Sky Shops case, and soon afterwards a meeting was held between Tarasofsky and Stamler, who was accompanied by Sergeant Pierre Gourdeau.

Stamler outlined the various cases: the Sky Shops kickback, the theft from the Liberal Party, and the senator's hidden involvement in the advertising company that was getting lucrative federal government contracts.

Tarasofsky, like Landry, said he thought that the Sky Shops case wasn't as strong as the others and that the Mounties should first develop the theft case and the one involving the advertising agency. Stamler was certain the kickback evidence against Giguère was good enough to gain a conviction, but it seemed that in Quebec the bar was set at a different height.

Ten days later, Stamler received a call from Landry. Landry wanted Stamler's brief of evidence, which, he said, Stamler had promised to show him. But Stamler had made the promise only because he had thought Landry would be involved in the prosecution. Now the changes in procedure had put Landry out of the picture, Stamler suspected that the real reason he wanted the details of the police case was so that he could brief his political masters. Stamler consulted with Kereluk, and they agreed not to hand over the brief. Kereluk called Landry to give him the news.

The next day, Stamler called Landry and told him that, as he was no longer responsible for prosecution of the case, it was improper for Stamler to provide him with details. Landry then asked Stamler if he could just read the evidence brief without copying it, before the charges were laid. Stamler said that might be possible – anything to neutralize him.

Both the federal and Quebec prosecutors were being too political for Stamler's liking. Tarasofsky, the Quebec prosecutor, called to let Stamler know a press release had been issued in Quebec City concerning the Quebec government's interest in the matter. The heat had been turned up another notch. Tarasofsky said he was extremely concerned about the matter and had to act quickly because of pressure coming from Quebec City.

In the week since their first meeting, Stamler, as instructed by Tarasofsky, had been gathering evidence on the theft and the advertising company cases. Suddenly, Tarasofsky was now demanding that Stamler submit all his evidence on Sky Shops, despite the fact that Stamler hadn't completed his work. Further, Tarasofsky told Stamler he couldn't proceed with his sworn information until the evidence was presented to a judge at a special hearing called a pre-enquête, which he said was a standard procedure in Quebec, but rarely used outside the province. Pre-enquêtes allow a judge, in private, to determine if there is sufficient evidence to warrant a complaint being laid. In a legal system to which everyone is supposedly allowed free and unimpeded access, it can serve as a check against nuisance prosecutions. The judge has the power to quash, endorse, or enlarge on the complaint. The Mounties were not upset about the requirement for a pre-enquête – all they wanted was to lay their charges and to have them dealt with in the usual fashion by a prosecutor who was willing to proceed. But there was a hitch. Quebec authorities recommended that everyone but Giguère – the key figure – be charged.

In Quebec City, Solicitor-General Fernand Lalonde baldly explained to the media that the pre-enquête was also used to assess charges involving such public figures as politicians. A spokesperson from his office told *Globe and Mail* reporter Peter Moon that the use of the pre-enquête wasn't all that common: in the previous eleven years it had been used only in three cases – all involving prominent Liberal politicians.

Having operated outside Quebec for his entire career, Stamler wasn't familiar with the use of the process. Worse still, when he was told the nature of a pre-enquête, he knew he couldn't go along with the plans of the Quebec prosecutors. The entire pre-enquête exercise was designed to assess information from a dubious informant, but Stamler was a professional peace officer with a track record of successful prosecutions. There was nothing dubious about him; he knew how to gather information. He sensed that the pre-enquête was a manoeuvre by Quebec's political élite to save Senator Giguère's hide and to skin his own. However, he had little choice but to go along. Ten days later he submitted an outline of his brief of evidence to RCMP headquarters and to Tarasofsky. A week after that, on April 6, Stamler and Gourdeau met with Tarasofsky outside a courtroom in Montreal. "I have to proceed with a pre-enquête in relation to Sky Shops because I have received instructions to do so," Stamler quoted Tarasofsky as saying.* Tarasofsky's superiors, whoever they were, had instructed him to proceed only against Giguère, and only with one charge. Tarasosfky wanted all the witness statements as soon as possible so that he could prepare his case.

Stamler, wary of what was happening, replied that he would comply. Then, as politely as he could, he expressed his concern that the Crown's case would be severely weakened by proceeding this way. Tarasofsky reiterated that while the evidence pointed to a conspiracy among all five suspects, including the senator, he had no choice but to proceed against Giguère alone.

Later that day, Stamler again confronted Tarasofsky in his office to express his concern about the manner in which the case was proceeding. He asked about the other cases the prosecutor had once seemed eager to pursue. Now, Tarasofsky said, they were on the back burner. "I'll do my best to proceed on all cases."

Did he plan to use the other cases as similar-fact evidence against Giguère?

"We're just doing the Sky Shops case," Tarasofsky said. "No similar-fact evidence will be called."

"That is a most unsatisfactory way to proceed," Stamler said.

"You must go along with me for now because I am acting under instructions from a superior and if I do not go along with them, I will be taken off the case," Tarasofsky replied. "If the situation gets tight and I feel I have to call similar-fact evidence, I will call it. I may even have to resign to establish my position."

---

* In an interview in January 1993, Tarasofsky, now a Quebec Provincial Court judge, categorically denied that any pressure had ever been put on him by his superiors over Sky Shops or related cases. However, Stamler made extensive contemporaneous notes of his meetings with all prosecutors. The accuracy of the notes were confirmed in 1993 by other Mounties who were present at various times with Stamler, Tarasofsky, and others. Based on that and other evidence, the author has relied on the Mounties' version of events to retell what happened during the meetings.

"That won't help the case very much if you do that," Stamler shot back.

Stamler wouldn't back down. He said he believed there was a conspiracy in the Sky Shops case and that the appropriate charge should be laid. Nevertheless, he and Gourdeau prepared a list of witnesses for a pre-enquête.

Stamler had never been more emotionally affected by a case. Stories were being written about his past exploits as the press began to pick up on this new breed of police officer. His picture had been in the newspaper a couple of times, but little of the publicity went to his head. He hadn't set out to prosecute politicians, but his investigations had led him to their doorsteps. No matter where he started out, he ended bumping up against the élite. For the first time in his career Stamler was afraid. Some people somewhere – the Quebec prosecutors called them their superiors – had identified Stamler as an enemy. Frightened he might be, but Stamler was determined not to give in. Somebody had to be a loyal servant of the rule of law, he thought, so it might as well be him.

The next day, April 14, Tarasofsky called to tell Stamler that he had met that morning with two of his superiors, Gérard Girouard and François Tremblay, and the Quebec minister of Justice. Judge Maurice Rousseau had been appointed to hear Stamler's information and Tarasofsky expected that Rousseau would order an inquiry. He told Stamler that his information would charge Giguère with only one substantive count of bribery, and that the press would then be informed by the Quebec Justice minister of the procedure adopted.

"Am I expected to sign this information?" Stamler asked.

"It has already been completed in your name," Tarasofsky replied. "That was the way it was decided at the meeting with my superiors."

"I cannot, in all conscience, agree with that procedure," Stamler replied. "First, I believe that a criminal charge must be laid against all the individuals that I have grounds for believing were involved in the conspiracy to set up the payment for Senator Giguère. The information I received throughout my investigation clearly indicated there would be evidence against Louis Giguère, Louis Lapointe, Clarence Campbell, Gordon Brown, and James Lavery, and I do not feel it is fair to select only one of the five and to proceed only against him."

"I cannot change the procedure, but if you hold the line, I will consult with my superior and get right back to you," Tarasofsky said. "My superior says you should lay the charge now prepared, and the judge will probably extend the charge to include others in a conspiracy with Giguère, but that I should proceed with this charge for the time being."

Stamler could not agree. He arranged to meet Tarasofsky at his office. As usual, he brought along a witness, this time Sergeant Klaus Gerhardt, who later confirmed the details that follow.

The meeting began at 2:25 p.m. They started going over the same ground. Why would only Giguère be charged and not Louis Lapointe, for example? Why should the Mounties not put the widest charge before the judge? "Instead, we are starting at the narrowest point, and fifty per cent of the evidence could be ruled inadmissible on an information charging Giguère alone," Stamler wrote in a detailed note to himself immediately after the meeting. The note continued:

> Tarasofsky responded by saying that he agreed that a conspiracy charge is the most appropriate way to proceed with this case. But that he had been instructed to proceed in this manner and he cannot really give me a reason why we should proceed in this manner, except to say that by going their way, I would not then be the person who accuses the other four persons involved.
>
> I said that I have just as great a duty to lay a charge against the others if I have the necessary grounds, as I do against Giguère, that I have a duty to deal with the matter in an impartial way. I am not doing that if I lay a charge

against Giguère alone, when I have as much grounds against the others. I told Tarasofsky that both he and I have a duty to the public to proceed on the merits of the case, alone; and since he was not acting on his belief, but acting on instructions from his superiors without knowing why, I could not adopt that same procedure blindly without knowing the precise reason in law policy or strategy that may be involved.

Mr. Tarasofsky replied by saying that it was true that he had received instructions from his superiors without any real reason, but that he was prepared to promise me that Judge Rousseau would expand the case into a conspiracy charge. That both Girouard and Tremblay would guarantee that conspiracy charges would result possibly several months from now, if the judge feels there is evidence of conspiracy present.

I told Mr. Tarasofsky I have absolutely no interest in the promises that those charges would result. My only concern is that an information that conforms to the facts is instituted at the outset. That is, a charge involving all the accused. Once I had done my duty, my responsibilities were over. It then became the sole responsibility of the judge or justice who received the information to call one or more of the accused to answer the charge, or to refuse to issue process completely. He may call evidence relevant to the case because we have provided him with jurisdiction to look at the case from its widest point. He may then proceed with one substantive count against Giguère, alone, or any combination of things. He may add co-conspirators to the information. He may seek advice of the Crown Attorney who may recommend one action over another. But that procedure did not in any way concern me, except that I may be called as a witness at the hearing.

The Crown prosecutor in turn has the power to intervene, once proceedings are instituted. He may amend the information or withdraw it. The prosecutor clearly has the power and the duty to act at this stage. So why should I not proceed in accordance with my belief and, thereby, exercise my duty to the public?

Mr. Tarasofsky replied by saying that there is nothing stopping me from laying a conspiracy charge by going downstairs and appearing before a Justice of the Peace and laying the charge of my choice, but that after that, I was on my own and I could not expect any help from the Crown's office. There would be no inquiry before a judge and the case would go directly to preliminary inquiry.

I said [if] there was nothing wrong with this procedure, why not then prepare this information and we will go downstairs to see Judge Rousseau who is waiting for us and lay a conspiracy charge. He could then listen to all my information and could then decide whether to listen to other witnesses and/or persons named in the information. In turn, Tarasofsky could make representations to the judge to proceed only with one count against Giguère. The judge then, after hearing all the information, could proceed with either one or with two informations.

Mr. Tarasofsky said we can't do that because it was not the way the entire procedure had been set down by his superiors. . . .

I asked Mr. Tarasofsky what would happen to the $20,000 theft case that I had presented to him in a recent letter, outlining facts.

Tarasofsky said he referred that case to his superiors and he was told that we would not proceed with that case. I asked, why? He said because his superior said "No." I asked him whether it was because there was a problem with the evidence. He said it was because the case was politically embarrassing to the Quebec Liberal Party and to the federal Liberal Party.

I said . . . I can't really become a party to a plan or procedure when I do not have the answers from the person who is making all the decisions. I told Mr. Tarasofsky that he and he alone should be dealing with the question of procedure in this case and only then would he be fulfilling his duty to the public; but instead, what we have here is a situation where the prosecutor is following orders without knowing the reasons for the particular procedure.

Mr. Tarasofsky said if he disobeys his instructions, he will be taken off the case. I replied by saying that in this situation that is developing all the power lies in one person, namely one of his superiors, as well as the power or duty of the judge to decide what action should be taken.

That person is deciding what charges are to be laid, and what the judge will do after he receives that charge. And yet, I don't know who that person is or why he is giving these instructions. I feel I am being pressured into making a decision by some unknown person in authority and I have no knowledge of why that position is being taken in law, procedure, or strategy.

Mr. Tarasofsky said he cannot change his position and there are major problems developing: 1) Judge Rousseau is waiting for us; 2) the Minister of Justice has the press release ready; 3) Both Tremblay and Girouard are at the Expos game and they can't be reached. In addition, they expect everything to go forward as planned.

I said I can't do anything about that except to formally advise Tarasofsky that I am not prepared to lay the one information alone, without the conspiracy charge. I suggested that he contact Girouard and explain my refusal to him. . . .

Mr. Tarasofsky called the baseball stadium [Jarry Park]. I said he should tell Girouard to call Chief Superintendent Duchesneau . . . if he could get hold of Mr.

Girouard at Jarry Park. I left the room and returned some-
time later.

When I returned, Tarasofsky and Klaus Gerhardt were
in conversation. I went over my position once again with
Tarasofsky and said I could not go ahead with the adopted
procedure without knowing the full reasons.

Tarasofsky said that this was clearly a situation where
an officer of the RCMP, unilingual from Toronto, was in
Quebec accusing some leading French-Canadian resident
from the province of Quebec. The Prosecutor's office
wanted to spare me the difficulty of accusing those people
directly, he said, so let the judge accuse these people after
hearing the evidence under oath.

I said, "That is the most unreasonable reason I have
heard so far. For one thing, it is my duty to act fairly and
impartially against all persons involved. Based only on the
information I have uncovered, I have reasonable grounds
to proceed against five persons ... yet you, Mr. Tarasofsky,
are not prepared to let me proceed against Clarence Campbell, Gordon Brown, and James Lavery. Why?"

Jos. Tarasofsky said that that is the way he was told to
proceed.

I left Tarasofsky's office again, both Sgt. Gerhardt and I
went to the cafeteria on the fifth floor. At 4:30 p.m., I
returned to Tarasofsky's office.

Mr. Tarasofsky said he believed that the whole question
that had to be answered was who had the final authority to
say what charges are laid, the police or the prosecutor.

I said when it comes down to that, that is, laying a
charge, it is the informant who presents the charge to the
judge or J.P., and neither the Crown Counsel, Attorney-
General, or anyone else, can tell the informant what to
affirm in an affidavit outlining the charge. Advising the
informant is proper, but instructing the informant is not

proper. Therefore, if the police are expected to lay a charge, the police decide what to put in the information.

I went on to say that I believe Tarasofsky should go before the Judge himself and lay whatever charge he believes is appropriate, or bring some other informant into the picture to do that; but don't instruct me what I must say in any affidavit that I am expected to lay before a justice.

Mr. Tarasofsky said that he would not personally lay the charge. Since we could not resolve the issue, we set up a meeting for 9 a.m., the following morning.

Tarasofsky absolutely denies Stamler's version of this discussion.

In 1976, Paul Drapeau was the RCMP assistant commissioner in charge of criminal investigations in Quebec and was about to be made deputy commissioner in charge of operations in Ottawa, working under his old friend Maurice Nadon, who was the commissioner. Nadon and Drapeau had made names for themselves busting drug dealers in Montreal. Drapeau particularly remembers one raid where he and Nadon found themselves alone in a room with hundreds of thousands of untraceable dollars. "It was funny. There was enough money there for us to retire on, but we believed so much in what we were doing that we never even considered taking it. We just logged it all in and continued on with our work. It would have been dishonourable to do anything else. That's the way we were."

When Henry Jensen had informed Drapeau months earlier that Stamler had an important lead into a case in Quebec, Drapeau could have insisted that his officers conduct the investigation, but he hadn't because he didn't think that territoriality was necessarily the way to go about policing. Drapeau hadn't paid much attention to Stamler's investigation, but now Stamler was refusing to co-operate with Quebec Justice officials, Drapeau was thrust into the Sky Shops controversy. He, Stamler, and Chief Superintendent Ray Duchesneau met with Tarasofsky and his superior, Gérard Girouard. Stamler had told him about the "orders from above" and Drapeau thought perhaps there might have been a misunderstanding, a mistranslation of a phrase from French to English. Drapeau went to the meeting to hear for himself.

Girouard told the three Mounties that Stamler's decision not to sign the information made out by Tarasofsky was a symptom of a larger problem. The question to be resolved, he said, was whose duty it was to commence criminal proceedings. Was it the duty of the attorney-general, who administers justice in the province, or of the police? Girouard clearly thought it was the attorney-general's. He said the job of the police is finished when a police officer delivers the brief of evidence or consults with the Crown prosecutor with respect to the charges.

Duchesneau countered by pulling out a policy letter stating that charges were to be laid by investigators who, afterward, would send a brief to the prosecutor's office. In exceptional cases, the officer could consult with a prosecutor prior to laying charges. The policy had been worked out with Girouard. Girouard said that in his opinion once the investigator elects to consult with Crown counsel, he must then be guided by his instructions as to which charge was to be laid.

"Doesn't that policy contravene the Criminal Code? Isn't it wrong?" Duchesneau asked.

Stamler interjected, "If you accept the position that the policeman's role is finished when he delivers the brief, then the Crown prosecutor should lay the charge. I have no objections if the Crown elects to proceed against Giguère alone and Mr. Tarasofsky lays the information himself. But I do object to being told what I must put in my affidavit which I swear before a justice. That seems to be the real issue here."

"I know you are concerned that a conspiracy charge will

not be laid," Girouard said, "but leave that up to the judge. Let the judge accuse the other people. We start small, let the judge expand it."

The Mounties couldn't accept that logic.

"Much of the evidence of conspiracy may not be admissible before the judge on an information that does not include everyone," Stamler argued. "If a witness is represented by a lawyer who objects to questions not relevant to the one specific charge before the judge, the evidence may not get before the court. Under these circumstances, how can the judge expand the case to include others when he has not heard the evidence? I suggest we proceed from the wider point with a conspiracy charge and then let the judge decide whether to cut it back."

"I cannot do that," Girouard said, standing firm. "We must start the case at the smallest point and let the judge expand it."

"Why?"

"You should not be the one who accuses the co-conspirators."

Stamler had been told by Tarasofsky that he shouldn't be seen to be charging a single French Canadian, now he was being told that the real concern was his charging the co-conspirators, three of whom were English Canadians. The excuses were getting weirder and weirder. Stamler turned to Tarasofsky and asked him if he believed, after reading the case outline and the statements of the witnesses, that the evidence supported a conspiracy charge against the five persons named, and whether, in fact, that was the best way to proceed.

Tarasofsky said there was no question about the fact that a conspiracy charge was the best charge with which to proceed.

"Why are you not proceeding with a conspiracy charge then?" Stamler demanded.

"Ask Mr. Girouard that question."

"It's best that you not lay the charge," Girouard repeated to Stamler. "Let the judge do that. There are many persons involved in this conspiracy. Where would you draw the line?"

Stamler said he could simply charge those named and let the evidence speak for itself. If others were shown to be involved, the judge or prosecutor could add their names later.

Girouard, who could see he was getting nowhere with Stamler, told the Mounties that he was following orders from above, a phrase that caught Drapeau's ear.

"Orders from above?" Drapeau repeated the phrase, asking Girouard to explain what he meant. Girouard did, as Tarasofsky had before, without specifying who made the orders. Perhaps, Drapeau thought, Girouard wasn't expressing himself clearly in English, so he asked him to explain his position in French. It came out exactly the same way.

The meeting ended with Girouard telling the Mounties they could lay their own charge, but that they would receive no help from the Crown Attorney's Office in prosecuting the case.

Stamler asked them to wait until the following Tuesday before briefing the provincial police on the matter. He wanted the weekend to think over his options. "I don't think I'll change my mind, but I will call Mr. Tarasofsky on Tuesday to arrange for a further meeting."

Stamler had already arranged to take all the documents on the case to Toronto so that he could prepare his brief over the Easter long weekend. Now, he filled out the necessary papers and presented them to Justice of the Peace Morand in Montreal, who stamped them with the time and date and placed them in the court file. The evidence was formally handed over to Klaus Gerhardt, who put the boxes of documents in the trunk of his police car.

Paul Drapeau was extremely disturbed by the meeting in Girouard's office. Drapeau had never before seen such blatant interference in the judicial system. He was pleased and proud of the way Stamler had stood his ground. What rankled Drapeau more than anything else was the same thing that had irritated Stamler: Girouard's insistence that he was only acting on orders from above. Drapeau was so incensed he was thinking of having Stamler lay the charge the next morning in Montreal, then calling the press to witness the event "so that everybody would know that we had done our work properly." But when he got back to his office from the meeting, the phone was ringing off the hook. It was Commissioner Nadon on the other line, eager to know the outcome of the meeting. After he listened to Drapeau's account, Nadon ordered him to drive back to Ottawa immediately, where a meeting would be held with federal Justice Department officials. Nadon and Drapeau weren't yet aware that the federal officials didn't exactly have clean hands on the matter, either.

Stamler returned to Toronto on Friday for a meeting about the dredging trial with Ontario Crown prosecutor Rod McLeod, during which Stamler brought up the jurisdictional haggle over the Sky Shops case. McLeod was convinced that there was sufficient evidence to proceed with the case in the Ontario courts, but he wanted to check first with his boss, Clay Powell, who had become Stamler's regular weekend tennis opponent.

The next day, Powell, McLeod, and Stamler met to discuss the matter. The two prosecutors, who had initially recommended the case be tried in Quebec, were now willing to take the case in Ottawa. According to Powell, whether the RCMP decided to proceed in Ottawa or Montreal was entirely up to the force; if the Mounties chose to go to Ottawa, Powell's office would vigorously prosecute the case. Stamler then briefed his superior, Bud Howe, who agreed to this plan.

The following Tuesday morning at a meeting held at RCMP headquarters in Ottawa between the Ontario prosecutors and the investigating officers, Powell outlined his reasons for believing there was sufficient evidence to show that criminal acts had been committed in Ottawa, which gave jurisdiction to local prosecutors. Later that morning, another meeting was held at the office of the federal solicitor-general. Present at the meeting were

Nadon, Drapeau, Superintendent Don Wilson, who had just taken over from Henry Jensen as head of the Commercial Crime Branch, Stamler, Landry, and Réjean Paul, who was replacing Landry as Montreal regional director of the Justice Department and who would represent the RCMP's interests in court. The meeting was chaired by Deputy Solicitor-General Roger Tassé. The intention of the meeting, as Tassé put it, was to discuss the differences in philosophies in respect to the laying of charges and to attempt to resolve the crisis.

Paul and Landry said they understood why Quebec wanted to proceed against Giguère alone, and that they felt comfortable with the pre-enquête process. If the RCMP laid a charge against everyone, Paul argued, the judge in the pre-enquête would not be able to call the co-accused as witnesses against Giguère.

But, Stamler explained, the Quebec prosecutors had indicated to him that they had no intention of calling Lapointe, Campbell, and the others; they planned to call only five or six of the more minor co-conspirators. Both Paul and Landry expressed surprise at the suggestion, but it was clear the meeting was going nowhere. It ended with Paul saying he would make inquiries among his Quebec Justice colleagues, and get back to Stamler.

Back at Mountie headquarters, Drapeau expressed concern about having Réjean Paul represent the force. It was finally agreed that the evidence brief would be delivered to Paul, but Drapeau advised Stamler to tell Paul that he was not to contact the Quebec officials until he met again with the Mounties to discuss the issues further. Drapeau headed back for Montreal, where, ironically, he was to be a guest speaker at Landry's going-away party that night.

The agenda in Quebec was played faster than the Mounties expected. At 1 p.m., before Paul got back to Stamler, *Globe and Mail* reporter Peter Moon telephoned saying that he had filed a story based on an interview with the deputy attorney-general of Quebec. Moon told Stamler that the deputy had gone on record as being upset with the Mounties over Sky Shops, calling their investigation unsatisfactory, the Mounties incompetent, and blaming delays in the prosecution on the Mounties' refusal to carry out further enquiries requested by the Crown prosecutor. The Mounties were publicly under attack.

Commissioner Maurice Nadon was well respected within the force for being an honest cop who knew the law. He listened to Drapeau and Stamler, then agreed that the Mounties should proceed with their case in Ottawa immediately. Nadon informed Roger Tassé that Stamler would swear the information within hours before a justice in an Ottawa court. Quebec authorities were alerted to the new plan. Stamler went to the Ottawa court and swore his information before Justice of the Peace Herb Woods, setting out his belief that the five men named in it had been involved in influence peddling and bribery with regard to the Sky Shops share transaction. Woods accepted the information, heard Stamler's sworn testimony, examined the evidence, and then issued warrants for the arrest of the five accused.

That evening, at Landry's going-away party, Drapeau realized he was being cold-shouldered. He finally cornered Landry.

"What the hell's wrong?"

"You son of a bitch, you double-crossed me," the lawyer shot back. "You said you weren't going to lay the charges in Ottawa."

Drapeau was shocked. No one had bothered to tell him.

The next day Quebec Solicitor-General Fernand Lalonde called a press conference saying the RCMP had double-crossed him, too, by laying charges in Ontario. As promised, the Quebec authorities announced that Judge Rousseau would be conducting a pre-enquête into a single charge of influence peddling against Senator Giguère. But the Quebec authorities faced a major problem. Stamler had all the evidence in his possession, and it was now under the jurisdiction of the Ontario court. They were furious.

The next day, Stamler was at the Alta Vista headquarters, preparing for the arrest and arraignment of the Sky Shops accused, when word came up from security that a member of the

Quebec provincial police force, La Sûreté, was in the lobby with a warrant commanding Stamler to appear before Judge Rousseau in Montreal. Drapeau and Chief Superintendent Duchesneau had already been served in Montreal. The Quebec courts were preparing to charge the Mounties with obstruction of justice if they didn't return the evidence against Giguère to Quebec. The world was getting even more bizarre, Stamler thought.

Stamler called Réjean Paul, who said he wanted to meet the next morning with Stamler in Montreal. He told Stamler to bring the order from the Ontario court granting him jurisdiction over the documents. In Montreal the next morning Réjean Paul opened the meeting by stating that the order issued by Judge Rousseau to produce all documents seized by the Mounties under the warrant issued by Quebec Justice of the Peace Morand had to be answered by 1 p.m., slightly more than an hour away. Then, for more than twenty minutes, he reviewed Stamler's stance in the various meetings that had taken place between Justice officials and the force, clearly trying to drive a wedge between Stamler and his superiors, but to no avail.

Then Paul dropped his bombshell on the Mounties: Stamler had illegal possession of the Sky Shops documents, was interfering with the administration of justice, and was therefore liable to charges. Paul said the Mounties had failed to obtain an extension from Justice of the Peace Morand to keep the documents in their possession, and that the court file had been examined and there was no court order in it allowing Stamler to have the documents. They were to be returned immediately.

For Stamler it was one of those moments a boxer probably savours, where everything moves in slow motion and he has a clear view of his opponent's chin and all the time in the world to mark the sweet spot with an X before landing the knockout punch. "But we do have such an order from the Justice of the Peace," Stamler said, raising his eyebrows ever so slightly.

"That is not a lawful order," Paul snapped back, not knowing what he was talking about.

Out of his briefcase Stamler pulled a copy of the signed order giving the Mounties possession of the documents for another three months. No dirty or illegal trick could beat that. A copy? Every lawyer knew that the procedure in Quebec was that no copies were made, but Stamler, the ex-bookkeeper, always made copies. He left nothing to chance.

The lawyer was flabbergasted. "This is most unusual," Paul said. "The court files do not show this document, that the order had been made. There is something wrong. I will have to check on this matter further."

Stamler then produced the Ontario court order. The game was over.

In June 1976, the fight between the RCMP and the Quebec Justice Ministry was the subject of a conference of Canadian attorneys-general. Not much was resolved. Prior to the meeting, an unidentified senior Justice Department official told Canadian Press reporter Gerard McNeil his view of the debate over who decides what charges will be sworn – the police or the Crown prosecutor. "There is nothing worse than a policeman who thinks he's a lawyer," the Justice Department official was quoted as saying, which seemed like a shot at Stamler.

The pre-enquête under Judge Rousseau eventually took place. In June 1976, the judge announced a single charge against Giguère of illegally accepting a benefit in the Sky Shops case. Observers remarked that it was a more substantial charge than the one laid in Ontario. If only they had understood the history.

With the laying of charges in two provinces, Giguère's lawyer complained about "abuse of process" and about how unfairly his client was being treated. Eventually, the dispute was resolved by transferring all the cases to Quebec, where Quebec officials acceded to the RCMP wishes to charge all the parties together. Louis Lapointe died before his case came to trial.

The new Quebec prosecutor was Bernard Beaudry, who, unlike his predecessor Tarasofsky, was impressed by Stamler's and Gerhardt's work. But even Beaudry found he was in for some surprises. Giguère, who suddenly could speak no English, requested and was granted a trial in French only. "It was most unusual," Beaudry says, "since all the evidence was in English, except for a few documents."

Beaudry had no trouble gaining convictions against Clarence Campbell, James Lavery, and Gordon Brown, but in the French-language case against Giguère, the judge threw innumerable obstacles in front of him. "It was extremely strange," Beaudry recalls. "For example, a key piece of evidence was whether Giguère had met in Florida with his co-conspirators. When I produced the chit from the Florida golf club, it was a big moment for the prosecution. But the judge immediately called a recess. The jury never got to appreciate the impact of the evidence. The entire case went that way."

Just as Stamler had predicted, by trying Giguère alone, there was not enough evidence to convict him. The senator went free.

To this day Beaudry and even Tarasofsky believe there was a miscarriage of justice. "He was as guilty as sin," Tarasofsky says.

Later, Stamler laid charges against Giguère in the theft of monies from the Liberal Party. Canadians received a rare treat when some of the Crown princes of industry – including Charles Bronfman and a number of bank executives – found themselves in the witness box, but that case, too, was doomed to fail. Thanks to the help of indifferent testimony from the victim and the novel defence from his lawyer that Giguère had not stolen the money as Stamler had alleged, but simply acted as a money-launderer, a strange argument believed by the Quebec judge, Giguère was acquitted.

Paul Drapeau's support of Stamler ensured that he would never become RCMP commissioner, even though his record had been spotless and splendid. But Drapeau has never regretted the decision he made. "I did what the law asked me to do, I couldn't be worried for myself." Drapeau ended his career a few years later as deputy commissioner of operations.

During the Sky Shops confrontation, four government lawyers had played key roles – Joseph Tarasofsky and Gérard Girouard in Quebec, and Philippe Landry and Réjean Paul at the federal level. By 1980, the Quebec government had appointed Tarasofsky and Girouard as judges in the Provincial Court, and Ottawa had appointed Landry and Paul as judges in the Quebec Superior Court.

Stamler would spend much of the last half of the decade in criminal court, helping to prosecute all the cases he had investigated. The fight with Quebec authorities over Giguère signalled both the beginning of Stamler's rise in the RCMP and the end of his career as an investigator.

George B. McClellan had wanted the Mounties to be more than a display police force, and that they had become. Stamler had only been on the streets five years and had investigated just a handful of cases, but the fallout from them had shaken the country's establishment. Stamler and his fellow Mounties had learned that in Canada the rule of law did not supercede the rule of politics.

Even so, the political problems caused by the single-minded investigators from the Commercial Crime Branch had to be addressed by the political élite. While everyone was distracted by Quebec separatism, the Mounties had managed to escape their confines and had been allowed to run wild. A way had to be found to corral the Horsemen, once again.

12

Handcuffing the Horsemen

The RCMP's Commercial Crime Branch made headlines throughout the 1970s, but its achievements were still largely ignored by most Canadians. It was all but impossible to capture the public's imagination with tales of bid-rigging, kickbacks, and influence peddling – all seemingly petty, victimless crimes.

This didn't stop some politicians from attacking the branch's investigators, suggesting their real intent was the overthrow of the democratic process and destruction of the country's political institutions. The era produced no clear-cut heroes for the force. Among all the Mounties, Stamler had risen to the highest public prominence, primarily because his cases had created the greatest continuing controversy. But a policeman who didn't carry a gun, whose chases involved not cars but paper, whose most climactic moments often came while flicking through a filing cabinet was not the stuff of legend. Rather, the most indelible impression of the Mounties of the 1970s was captured in one startling and dramatic image – barn-burning.

Since the 1970 October Crisis in Quebec, the Security Service had been preoccupied with a recurrence of terrorist activities. Following the recommendations of the 1968 Mackenzie Royal Commission on Security, Trudeau had appointed John Starnes as the civilian director-general of the Security Service. Starnes had undertaken a massive counter-intelligence operation, whose purpose was to thwart the growth of terrorist groups in the province. The RCMP commissioner between October 1969 and December 1973 was Len Higgitt, who had spent almost his entire career within the Security Service. He was followed by Maurice Nadon.

During the last week of July 1974, the same week that the U.S. Congress approved three articles of impeachment against President Richard Nixon, the Security Service was caught *in flagrante delicto*. A man was injured after a bomb outside the Montreal house of Steinberg supermarket executive Melvyn Dobrin exploded prematurely. The injured man was soon identified as Robert Samson, a member of the RCMP's Security Service, whose duties involved following the activities of the suspected radical separatist group, the Agence de Presse Libre du Québec (APLQ). The Security Service soon found out that Samson had been working freelance for a Montreal crime boss who wanted to send a message to Dobrin. Samson was turned over to the Montreal police, dismissed from the force, and the scandal quietly receded into the background.

Samson's arrest didn't shock many in the RCMP's Criminal Investigation Division. Former Mountie George Wool says, "The people who went into the Security Service were implicitly saying by that very act that they didn't want to be peace officers, that they didn't like law enforcement. That they would get into trouble and break the law didn't surprise most of the real policemen at all."

In March 1976, Samson's case went to trial for the second time, the first having ended in a mistrial. When he was arrested, Samson had been a Mountie for less than five years, almost all of them as an agent in the Security Service. He had little experience as a policeman. Testifying in his own defence, Samson said his assignment had been to follow and plan operations against the APLQ and that he had done much worse things than bombing Dobrin's house while a member of the Security Service. "Let's say that at a certain time I committed a break and entry," Samson testified, naming as his accomplices the Montreal police, the Quebec Sûreté and the RCMP, meaning the Security Service. "It was to take documents, which were files of the most militant members as well as pertinent documents. L'Agence Press Libre always had a fairly big list of Quebec leftists."*

Samson was convicted of the Dobrin bombing and sentenced to seven years in prison. The federal government considered holding a public inquiry into the APLQ break-in, but decided against doing so after Commissioner Maurice Nadon and the new SS director-general, Michael Dare, assured the government that the incident was isolated.

The Quebec government, however, did set up its own investigation – the Commission of Inquiry into the RCMP – under lawyer Jean Keable. Keable's insistence upon seeing confidential federal and RCMP documents immediately provoked a confrontation with Ottawa. In retrospect, considering the heated Sky Shops jurisdictional dispute, it should have come as no surprise that Keable picked a public fight with Ottawa. Eventually, the Quebec Department of Justice laid charges of authorizing a search without a search warrant against one member from each of the three forces. The three pleaded guilty, were given unconditional discharges, and returned to their police duties. There was virtually no public outcry, and the APLQ matter slipped out of sight.

Solicitor-General Francis Fox told the Commons, "In a democratic society, Mr. Speaker, it is essential that those on whom, like the RCMP and the Security Service, falls the task of enforcing the law and protecting our basic civil liberties, can count upon the

---

* Reported in the *Montreal Star*, April 1, 1976.

complete support of the people. This support, in return, must be based on the faith that those protecting these rights do themselves feel bound and indeed are bound by our laws in fulfilling their duties."

When he said this, Fox already knew that trouble within the Security Service was still brewing.* Two former ss officers were protesting their dismissal from the force in 1973. The two, former staff-sergeant Donald McCleery and former sergeant Gilles Brunet, had come under scrutiny from the RCMP's intelligence unit. There were serious questions about the quality of the evidence against the two men, but the Mounties remained sure they had done wrong.

In late May 1977, McCleery and Brunet brought their case to Fox's deputy, Roger Tassé, and the assistant deputy attorney-general, Louis-Philippe Landry, both of whom were smarting over the Sky Shops affair still before the courts. During their discussions, McCleery and Brunet made allegations, of a general nature, that members of the RCMP had committed criminal offences. "It was the biggest cover-up since the blanket was invented," McCleery told them. "I asked if opening mail was illegal, without going into specifics. I asked if possession of stolen dynamite was illegal, without going into specifics."† Later, McCleery and Brunet gave Landry details of their allegations against the Security Service, some of which indicated unlawful practices in the force.

The directors of the Security Service were naturally concerned about the allegations. If the story was to come out, they wanted it

---

* For a detailed look at the Security Service, see John Sawatsky, *Men in the Shadows*, Doubleday, 1980, and *For Services Rendered*, Doubleday, 1982.
† Quoted in Jeff Sallot, *Nobody Said No: The Real Story about How the Mounties Always Get Their Man*, James Lorimer & Company, 1979.

to be told completely and not in a piecemeal fashion. "There is a great need to bring some significant reform in the country and that perhaps this is the time and the opportunity to do that," four anonymous senior members of the ss wrote in a memorandum to Director-General Dare. "We wish here to reiterate and emphasize most strongly the need for a co-ordinated and total review of former Security Service operational techniques." The Security Service members felt as if they had been left out on a limb. In the wake of the Quebec crisis, the political desire to fight Quebec terrorists had placed the Security Service in an awkward position. But the ss members knew that they must abide by the laws of Canada and the provinces and pay for their sins. The four asked in their memo that the police force be exempted from any investigation because it had not been involved in the possibly unlawful actions of the Security Service.

After meeting with Tassé and Landry, McCleery and Brunet found that their case was suddenly being taken seriously.* Upon hearing of their allegations, Commissioner Nadon concluded that he had been misled by the Security Service and that, consequently, he had inadvertently misled his political masters. He asked Fox to set up a public inquiry.

Soon afterward, Fox announced the appointment of Mr. Justice David C. McDonald of the Alberta Supreme Court as head of the Commission of Inquiry Concerning Certain Activities of the Royal Canadian Mounted Police. In his speech to the Commons setting up the commission, Fox explicitly said that national security and the role played by the Security Service was the primary issue. He took pains to point out that, as far as he knew, the police had done nothing wrong, but that the commission should

---

* Little did they know that Brunet was probably a longtime KGB agent who was paid to disrupt the Security Service. This information only came to public attention in early 1993 in a report by Victor Malarek on the CBC-TV program "the fifth estate."

nevertheless try to detect any unlawful practices on the policing side. The government was in no position to do otherwise. Considering that the Opposition was already accusing the government of operating a cover-up, it would have been politically disastrous for the government to restrict the commission's scope.

In taking up his new role, Mr. Justice McDonald said, "Our mandate stresses the role of the RCMP in protecting the security of Canada. It correctly notes that unless the RCMP has and deserves the trust of Canadians, it cannot perform that task effectively. Without the full co-operation of citizens, confident that the task is being performed competently and lawfully and with due regard for the freedom of the individual, it will not receive from government the material support which it needs, whether for its work collecting security intelligence or its law-enforcement duties."

The McDonald Commission was slow to get into gear as McDonald took more than four months to hire a chief counsel. During this time newspaper reporters began to ferret out more stories about the Security Service. A *Globe and Mail* series about police attempting to obtain confidential medical records resulted in yet another commission being set up, this one in Ontario under Mr. Justice Horace Krever. With four active commissions – McDonald's at the federal level, Krever's in Ontario, Keable's in Quebec, and another in Alberta headed by Supreme Court Justice James Laycraft – it seemed to the casual observer that everywhere in Canada the police were out of control. Then the Keable Commission found out about a barn-burning.

The barn had been located on a farm at Sainte-Anne-de-la-Rochelle in the Eastern Townships. The farm was owned by relatives of Jacques and Paul Rose, two of the FLQ kidnappers involved in the October Crisis. The farm and its buildings had been used as a kind of community centre and weekend retreat for poets, musicians, and their families. In the spring of 1972, McCleery believed he had good intelligence information that the farm was to be used as a meeting place for members of the FLQ and the militant U.S. group the Black Panthers. The Mounties found they couldn't put a listening device in the barn, so they decided to burn it down and so thwart the meeting.

When the story became public, long-time police officers such as Stamler and Henry Jensen shook their heads over the false logic of the Security Service agents. The problem they faced – the meeting in the barn – was akin to those faced by police officers all the time. As Stamler says, "There might be reasons for burning down the barn – such as having the reasonable belief that such a meeting would bring together forces who would end up bombing airplanes or killing hundreds if not thousands of people. But how do the police go about it? Do they make a deal with the barn owner to pay him for the barn afterward? Do they rebuild it themselves? Or do they do nothing? What the ss did was the worst of the choices: even though its concerns were legitimate, it burned down the barn and then tried to cover up the fact that it did so."

The barn-burning was typical of the kind of crime prevention philosophy that had been common among peace officers from the Wild West days almost up to the present: heavy on rough justice. Remember the cowboy movies where a municipality was suffering under a plague of bank or stage-coach robberies? Instead of investigating the robberies, the sheriff would survey the criminal world. If he learned that bank robbers were coming to town on the next train, the suspects would be rounded up at the station. Sometimes they were sent home on the return train, other times they were taken somewhere quietly down to the waterfront, taught a lesson in municipal inhospitality, and then sent home on the return train.

"There are cops who adopt this kind of attitude, but in the long run a force can't operate out of such a system," Stamler says. "Sure, there might not be any bank robberies, but the trade-off is unacceptable – the police are taking the law into their own hands and there is no way to check if the right person was taken down to the waterfront. In such a system, eventually somebody gets dunked into the water a moment too long and drowns and then what do you do? Now, you've killed someone. That certainly stops the robbery problem. Then, the next step is for the policeman to say, 'It is more efficient to kill these bastards than to pay all the expenses in chasing them down.' That's not the way to go. It's morally wrong and unlawful, and if the police chief condones such actions, he will lose control of his force."

Soon there were other revelations about the Security Service's activities: the SS had opened mail; a phony communiqué had been sent to discredit an FLQ member; there had been break-ins, including one at the headquarters of the separatist Parti Québécois in search of a list of supporters; a potential informant had been kidnapped; and some electronic surveillance had been illegal. Clearly, poor judgment had been exercised by Security Service members, but every action taken by them had been in response to either a real or perceived threat to national security. That they ended up skating on the edge of the law was due more to the fact that the law was totally inadequate.

From its inception, the McDonald Commission and the reporters covering it rarely distinguished between the police and Security Service branches of the RCMP in their public statements, using both interchangeably – "RCMP" fit nicely into headlines. There was still little public concern about the Security Service's *faux pas*, but opposition politicians, civil libertarians, and Quebec separatists alike were whipping themselves into a frenzy about the problems with "the police." The RCMP were called anti-democratic and abusers of the rule of law.

The tables turned so quickly on the police, many couldn't believe what had happened. Throughout the 1970s the RCMP had seen powerful politicians at all levels of government control the enforcement of the law in a number of serious criminal cases, yet their actions had been rendered down to little more than the stuff of jokes, provincial idiosyncrasies, and the like. Now the police were being pilloried for being corrupt and subject to special measures.

Jeff Sallot's 1979 book *Nobody Said No* showed just how confused people were about the separate roles of the RCMP and the Security Service. The dust-jacket alone propounded the grand misperception:

Who could have imagined that the RCMP, those clean-cut men in red pacing their horses through the Musical Ride, steal dynamite and destroy private property, break and enter, wiretap at will and generally behave as if the law of the land applied to everyone but themselves?

Jeff Sallot, who covered the McDonald Commission of Inquiry Concerning Certain Activities of the RCMP for a year, has written a gripping account of the force's illegal activities. Burning down a barn in Quebec to prevent separatist meetings, breaking into offices and stealing Parti Québécois membership files, intimidating people suspected of FLQ affiliations into informing on their friends and repeatedly opening private mail in flagrant violation of Canada's laws on personal privacy – *Nobody Said No* tells it all. It is the story of a police force that took the law into its own hands and of a government that looked the other way.

That Sallot in the book chose not to distinguish between the Security Service and the police was typical of the hysteria of the times. All polices forces were alarmed about what was happening, none more so than the Mounties, but there was nothing they could do or say about it. To make a comment, to ask that greater care be taken or for added perspective or context would have been deemed to be self-serving, at best, and political, at worst.

Only Trudeau rose to the defence of the police. He made the following poignant observations regarding ministerial responsibility at a press conference on December 9, 1977, in the midst of the barn-burning storm:

I would be much concerned if knowledge of that particular investigative operation by the Security Service were extended to all their operations and, indeed, if the Ministers were to know and, therefore, be held responsible for a lot of things taking place under the name of security or criminal investigation. That is our position. It is not one of pleading ignorance to defend the government. It is one of keeping the government's nose out of the operations of the police force at whatever level of government.

On the criminal law side, the protections we have against abuse are not with the government. They are with the courts. The police can go out and investigate crimes, they can investigate various actions which may be contrary to the criminal law of the country without authorization from the Minister and indeed without his knowledge.

What protection do we have then that there won't be abuse by the police in that respect? We have the protection of the courts.

His comments were written off by a number of observers as being somewhat naive and out of touch with Canadian realities, all part of his cover-up of the government's activities. Trudeau was soft on the police, they said. He didn't understand the rule of law and how a democracy should operate.

With the inception of the McDonald Commission, Maurice Nadon, much beloved by his police underlings, stepped down. Many journalists had portrayed him as a failure, a man who had lost control of the Security Service either through negligence or incompetence. But the Security Service had never been his to run. To the police, Nadon had been the perfect commissioner. He knew the law and had enough sense to let the police do their job. Usually, the end of a commissioner's reign was marked only by stylized, formal affairs. This time virtually every detachment took up a collection to purchase gifts for the outgoing commissioner. It was a rare display of affection for a boss seemingly so removed from the streets.

Nadon was succeeded by Saskatchewan-born Robert Simmonds, who began his tenure as commissioner of the RCMP at almost exactly the same time the McDonald Commission was appointed. Over the next four years, much of Simmonds' attention would be focussed on the commission's agenda.

A well-respected career policeman and probably the force's best homicide investigator, Simmonds had risen slowly through the ranks until 1973. Then, at age forty-seven, he was appointed superintendent in charge of the lower mainland of British Columbia. Unilingual, he had served all but one year of his career in Alberta and British Columbia. Simmonds began to make his name during a protest by a Native Indian band in June 1975. For a month the band had been blocking a road north of Vancouver to protest the seizure of their fishing nets. The RCMP were called in to defuse the situation, and instead of using force, Simmonds applied a mix of firmness and compassion that wilted resistance and allowed the dismantling of the barricade within twenty-four hours. Simmonds followed up with what Southam News reporter Peter Maser described as a "thoughtful report that not only examined Indian problems, but urged the government to try new avenues in addressing them. The report found its way to then solicitor-general Allmand who believed RCMP headquarters in Ottawa was in need of people with recent experience in the day-to-day problems of policing and policemen." The next year, Simmonds was appointed deputy commissioner, and fourteen months after that, commissioner. It was the most rapid rise in RCMP history – from superintendent to commissioner in little more than four years.

When he arrived in Ottawa, the force was under attack. Internally, his deputy commissioners were squabbling over turf and policy. Soon, one by one, the commissions and inquiries published their reports. To battle the storm, Simmonds drew the force into a shell, stripping his deputies of much of their line authority and centralizing control to ensure that headquarters – mostly meaning Simmonds – had a say in every major operation. He ran the force as if it were a small detachment, leading more than one senior member to describe him as a good corporal. Simmonds was the first to arrive at work in the morning and the last to leave at night. He lost weight and his marriage fell apart. He was deeply wary of the media and refused to talk about the force and its future. Simmonds was the perfect leader for what was about to take place. As *Globe and Mail* reporter Mary Trueman observed in a telling profile of Simmonds on his appointment, "The new commissioner will... have to quash the suspicions that the federal Government, in searching both within and outside the force for candidates for the top job last spring, was seeking a yes man who might allow more Government control."

When it made its report in August 1981, it came as no surprise to anyone that the McDonald Commission recommended that "the Cabinet make its decision quickly to separate the Security Service from the RCMP." The same recommendation for a civilian security service had been made in 1968 by the Royal Commission on Security, chaired by Maxwell Mackenzie. At that time, Trudeau had taken the half-measure of appointing a civilian director of the Security Service, but had left the service under the ultimate control of the RCMP. Now Trudeau was left with few options but to separate the SS and the RCMP, considering how much weight McDonald had given to problems within the Security Service in its report.

The primary mandate of the commission had been to investigate the failings of the Security Service. Almost as an aside the commission had said it would peek over the RCMP's wall and take a look at the administration and operations of the police. Lost in the hurly-burly that greeted the release of the commission's report were recommendations seriously affecting the police. The commission seemed to have used the Security Service tempest to take control of the Mounties' criminal investigators.

In their reading of the McDonald Commission report two things stood out for Stamler, Jensen, and many other policemen. First, and most significantly, was the commissioners' conclusion there had been no criminal conduct by the Mounties. The commissioners clearly stated that neither the police nor the Security Service had wilfully broken any laws. It found that many of the problems were the result of shortcomings in either the law or the established techniques and administrative policies of the force. The Charter of Rights, which was soon to be implemented, would help to clarify some of the problems, they wrote.

"What the commission was saying after such a long and thorough investigation was that there were flaws in the techniques of the police and improvements in policy were required, which is a tacit admission that the legal system was operating as it should," Stamler says. "But then McDonald turned around and said the courts weren't strong enough to control the illegal actions of the police, of which there was no evidence. To most of the policemen, it seemed like a terrible leap in logic."

When the McDonald Commission was set up, Trudeau went to great lengths to delineate what he believed was the role of politicians in relation to the day-to-day operations of the police. When he spoke, Trudeau borrowed from a long line of legal wisdom which the McDonald Commission subsequently investigated on its own, then chose to ignore. The commission dealt with Trudeau's warning that politicians should not know the details of police investigations by stating:

We note that the Prime Minister . . . assigned the source of protection against police misdeeds on the law enforcement side of the RCMP to the courts and not to the government. Such a policy implies two things. The first is that the courts will become aware of police misdeeds during the course of criminal trials on other matters and will make their views known from the Bench, and the second is that those views will have a salutary effect on the police. This procedure is considered by the RCMP to be a significant control over their activities, but we have come across situations in which the failure of a judge to express disapproval of an objectionable investigative procedure disclosed in evidence has been interpreted by the RCMP as judicial approval. . . . In our view, reliance on comments from the Bench is an entirely haphazard and unsatisfactory method of control, depending as it does on the almost accidental disclosure of a misdeed in the course of other proceedings, and the inclinations of the judge to comment on it or not, usually without the benefit of any background evidence or argument. Moreover, judges are unlikely to comment on the lawfulness of an investigative procedure if, as at present, the law holds that evidence is admissible if relevant, even if illegally obtained.

The commission members seemed entirely cynical about the independence, impartiality, and integrity of the judiciary, which didn't come as much of a surprise to the police, who had become just as cynical. But while the commission seemed to think that the courts bent over backwards to the police point of view, the police knew that the scales of justice weren't always tipped in their favour. They had seen how political and malleable judges had been allowed to become through flagrant patronage appointments. But the police, being public servants, couldn't say what they thought.

Further adding to the controversy were the old unsubstantiated allegations made by politicians that were still in the air, such as Jean Marchand's complaints that the Mounties had leaked word to the media that he was involved in the Sky Shops affair and that the force had become a law unto itself. *Maclean's* reported the rumours in its coverage of the McDonald

Commission report: "Ministers have also quietly wondered about a series of damaging stories that have beset a long line of solicitors-general responsible for the RCMP: [Warren] Allmand for travelling on a government plane to Bermuda; [Jean-Pierre] Goyer for a U.S. trip with a woman; and Francis Fox for signing an abortion form for a friend."

None of these allegations was addressed by the McDonald Commission, but the impression its report left was clear to the casual observer: the Mounties were out of control. When it came to the Security Service, this was partly true; it was not at all true for the police. "If the police [rather than the Security Service] had just been blamed for blowing up a barn, committing other unlawful acts, and covering them all up, that would be one thing, there would have been some justification for what McDonald decided to do, but the police didn't do anything wrong," Stamler says.

The McDonald Commission had just opened a door through which politicians could creep and gain a level of control over the police that is unprecedented in modern Western democracies. The commission concluded that what "might well be the most serious charge" to be made against the RCMP was "a willingness on the part of members of the RCMP to deceive those outside the force who have some sort of constitutional authority or jurisdiction over them or their activities."

The commission was of the opinion that there was "an unwarranted disinclination on the part of government to interfere in RCMP affairs, even when serious questions of ultimate government control of the force arise. The reluctance has been increased by three other factors – an ill-defined principle of non-intervention by the government in the decision-making processes of peace officers, the long-standing ambiguity surrounding the legal status of the Deputy Solicitor-General and the RCMP Commissioner vis-à-vis each other, and the monolithic character of the Force arising from its organizational structure and the common ethos imbued in each of its members by its internal systems."

At a time when Canadians were being led to believe that all their rights should be written down in a charter, the McDonald Commission was heading down a popular path. Nothing was to be left to discretion or chance. Anything vague, even deliberately so, or *ad hoc* was to be eliminated. The commissioners wrote:

> We take it to be axiomatic that in a democratic state the police must never be allowed to become a law unto themselves. Just as our form of Constitution dictates that the armed forces must be subject to civilian control, so too must police forces operate in obedience to governments responsible to legislative bodies of elected representatives. This important doctrine in our system of democratic government has often been overshadowed by the parallel concept that the best interests of the state are served by keeping at bay any attempts to interfere with the making of police decisions relating to investigation and prosecution in individual cases.
>
> The concept of independence for peace officers in executing their duties has been elevated to a position of paramountcy in defining the role and functions of the RCMP, thus setting the norm for all relationships between the government and the Force. We believe, on the contrary, that the peace officer duties of the RCMP should qualify, not dictate, the essential nature of these relationships. The government must fulfill its democratic mandate by ensuring that in the final analysis it is the government that is in control of the police, and accountable for it. There is no inconsistency in asserting simultaneously that every member of the government, and above all the minister responsible for the RCMP, has an essential obligation not normally to become involved in the decisions to be made by members of the Force, including the Commissioner himself, with respect to investigation, arrest and prosecution in individual cases.

Over the years, in British parliamentary and administrative law, a system had developed whereby those who were responsible for administration and those responsible for policy were kept separate and apart. This was especially relevant to the relationship between the police and the politicians. It promoted a system of checks and balances that the police, schooled in the rule of law, liked to believe existed in Canada. Governments made laws and set policy, while the police had the authority to administer and enforce those laws. Because of the natural sensitivity of their work, the Mounties depended on internal, and later, external review committees to monitor their performance. Meanwhile, the integrity of the legal system was the responsibility of the courts.

In Canada, however, the system of checks and balances had broken down, mainly, as the Mounties saw it, because governments insisted on using political imperatives to intrude into the realms of both the courts and the police. The police could no longer implicitly trust the courts and were cautious, with good reason, about the growing number of politicians eager to get close to delicate police investigations. The police wariness, naturally, made their motivations and intentions more suspect to both the politicians and the ever more politicized judiciary.

Into this gap were thrust the members of the McDonald Commission, inspired by legal insights that seemed to have bypassed far more distinguished jurists and observers. McDonald's solution was little more than a gerrymandering of the legal system to enforce the co-operation of the police for only one reason, as the police saw it: to thwart and usurp the rule of law with the rule of politics. This fusing of responsibilities seemed uppermost in the minds of the McDonald Commission members, who did not think internal and external review committees or ombudsmen were adequate watchdogs of police activities.

The McDonald Commission noted that the Canadian system of law was fundamentally different from the British one because

Canadian legislation "empowers the minister to give direction to the Commissioner in regard to the control and management of the force and all matters connected therewith." In Canada, that had been interpreted to mean control over the administration of the force, not the enforcement of the law. Therefore, the commissioners recommended:

> In examining earlier in this Report the role of the responsible Minister in relation to the security intelligence agency, we set out our views on the extent to which the Minister ought to be involved in its operations. In our view, the methods, practices, and procedures used by the RCMP in executing its criminal law mandate – "the way in which they are doing it" – to borrow the Prime Minister's words – *should* be of continuing concern to the appropriate Minister. We believe that the Solicitor General of Canada has not only the right to be kept sufficiently informed but a duty to see that he is kept sufficiently informed.

The commissioners took one more critical step by addressing the formal role of the deputy solicitor-general, the principal adviser of the minister, who is appointed to the position directly by the prime minister. A deputy minister's job is to advise his or her minister but, more importantly, to act as the prime minister's watchdog to make sure that the minister toes the party line. "Any doubts about the Deputy Minister's right to be kept informed and to look into all matters must be removed. The Deputy Minister is not a member of the Force itself and thus should be able to give the Minister informed, independent advice on policy matters relating to the Force, something which has not been possible in the past," the McDonald Commission recommended, adding, "One final note needs to be made in this regard. On no account should the Minister or his Deputy give direction based on partisan or personal considerations. If the Deputy Solicitor General does so, the Commissioner should take the matter up with the Minister and if necessary with the Prime Minister. If the Minister gives such an improper direction the Commissioner should speak to the Prime Minister directly."

It was a salve designed to ease unrealistic concerns about a growing police state. To almost every ear conditioned to the "atrocities" committed by the Security Service, it all sounded reasonable. The government was finally going to take care of things and get control of the lawless Security Service men. The McDonald Commission, like the Glassco Commission and so many others before it, had set out to construct a model for a perfect world peopled by disinterested and honourable men and women.

As they read the McDonald Commission report, the police couldn't help but wonder if the commission had paid any attention at all to the very public conflicts between the Commercial Crime Branch investigators and the political and business élite. The commissioners knew the difference between the Security Service and the police – apples and oranges – but by mixing them into a fruit salad, as it were, in its report it was virtually impossible for the public to distinguish between them.

Some police officers thought it was no accident. They were certain that the fix was in. For them there could be no other explanation, short of naivety or negligence, to interpret the commission's findings. Disheartened and mute, they could see the logical implications of what the commission proposed. It was so simple that for an army of lawyers and politicians to miss it seemed inconceivable.

The commission's recommendation was that the commissioner of the RCMP be a deputy minister. Since deputy ministers are the prime minister's appointment and directly serve the prime minister, the net effect would be to convert the RCMP from a police force into a government department.

"The flaw in the McDonald Commission's plan was evident

from the very beginning," Stamler says. "One only had to ask a single question to test the validity of its central premise about ministerial responsibility for police actions – that is, how safe would the integrity of the institution of the police be if the prime minister were, in fact, unethical or corrupt?"

In effect, the McDonald Commission had recommended giving the prime minister extraordinary powers that had never been contemplated by the Fathers of Confederation or the electorate. There would be no checks and balances against corrupt practices by or on behalf of the chief executive of the government. What had attracted men like Stamler, Jensen, Drapeau, Nadon, and so many others to police work was the pride they gained from enforcing laws according to the rule of law. They held that the law was for everyone and everyone was equal under the law. As officers of the law they had the discretion to do what they believed was right, their powers held in check by the courts, the final arbiter.

"Policing from the bottom up," Stamler calls it, contrasting it with the top-down structure of the Security Service, where everyone is an agent of the director. But now bottom-up policing was imperilled. The Mounties, who may have caused many of their own problems by being arrogant, politically insensitive, and inept in getting across their point of view, seemed on the verge of being converted into an agency – just like the Security Service.

If the system were to be adopted, Stamler knew, it wouldn't be long before investigations would be directed by some unseen hand at the top. So much for the rule of law.

The only saviour for the police seemed to be Trudeau. The McDonald Commission report had been commissioned under Trudeau, who had gone on to suffer a humiliating defeat to Joe Clark in the federal election held in May 1979. That November, Trudeau announced he was stepping down as Liberal leader and called a leadership convention for March. But when Clark saw his minority government go down to defeat in Parliament on

December 13, 1979, Trudeau was coaxed out of retirement and his Liberal Party managed to win a majority in the February 1980 election. Surely, Stamler thought, once the Security Service was split off from the force, Trudeau would move to prevent the police coming under political control. To an extent, Stamler was right about Trudeau because he stalled on making changes. The Security Service wasn't formally split off from the RCMP until May 1984, a little more than two months after Trudeau decided to leave politics.

Trudeau took with him his philosophy and strong convictions about the independent role of police in Canadian society.

The 1970s had been the most invigorating decade of Stamler's life. He would never again feel such highs and lows. At its end, however, his victories, great as they might have been, paled in comparison to what had been left undone. The Commercial Crime Branch had not yet won its battle to establish its credibility both outside and inside the force. Inside, incredibly, there was still resistance to the notion that business fraud was a criminal, not a civil, matter. As late as 1982, a group of Mounties in Vancouver were discovered holding shares in a company whose stock was being manipulated. They were the latest in a long line of cops Stamler and the other fraud investigators had arrested over the decade. RCMP cruisers still were being used to scout out likely mines, Mountie investment clubs were still operating on the fringes of the securities law, and to many policemen, fraud was still just a five-letter word.

In 1978, Stamler, whom Maurice Nadon once described as "born to be an investigator," had been promoted to a desk job, as superintendent in charge of twenty Ontario detachments between Windsor and Niagara Falls. Moving off the streets was a mixed blessing for Stamler. He had only wanted to be an investigator, but in the RCMP system, as in most, moving up was the only tangible recognition of success.

Stamler had grand plans for his detachments, but never got the chance to implement them. He spent most of his first year as superintendent in courtrooms where his various cases were being tried. Then, in January 1979, he received word that he, like Henry Jensen before him, had been selected to attend the élite course in public administration at the National Defence College at Kingston. It was a singular honour to be chosen for the year-long program, a sign that he was being considered for greater responsibilities. The course was world-famous for the study of world politics and governments required for executive duty in the public service. It was a year of learning and travel, of analyzing public administration problems both in theory and first-hand. Half of Stamler's class of forty were members of the military in the United States, Great Britain, Australia, and Canada, and the rest were Canadian civilians, public servants, lawyers, and the like. Stamler was the only police officer but was classed as a civilian for the course.

After all those years of studying at his homemade desk in his spare time, Stamler welcomed the opportunity to have no other responsibility but to learn. For the first time in his life he felt pampered. The Defence College students were entirely removed from their everyday lives, and Stamler's only contacts with the RCMP during the year were friendship calls or to sort out personal administrative problems. The force could go to hell in a handcart; it was none of his concern.

Travel was one of the benefits of the course as the students studied problems in forty countries. Stamler travelled across Canada, meeting with business people in Toronto, civic leaders in British Columbia, oil executives in Calgary, ranchers in Alberta, and ex-FLQ members in Quebec. The class then visited the United States, Cuba, and Brazil. There was a trip to Africa, where they visited Zaire, Tanzania, and South Africa. They met with Prime Minister Menachem Begin on the eventful day that the border was opened between Israel and Egypt, and with Egyptian officials afterward. For Stamler, the course was a wonderful opportunity to learn about the wider world and to develop important contacts, which he did.

While Stamler jetted around the world, some of those left behind wondered about the timing of his promotion, especially after all the controversy over his cases. Mounties such as George Wool thought it a bad omen when the best cops on the street were being taken off the beat. The two strongest Horsemen in the Commercial Crime Branch – Jensen and Stamler – had been moved on, and in the wake of their leaving, the branch began to change.

After Jensen completed the Defence College course, he took over as commanding officer of RCMP District Number One in British Columbia, in Vancouver. Under others, his vision that the Commercial Crime Branch be based on functional priorities had been set aside, and the branch had been divided into territorial units. This made a substantial difference both in the way its investigators approached their task in the future and in their increasing lack of success.

Stamler's rise to the upper echelons of the RCMP and into other areas of work took him away from many of his best contacts, particularly Cliff Kennedy, the old Transport Department lawyer who had led Stamler to his biggest cases. Kennedy knew that the Mounties' work in general, and Stamler's in particular, had led to a political backlash. Their attack on white-collar crime had been ferocious but not fatal; corporate criminals had survived to fight another day. As Kennedy ruefully said, years later, "Our successes were our failures, too."

13

The Drug Years

Commissioner Robert Simmonds took to politics like a hungry horse to a bag of oats. "I'm a senior deputy minister," he told his underlings, and he was determined to live the part. One moment he was part of the social whirl in Ottawa, the next he was a guest of the Canadian ambassador, Allan Gotlieb, at the embassy in Washington. There were serious concerns among senior officers in the force about the increasing political control of the force, but Simmonds was the last man to raise questions; it wasn't in his nature. First and foremost he was a controller; chain of command was one thing, but Simmonds believed in hands-on management to the point where he hardly let his underlings breathe.

One incident which typifies Simmonds' style occurred in the early 1980s. An inspector who had worked for two years on developing a computer program designed to help the force better manage its staff and workload was invited to make a presentation to every senior officer in Ottawa above the rank of superintendent. Simmonds chaired the meeting. "What's this all about?"

he interjected, as the inspector began to explain the computer program. "I don't want to hear about this, I don't want to hear any of this. Close this down." The assembled Mountie brass could only give knowing looks to each other. Later, many of them agreed that Simmonds didn't like the system because he feared it would be used to outmanoeuvre him and take him out of the loop of control. Simmonds's antipathy toward computerized systems set the Mounties back years in the fight against crime, especially the economic and commercial variety.

Paul Drapeau left the force, partly to get away from Simmonds. Jensen, Stamler, and others made their points when they could, but mostly they decided to bide their time.

In August 1980, while on a trip to Samoa, Australia, and Indonesia on the Defence College tour, Stamler heard from a friend in the force the rumour that he, Stamler, was destined to head up the RCMP Drug Enforcement Branch, in spite of the fact that he hadn't done a drug case in his career. By the time he got back to Canada, Stamler learned that the rumour was true: drug enforcement was his future. His superiors wanted Stamler to design programs to shift the branch's focus from street-level buyers to the conspiracies that drive the illegal business. The RCMP wanted both a higher level of enforcement and the development of police skills to trace the money flow of the drug lords.

Stamler was somewhat soothed by this rationale as, after all his work in commercial crime, he was well schooled in detecting money flows, offshore bank accounts, and conspiracies. Running the Drug Enforcement Branch was a highly sought-after position in the force, at least in part because the director was expected to make a yearly visit to each RCMP liaison officer with drug enforcement responsibilities stationed at embassies around the world, as well as to attend numerous international conferences. Stamler took to the travel so well he wore out his passport and soon earned the nickname the "Rocket," not always said with affection by those left behind.

When Stamler took over the Drug Enforcement Branch, he felt like he was a master of the universe. He knew Simmonds only by reputation, and he feared nothing or no one. Stamler had already shown his independent nature and the depth of his will power in the Sky Shops dispute, and it was only a matter of time before Stamler and Simmonds were bound to have a blow up. If there was one thing Simmonds had made clear to everyone on the force it was that he didn't want to be seen to be critical about or negative toward any government policy. Many Mounties recall Simmonds telling them at one time or another over the years: "We are public servants and we have to accept the decisions of our political masters."

Political masters was a phrase that stuck in the craw of many members of the force, including Stamler, but Simmonds didn't seem to mind. The master of the police was the law and the courts, not politicians. Politicians were supposed to be responsible for the administration of the police force, not law enforcement. However, after the McDonald Commission, having political masters was part of Simmonds' mandate, as would have been the case for any individual appointed to that position. Perhaps the major difference between Simmonds and anyone else was his apparently absolute lack of resistance to the political will of the day. There was no way that he would brook criticism of the government from an underling.

Simmonds was "in charge" and made sure everyone knew that both implicitly and explicitly. Mounties describe him as being extremely hard on his immediate underlings, his potential heirs-apparent. As he peered over his reading glasses, he was frequently stern, even hectoring in attitude. He made it clear that he was a thoroughly uncompromising man. Many on the force joked that he paid more respect to lowly constables than to his deputy and assistant commissioners, and often seemed to place a higher value on the opinions of constables than on those of the commissioned officers.

Shortly after moving over to drug enforcement, Stamler was confronted by one of his first policy problems – a move by the government to liberalize the country's marijuana laws. Politicians and civil libertarians were criss-crossing the country campaigning for the new laws, even for the legalization of marijuana, but there was virtually no articulate opposition to the plan. The proposed legislation was circulated to the Drug Enforcement Branch, complete with Simmonds's stamp of approval. Simmonds and his deputy at the time, Raymond Quintal, each had a reputation for being completely uninterested in what they called morality work – drugs, prostitution, and gambling. Their attitude, as former senior officer Don Docker later described it, was that "they couldn't care less about the lowlifes on the street, all they wanted the RCMP to do was pursue traffickers. They couldn't get it through their heads that to arrest drug traffickers, the police had to know who the users were and that users led to traffickers."

At one point, Stamler was asked to help sell the new legislation to the public, but he refused. As he put it later: "I didn't want to be part of some dog-and-pony show. I wouldn't have anything to do with it, and I told them so." Stamler agreed with the principles espoused by the proposed marijuana laws, but two key members of his staff, Dick Dickens and Bob Sturgeon, voiced their serious concerns about it to their new boss, Stamler. In their opinion the proposed legislation was flawed because it failed to address or strengthen the laws and penalties dealing with the sale and distribution of hard drugs, such as heroin and cocaine, which were escalating dramatically. They believed that mere liberalization of the marijuana laws would send a confusing signal to the public, making the work of the police even harder. Stamler analyzed the shortcomings of the legislation and soon found himself in philosophical territory markedly different from that apparently held by the commissioner and his political masters.

Stating the force's position about proposed legislation was

nothing new to Stamler. In the late 1960s, his work helped to convince the government to give the Mounties sole jurisdiction for the enforcement of bankruptcy laws. This time around, though, the landscape was decidedly different. Dickens drafted a position paper in which he concluded that the proposed marijuana legislation was too one-sided. It suggested that laws should be drafted so that the police could seize the profits and assets of drug traffickers. Stamler circulated the document among senior members of the force, including Simmonds, who was dealing with the government on the drug question. At the heart of Stamler's concerns was his belief that police officers must respond to community needs and community requirements, a philosophy which was gaining currency in the late 1970s and early 1980s in police circles. "The responsibility of the police is not to govern, but to serve the interests of the public," Stamler says. "For the police to be successful, the public must be included in policing. The public has to know what's going on and what the intentions of the police might be. That's the only way the police will get support for their actions."

Stamler, mild-mannered as he might have been, never perceived himself as being a troublemaker, but always managed to stir up controversy. He was eventually called to a meeting with Simmonds and Quintal over the circulation of the position paper on marijuana legislation within the upper echelons of the force. The only other witness to what happened in the commissioner's office that day was the stuffed buffalo head on the wall, and it won't talk about what happened, either.

Others within the force at the time, however, remember there was an air of tension over the issue, which dissipated after the meeting in Simmonds's office. Whatever transpired, Mountie insiders say Stamler must have convinced Simmonds to listen to the concerns of the experts within the force because the commissioner agreed to carry the case being made by the Drug Enforcement Branch forward to the government.

Although Simmonds might have come on side, neither Stamler nor many other police officers were under any illusion that the victory was a permanent one. Simmonds's staunch conviction about the subservience of the police to the politicians made him a commissioner who had to be watched and dealt with carefully.

Soon after the meeting, Stamler attended a conference sponsored by the United Nations in Vienna. Representatives from forty-five countries attended the four-day meeting on exploring ways to recover the proceeds of illegal drug traffic. Stamler had expected that the Canadian ambassador or someone else important would be attending the conference with him, but he found himself sitting alone behind the Canada name-plate. After listening to speech after speech, he concluded that the meeting was going nowhere. Almost every country had sent either an academic or a bureaucrat who wouldn't take either risks and responsibility, lest they irritate someone and have their necks and expense accounts chopped off. Each representative expounded on his or her country's fiscal policies or financial and tax investigations, but no one addressed the matter at hand.

Stamler had no prepared text, so when his time came to speak for Canada, he told the audience what his experience in the Hamilton Harbour, dredging, and Sky Shops investigations had taught him. What was needed to fight drug trafficking was international co-operation, he said, which meant more than talking about the problem. Legal issues needed to be overcome. Countries would have to give up some of their protective sanctuaries, such as the overly secure banking systems of certain countries. The secret to fighting drug trafficking, Stamler said, is to discover the money flow from drug deals, to identify it, trace it, and seize the assets which represent the profits.

Stamler's performance was sufficiently impressive that Canadian diplomats were soon hearing rave reviews, which seemed funny to him. All he had done was talk about what he knew, but obviously he knew more than anyone else. During much of the next decade, Stamler was a fixture at the United Nations and a leading force in the international fight against drug trafficking.

Back at home, however, he still had to whip the RCMP Drug Enforcement Branch into shape. The Mounties had a terrible public image. It seemed that every time the force executed a search warrant, tearing apart a house looking for contraband, the press would follow them through the door. Stamler says, "The accused would be portrayed as a poor victim, while the RCMP members would go home with their tails between their legs with a handful of seized drugs. Then they would have to mount a prosecution amid all the negative coverage."

Stamler concluded that one of the reasons this was happening was that the public didn't understand the extent of the problem of illegal drugs and the difficulties the police had in dealing with traffickers. The public seemed to think that the police were only after marijuana, and few seemed to appreciate the amount of hard drugs, such as cocaine, heroin, and speed, on the streets or how much money was involved in the highly profitable drug trade.

Stamler's solution relied on his basic philosophy – win over the public by informing them exactly what the police were up against and what they needed to do. Contemporary writings by academics also were beginning to espouse the same theory, and police in the United States were already moving in that direction. The vehicle for Stamler's plan would be a booklet titled "National Drug Intelligence Estimate," an annual report of the Drug Enforcement Branch. His plan was for the booklet to outline the extent of the illegal drug problem in the country, based on arrests, convictions, and police intelligence. Stamler tried to get his superiors interested in the idea, but to no avail. Eventually he decided it was within his mandate to produce the document, and he approached John Bentham, a veteran and well-respected Mountie, who was then in charge of public relations for the force, who liked the idea. But, to publish such an undertaking, the force's publication branch, which had all but died, would have to be resuscitated and all government requirements would have to be met.

Stamler didn't tell Simmonds about his plan, fearing Simmonds's first reaction almost certainly would be to give politicians the opportunity to vet the booklet, shaving the edges off the harsh spots, and delaying the process for years or, perhaps, for all time. As well, Simmonds's almost pathological aversion to the media and publicity would be excuse enough for the commissioner to quash a public accounting.

The day the "National Drug Intelligence Estimate" was published in late 1981, Stamler sent copies to the press, and Bentham hand-delivered one to Simmonds. What exactly happened in the meeting is unknown, although members of the drug squad of the day still joke about Simmonds heaving the book across the room.

The "National Drug Intelligence Estimate" was a huge news story, and Canadians finally learned just how pervasive was the nation's illegal drug business. Stamler never heard from Simmonds, but he received "negative feedback," he says, from the Solicitor-General's Office, among other places, and was chastized for releasing news about a problem about which the government had no advance knowledge or time to prepare its responses.

"That's too bad," Stamler says he told one bureaucrat. "I did it the way I thought I had to do it, and I guess I forgot to tell you about it."

The booklet was such a hit, in fact, that the next year the responsible minister asked to be involved in the project. So did Simmonds. Each had his picture in the 1983 publication.

The 1980s began to pass by in a blur for Stamler. He found himself in charge of both the obvious and the obscure. His mandate included, among other things, improving drug law enforcement by the police, as well as overseeing all undercover operations and developing a witness protection program. At the same time, he was called on frequently by the United Nations to apply his expertise and common sense to finding solutions to the international trade of illegal drugs. Being a leader on the international war on drugs brought him fame and innumerable frequent-flyer points.

The former traffic cop had come a long way. He was now considered a leading expert on drug enforcement. This eventually led him to a memorable television debate with the American right-winger William F. Buckley about legalizing marijuana. Buckley was slick and masterful, arguing that the world would be better served if illicit drugs were sold legally at corner stores.

Stamler played it for fun, sticking to what he knew – the real world. "Okay, now a sixteen-year-old is depressed because he just had a fight with his mother or parents and is now out on the street. The corner store is there and he walks in and sees a Buckley's cocaine and, he says, 'I'll try that' and he goes from the worst low to the biggest high. Where does he go from there?"

Stamler loved the travel and the United Nations work his job involved, but over time he found that drug enforcement was relatively easy and largely superficial work compared to what he had been doing in commercial crime. There was always a plentiful supply of cases and suspects in drugs – headlines were a dime a dozen – and it was the kind of assignment that captured the imagination of the masses. But he doubted the ultimate importance of his work. The success of the commercial criminal depended on his ability to create credible illusions, but in the world of illegal drugs it was the police who had become experts at make-believe. The RCMP had been investigating the illegal drug trade for more than three decades, but the force's philosophy and techniques had not kept up with the times. The quality of the police work was judged only by the quantity of arrests – law enforcement designed to please number-crunchers.

In the typical drug case, an investigator would move from city to city and town to town, collecting evidence against street-users and traffickers, then, after six months or so, the police would conduct sweeps and arrest everyone. It was exhilarating work, just like being a TV cop, an endless cycle of surveillance, small buys, busting down doors, charging suspects, new surveillance, more small buys, more broken doors, and even more insignificant suspects. Rarely did the police get past the pusher to the next level of trafficker. However, the force always had great statistics to trot out before the politicians who controlled the public purse.

With his mentor Henry Jensen as deputy commissioner of operations behind him, Stamler was poised to make changes. He knew that judging the value and effect of police work by volume of arrests and other statistics was misleading. Whatever benefit five-and-dime drug arrests had as a deterrent was offset by the negative image of police picking on small-time and mostly recreational drug users. It all smelled like police harassment, even to the courts.

Both Stamler and Jensen were determined to find ways to wean the police off quick-hit arrests and to concentrate higher up the drug chain on the serious criminals, the importers and large-scale traffickers. Stamler wanted to professionalize the drug cops, including the way they conducted undercover work and used informants. He wanted to bring to drug investigations the same long and painstaking approach that had worked so well in the Commercial Crime Branch. All the small cases of a decade didn't add up to the message sent to crooks by prosecutions such as Hamilton Harbour. These long, difficult, and noisy affairs provided the best publicity the police could buy and, more important, best served the public interest.

Stamler worked with Jensen on setting up a unit within the Drug Enforcement Branch to specialize in assessing the assets of suspected and known major drug dealers. This way they could determine the targets for major police operations. They envisioned a team approach directed from headquarters, much like the early days of the Commercial Crime Branch – function over territory.

During the dredging trial Ontario prosecutor Rod McLeod had impressed Stamler with his system of coding evidence so that the court and jury could easily understand the significance of each piece of paper. Stamler decided to adopt a similar system to identify drug traffickers across the country. Drug squad officers would identify each trafficker by the drugs involved – A for heroin, B for cocaine, for example – the amount of drugs the trafficker's organization could handle, and how much money the trafficker had accumulated. Once a trafficker was identified, the anti-drug-profiteering unit would move in and undertake a net worth of the suspect's assets.

As soon as the new policy was implemented, many in the force complained that the arrest statistics would drop off. "That's what we wanted," Stamler says. "We were more interested in the level of violator. When departmental auditors looked at our operations, I had a simple message for them: 'Don't count beans, count the size of the beans.'"

On the street the policy was slow to take hold. Many drug investigators viewed it as more paperwork from an idealistic boss who knew diddly-squat about busting traffickers. Soon Alta Vista was swamped with details of top-level cases; suddenly everyone was a top dealer. One Vancouver case was typical. The RCMP drug squad said it had identified a "Mr. Big," who was bringing in shiploads of marijuana from Thailand. Taking the policemen at their word, Stamler okayed a major operation, including the use of undercover police officers. The anti-drug-profiteering unit then assessed the net worth of the suspect. Mr. Big, it turned out, was anything but. He drove an old, rusty car and rented a cheap apartment in one of Vancouver's roughest neighbourhoods. "Not even the shoes on his feet were worth anything," Stamler says. "He had not a cent of net worth, and they were dealing with him in an undercover capacity." Still, it was a useful exercise. Caught out so badly once, the Mounties on the streets would be more careful in their assessments of prime suspects.

In 1983, the first full year of the anti-drug-profiteering program, convicted dealers forfeited $10 million in illegally gained assets to the government. The program was not only effective, it was also a political success.

Although Stamler came into the Drug Enforcement Branch at the top, he wasn't content just to fly his desk to fame and glory. He made it his business to understand how drug enforcement was carried out in Canada. But the deeper Stamler immersed himself in the drug world, the more disturbed he became about the Mounties' methods. Stamler found that informants and undercover agents had wormed their way deep into the drug trade around the world. Drug trafficking was a dangerous enough business, but the proliferation of police informants had made it treacherous.

Informants were the grease that made drug investigations run smoothly and effectively. Almost everywhere in North America, drug enforcement units used the same tactics. The usual procedure was for an informant, often a low- to mid-level trafficker, to work hand-in-hand with an undercover agent. One covered the other. That was the theory, and it was treated as gospel. But in practice, the system was a nightmare. Almost without exception the relationship with an informant began with his or her arrest by the police. To avoid jail the informant would agree to co-operate with the police and act as the force's agent on the street. After their arrests, it didn't take the dealers long to figure out who had fingered them, and then the informant's life would be in danger. The Mounties usually left the informant to fend for himself or herself, neither admitting nor denying that the person was an informant. Nor was there a witness protection program to provide the informant with a new identify. Too often, he or she would end up the victim of a gangland slaying or as a derelict found dead in the gutter. The police would hold their noses and carry on, never admitting a thing. It was bad for business.

Stamler and some of his wiser colleagues were appalled by this abuse of informants. "It was extremely unfair and inhumane. We could not do that kind of operation. We had to bring in these people after they testified. We had to protect them," Stamler says.

Stamler pressed for a proper witness protection program, a concept that has received much lip-service, but still has not been widely adopted across the country even today. Being a police informant is still a dangerous occupation in Canada.

In all aspects of drug enforcement Stamler found sloppy and unprofessional practices. Just as he took over the branch, the crimes of a drug squad member in Montreal came to light. Staff-Sergeant Paul Sauvé had been a Mountie for twenty-five years and had risen to become the number-three man in the RCMP's Montreal drug squad. Sauvé had helped put mobster Frank Cotroni and the drug smuggler Lucien Rivard behind bars. He had helped to break up the French Connection. His credentials seemed impeccable. In 1977, he had been promoted to director of operations and put in charge of twelve major informants. Sauvé, however, was corrupt – a pitfall for drug cops.

Having a trafficker as an informant makes operational sense as it provides the police with a window on the drug world. The trafficker–informant also benefited by gaining valuable inside knowledge of police operations and methods. To keep up a credible front, the trafficker continued to deal drugs, with virtual immunity from police investigation. He was allowed to keep all his profits and he was in the position of putting his competitors out of business.

"Inevitably, what we found," Stamler says, "where a policeman and an informant worked together for a prolonged period of time, is that the informant usually grew to become the largest trafficker in the region. The police statistics looked good, yet the flow of drugs was never really impeded because the trafficker was operating with almost total impunity." The considerable flow of dollars generated by the informant would be eyed enviously by the cop. In the case of Staff-Sergeant Sauvé, the temptation to profit was irresistible.

Sauvé and his informant were running a lucrative business built up by reinvested profits. When the police finally arrested Sauvé, they found hashish in the kitchen ventilator of a rented apartment, $206,990 in a briefcase in the bedroom, $20,000 in one-hundred-dollar bills in an envelope in the kitchen, $2,695 in a wardrobe, and $1,500 in the informant's clothes. At Sauvé's home they found $78,310 cash in a safe. Sauvé argued that the money was to be used to help him infiltrate drug networks, but the courts didn't believe him. He was ordered jailed in 1986, but his appeals were still before the courts in 1993, by which time he hadn't served a moment in prison.

Stamler implemented new rules and authorized a new manual that included detailed regulations on dealing with "confidential human sources." The police were no longer allowed to aid informants in any lawlessness. But legalized lawlessness was the custom. In the United States in 1985, President Ronald Reagan had declared a war on drugs, and Prime Minister Brian Mulroney had quickly responded with one of his own. An international war on the drug trade made great headlines, but it wasn't long before Stamler saw how much fiction was involved.

Through his normal police contacts and his work at the United Nations, Stamler studied the international drug enforcement agencies, and he didn't like what he found. In many cases their systems were simple; they relied on hundreds of agents and tens of thousands of informants strategically placed around the world, including, Stamler suspected, in Canada. Within them, promotion and respect were solely dependent upon breaking big cases. If there were no big cases, they had a way of making them appear. Stamler believed that, with rare exceptions, these agencies didn't play fair within the rule of law.

In a typical case the agency would get a tip that there was a buyer in the market for, say, fifty kilograms of heroin or cocaine. The agency would introduce its agents, arrange the deal, put up money, if necessary, and even help to transport the drugs. After the arrests were made, all the agents and informants would disappear, usually with the money.

One of the best examples of such a case involved sports-car maker John DeLorean, who was arrested in Los Angeles in 1982. At the time, DeLorean was in severe financial trouble. A longtime police informant – a professional informant – who knew about DeLorean's cocaine use pitched him the idea of financing a huge drug deal. The return for DeLorean would be a quick $1-million. Hungry for the money, DeLorean took the bait. The informant then turned around and told the police that he had information that DeLorean was planning to bring in a huge shipment of illegal drugs. The informant charged the police about $300,000 for his services.

To the police it was an ideal big case – a large quantity of drugs and a high-profile suspect. DeLorean was arrested and charged with conspiracy. The case was thrown out of court for the obvious reasons. "The police can't operate like that," Stamler says. "It is wrong for the police to provide the opportunities for a desperate person to commit a criminal act. Given time, the desperate person may well have gone on with some other lawful venture."

In the early 1980s, when Stamler found that similar practices were prevalent in Canada, he moved immediately to stop the Mounties from acting as go-betweens and facilitators in drug deals. "The police cannot be seen to be setting up the deals and selling the drugs. It's wrong. By operating in this fashion, the police are actually teaching the people at each end, in Thailand and Hamilton or wherever, how to distribute drugs. It is a shortsighted way of policing because no police force can keep all these informants under wraps forever, telling them who the contacts are, how to do it, how to come through the border, how to do this and how to do that." Stamler was convinced that this style of investigation was often nothing short of entrapment. But, for all his reforms, some Mounties still got too close to their informants. In December 1992, former head of the Montreal drug squad, Inspector Claude Savoie, shot and killed himself in his office at RCMP headquarters, the night before a "fifth estate" story about his connection to a Montreal drug dealer.

The eight years Stamler spent in the Drug Enforcement Branch did not sour him on his first love, commercial-crime work. In fact, during those years he gained a perspective about commercial-crime policing in Canada that disturbed him. A great deal of time, effort, and resources went into catching drug dealers while the most lucrative and insidious crimes – those by white-collar criminals – were no longer being investigated in any depth. At the very moment Canadian newspapers were being filled with the horror stories about Mafia activities, the country's treasury was being plundered by a scheme known as the Scientific Research Tax Credit.* The SRTC was a tax-avoidance measure concocted by the private sector in 1981 and formalized in 1983 by then finance minister Marc Lalonde. Under the program, companies were allowed to sell their research-and-development tax breaks. The intention of the plan was to foster an atmosphere of scientific research in Canada. What resulted was an unprecedented criminal raid on the treasury which eventually cost the Canadian taxpayer between $3 billion and $4 billion lost in outright tax frauds. Meanwhile, caught between the country's tax privacy laws and a lack of concern on the part of politicians, the Mounties were able to mount only a handful of cases. In 1993, four Vancouver-area men received jail sentences for stealing $17.5-million through the SRTC program, and two Toronto men were

---

* A description of the scheme can be found in Linda McQuaig's book *Behind Closed Doors, How the Rich Won Control of Canada's Tax System*, Penguin Canada, 1987.

convicted in 1994 for stealing $15 million. Although many members of the traditional Canadian establishment benefited from the SRTC scam, not one was brought to justice.

Many observers thought that decades of illegal drug trade didn't measure up to the economic and moral damage done to Canada during the few months the SRTC program operated. The rule of law was seen to be an illusion, and the Mafia and drug dealers were the smoke and mirrors. To some, the real bandits were on Bay Street.

14

The Bryce Mackasey Affair

Without Henry Jensen, Rod Stamler, and the others who had left, the Commercial Crime Branch was no longer as effective as it had been. Its achievements diminished markedly after regional commanders were placed in charge of investigations, and the nature of the squads had changed after personnel policies had been changed. A supervisor's instinctive feelings about a potential candidate were no longer considered within the new structure of committees empowered to ensure fairness in hiring and equality in promotion. Finally, Commissioner Robert Simmonds, who had committed himself to keeping his political masters informed about important developments, now controlled major cases directly. Well-intentioned as these policies were, they had ushered in a climate of caution, careerism, and, some thought, outright cowardice.

By 1982, seven years after the Sky Shops affair first erupted, six years after Robert Simmonds took the helm, the once buoyant

Commercial Crime Branch had been crippled. Its bright lights had been shipped out, bumped upstairs, or had quit in frustration. Many of those left had developed a severe allergy to controversy, especially if it involved politicians or their business allies. It was a disease made all the worse by easily corrupted, self-serving, and dysfunctional political and judicial institutions. There would be no more long, deep probes like Stamler's trio of cases that began with his Hamilton Harbour investigation. The subtle message from RCMP headquarters was that feathers were not to be ruffled.

After the McDonald Commission the Mounties no longer actively investigated commercial crime. The only people who did any investigation were a handful of journalists, and without the search powers of the police, they could only sketch the picture in broad strokes. Now the police were out of the game, journalists became sitting ducks for attack from those people whose questionable activities they were reporting. The case of Bryce Mackasey illustrated the vital role of journalism now that the commercial-crime investigators had been handcuffed.

In September 1982, Robert Harrison, a prominent accountant and president of the Montreal Board of Trade, gave testimony at a hearing into the bankruptcy of an obscure machine-tooling firm known as Les Ateliers d'Usinage Hall. At one point in his testimony, Harrison was questioned by Joachim Normand, the lawyer for the bankruptcy trustees. Normand wanted to know the identity of a lobbyist for Les Ateliers who had been paid through a numbered company, 109609 Canada Ltd., to lobby the federal government for contracts.

Harrison was reluctant to name the person but finally agreed to give the information "off the record." The stenographer's recorder was turned off, and Harrison gave the court the name of Bryce Mackasey, a longtime Liberal MP. Harrison's association with Mackasey went back a long way; his father had organized Mackasey's first political campaign, and when Mackasey was in the cabinet, Harrison had administered his blind trust. If the news got out about Mackasey, it would be a bombshell, so those attending the bankruptcy hearing vowed to keep it secret.

The amiable, blustering Mackasey had spent the past two decades caught up in one political storm after another. First elected to the Commons in 1962, he had overseen a string of ministries and had resigned twice. In 1976, after Conservative businessman Brian Mulroney introduced him to Quebec Liberal leader Robert Bourassa, Mackasey served a short stint as a Liberal member of the Quebec National Assembly. But almost as soon as he arrived in Quebec City, he resigned and returned to Ottawa looking to get back into Parliament. In 1978, he won the Liberal nomination for Ottawa Centre, but unfortunately anti-Trudeau sentiment was high at the time and Mackasey and a dozen other high-profile Liberals running in simultaneous by-elections were slaughtered at the polls.

As a reward for carrying the party's banner, Mackasey was appointed a few weeks later as the new chairman of Air Canada. His seven-year contract, which paid him $90,000 in the first year, enraged the public. Eight months later, with Trudeau and the Liberals out and Joe Clark's Conservatives in, Mackasey was asked to resign. He refused and was summarily fired, complaining loud and long about the vindictiveness of the Tories. However, Mackasey bounced back in the surprise 1980 federal election, winning a new seat in the Hamilton riding of Lincoln, next to the riding of his long-time friend and colleague John Munro, whose supporters helped push Mackasey over the top. Though he wasn't in the new cabinet, Mackasey was still given important responsibilities, including a membership on Parliament's banking committee, which reviewed and recommended changes to the Bank Act.

Enter William Marsden, a reporter for the Montreal *Gazette*. In late January 1983, Marsden received a tip about a company called Labec. Marsden checked out Labec in the Dun and

Bradstreet business directory where he found a cross-reference to Hall Engineering Ltd. of Cambridge, Ontario, which, in turn, had a Quebec subsidiary, Les Ateliers d'Usinage Hall. Checking further, Marsden found that Les Ateliers had declared bankruptcy eight months earlier. He called up the trustee in bankruptcy to inquire about the circumstances of the company's demise. The trustee told Marsden that there was "something interesting that was political." He refused to elaborate, which was enough to provoke Marsden to order a transcript of the bankruptcy hearing.

As Marsden waded through the all-French transcript, he came across Robert Harrison's testimony. Harrison's use of words was bizarre, Marsden thought, as if he were deliberately making it difficult for anyone to understand what he really meant. Harrison seemed to have been talking about a company set up only to mask the fact that someone's bills had secretly been paid off. But whose bills?

Marsden contacted some of the other parties involved in the bankruptcy hearing but found that they were all afraid to talk: "Actually, they were scared out of their goddamn minds," Marsden says. "It was all incredibly hush-hush because politicians were involved. I always found it interesting that politicians in this country can scare people so much."

Eventually, Marsden managed to wheedle out the secret that Mackasey had lobbied on Les Ateliers's behalf. Next he tried to approach Harrison about what he had said at the hearing, but Harrison refused to see him. Mackasey would say only that he had nothing to hide, everything was above board, and it would be a simple matter to explain. But Marsden couldn't get Mackasey to agree to a time for a meeting where the matter could be explained. Marsden knew he was being stonewalled.

Marsden had heard that a Mountie had sat in on the bankruptcy hearing, but had left before Harrison had testified, so he paid a visit to the Commercial Crime Branch offices in Montreal.

The senior officer he talked to made it clear that, while his squad was aware of the Les Ateliers bankruptcy, it wasn't conducting an investigation. "I hate these political investigations. We don't want to touch them because they are a big pain in the ass. They just cause problems for everyone and, in the end, the guy is always protected," the Mountie complained. The controversies of the previous years had taken their toll, indeed. The fact that the Mackasey case involved a forgiven loan by the Bank of Montreal didn't help either: the police also hated dealing with the banks. "They are all a bunch of whores," the policeman told Marsden. Experience had taught the Mounties that Canadian banks would not co-operate with criminal investigations. If a police officer armed with a search warrant was looking for a document, bank officials were more likely to point at a multi-storey office tower and say, "It's somewhere in there," than to hand the document over.

Marsden was dismayed by the unaggressive attitude of the Mounties, but went on chasing the story. The police might be afraid of politicians and the business élite, but he wasn't. Prior to uncovering the Mackasey story, Marsden had had occasion to call Mackasey. Mackasey had been friendly and courteous and had even invited the reporter to visit him in Ottawa. Now that Mackasey was being pursued, however, his manner changed. The night the story about Mackasey's hidden ownership of the numbered company was going to press, Mackasey showed up unannounced at the *Gazette*'s offices. There he met with the managing editor, Mel Morris. For half an hour Morris listened to Mackasey's insistence that Harrison's allegations were much ado about nothing. "It can all be explained. It's a simple matter," Mackasey told Morris, but, no, he couldn't be any more specific than that; he didn't want to go into it right then. If Mackasey wouldn't make his case now on the eve of the story's publication, Morris wondered, then when would he? There would never be a more important time for Mackasey to come forward. Morris didn't tip his hand one way or the other. "Bryce was a nice fellow. He'd done many great things for the country, it was true, but this time we had caught him dead to rights."

On March 10, 1983, the *Gazette* published Marsden's story about Harrison's disclosure at the bankruptcy trial and about how Mackasey was the secret owner of 109609 Canada Ltd., which was registered in Harrison's name. Quoting Harrison's testimony, Marsden wrote that 109609 Canada had received a $400,000 guaranteed loan from Les Ateliers to cover Mackasey's lobbying services, plus $22,500 in cash. The story was corroborated by two unnamed people who had attended the hearing, and Mackasey was quoted as denying any involvement with either company.

The *Gazette* expected that the story would cause a storm, but Marsden says no one realized how big it would become. "Ultimately, I was quite surprised at the forces that rallied around Mackasey," Marsden says. The story caused an immediate and, for many experienced observers, expected reaction: Marsden and the *Gazette* were attacked for publishing it.

Harrison, who had refused to talk before, now claimed that Marsden had misrepresented what had been said at the bankruptcy hearing. He charged that the paper had "no right to interpret my testimony." He launched the first of two libel suits against Marsden, the *Gazette*, and its owner, Southam, claiming $1.3 million in damages. Then he told everyone who would listen and write about him that he had not a worry in the world. Later, he launched another suit claiming an additional $1.5 million in damages.

Mackasey sought the haven of the House of Commons Privileges and Elections Committee. He said the *Gazette*'s story had infringed on his rights as a parliamentarian and he denied owning the numbered company or acting as a lobbyist for Les Ateliers. He argued that because the *Gazette* story was based on unnamed sources and was quoting from an off-the-record statement, his privileges had been breached. Therefore, he claimed, the *Gazette* was in contempt of Parliament for bringing the reputation of the House into disrepute. It was all silly, but the powers of the committee had to be taken seriously.

Gazette reporter Hubert Bauch pointed out, "What it comes down to is that to protect its collective sense of integrity, the country's legislative branch can transform itself into a high court, against which there is no recourse except to have the administration of the day thrown out by the voters. The members of the court can, at once, act as judge, jury, and prosecutor and impose any penalty short of capital punishment without having to follow procedures or recognize the elementary rules of evidence that Canadians take for granted in their judicial system. Why? Because it is Parliament's privilege. In short, Parliament, in the British tradition, had the right to set itself somewhat above those it governed."

Marsden had no objections to being questioned about his story: he had nothing to hide. The story wasn't perfectly executed, but he could defend everything he had done. His only worry was the nature and mandate of the committee which he described as a "kangaroo court."

When the committee hearings began, the *Gazette* was holding an ace up its sleeve. Harrison had accused the *Gazette* of "interpreting" what he had said in the bankruptcy hearing, knowing that the stenographer had switched off her recorder, but the *Gazette* knew there was a master taping system in the court house which was never shut off. The paper's publisher, Robert McConnell, went before a judge and argued that he should be given a copy of the tape. The judge agreed that it was a public document and ordered it released. McConnell insisted on playing the tape to the committee so that all of them could hear Harrison identifying Mackasey. McConnell thought this evidence would clear the *Gazette*. But Harrison immediately called a press conference in the corridor outside the committee room. He denounced the tape as "absolute garbage" and questioned its relevance and authenticity. "My suit against the *Gazette* is still very good," Harrison said.

The tape did force Harrison's hand. In his testimony the next day he said that Mackasey was paid $400,000 by 109609 Canada for shares, mostly in penny mining stock. When the numbered company turned around and sold the shares, it could only raise $150,000, meaning that Mackasey had somehow pocketed a quick $250,000. Harrison's testimony differed substantially from what he had said at the bankruptcy hearing. Harrison then told the committee that businessman Christian Joly, not Mackasey, had been the lobbyist for Les Ateliers. The story got murkier and murkier with denials by Joly, the revelation about connections to Bermuda banks, testimony from two former presidents of Les Ateliers who believed Mackasey was acting as a paid lobbyist, and evidence of some bizarre business transactions, including one in which $40,500 was spent either on a painting by an unknown Boston artist or on a piece of machinery called a power rotary turntable, depending on whose evidence one chose to believe. There were Bermuda connections, but in place of chains, grapnels, and ghost ships, the currencies were fine art, penny stocks, and power rotary turntables.

Finally, officials from the Bank of Montreal testified that they and Harrison had worked out a deal to help Mackasey with a $400,000 loan he had taken out but could not repay. In fact, the bank conceded, Mackasey had owed the bank $625,000 at one time. He had used money, with the knowledge of the bank, to invest in the penny stocks – an extremely unusual loan on the part of the bank, especially since the money was lent during a recession. The bank had agreed to finance Les Ateliers's purchase of Mackasey's shaky stock portfolio on the condition that Les Ateliers signed a five-year promissory note as collateral. However, when Les Ateliers went into bankruptcy, the bank made no attempt to recover the loan. Other Canadian borrowers had to wonder why their bank managers were not so generous to them. That the bank's largesse could easily be construed as bribing Mackasey, a member of Parliament's banking committee, didn't seem to concern the parliamentarians, who never pursued that line of questioning.

Also called to testify before the committee was RCMP Commissioner Simmonds. In what was called a "startling revelation," Simmonds told the committee that the police were investigating possible offences involving theft, fraud, and influence peddling among all those involved in the Les Ateliers bankruptcy, including Mackasey. Simmonds told the committee that the police would complete their investigation in ten days. The news of the police investigation was a relief to Marsden, public confirmation that his work was not a fairy tale. However, he also knew from his confrontation with the investigator in Montreal, and from the short timetable, that the RCMP was not going to strain a muscle in gathering more evidence than he had already handed to them on a silver platter.

True to the commissioner's suggestion, Mackasey was subsequently charged with influence peddling and fraud upon the government. Harrison and another man were charged with attempting to bribe a public official in relation to the $400,000 payment to Mackasey. The Bank of Montreal's role was completely ignored.

Three months later, in what many observers, not only the police, consider to be one of the most curious judgments in the history of Canadian jurisprudence, Quebec judge Benjamin Schecter threw out the case against Mackasey. After hearing fifteen witnesses and reviewing two hundred documents, Schecter ruled that the evidence against Mackasey was "flimsy." Furthermore, he described the liquidation of Mackasey's stock portfolio as a "good business deal," which was a gross understatement. Anyone who can get a bank to put up $400,000 for $150,000 worth of questionable stock in the midst of an economic recession is getting more than a good business deal. The judge said there was no evidence of influence peddling by Mackasey, even though the money had been paid to him and even though Mackasey admitted at one point that he had lobbied another minister on behalf of Les Ateliers. Finally, the judge wouldn't let the case be heard by a jury, saying that it would be unfair to a jury, since he himself was confused by the evidence.

The result didn't surprise Stamler, who had been face to face with justice in Quebec, but for Marsden and his colleagues at the *Gazette*, it was one of those rare moments when they felt what good policemen feel when they see justifiable cases disappear into the ether.

Marsden thought the decision incredible, but not surprising, considering what else had gone on behind the scenes. While Schecter was getting ready to hear the Mackasey case, one of his aides had phoned Marsden and told him the judge had a story for him. The judge had made what he thought was an important decision on a rape case and wanted Marsden to have the story first. Marsden took the judgment and did nothing with it. Later, based on his own observations and those of a Mountie attending the Mackasey hearing, Marsden bet fellow reporter Rod Mac-Donell that Mackasey would not be committed for trial. The outcome didn't really matter to Marsden. "My job is to raise issues, not to put people in jail. We were able to bring light on the subject, and no matter what the courts decided, the people knew the truth of what had happened. We served the public interest."

Judge Schecter's decision was never appealed and the RCMP did not bother to pursue Mackasey again, but the story did not end there. The truth did eventually come out.

With Schecter's ruling, the heat was back on the *Gazette*. Not content to leave well enough alone, Mackasey launched his own libel suit claiming $1.92 million in damages, then he took his case back before the Commons Committee on Privileges and Elections. He asked the committee to censure the *Gazette* for what he called sloppy and malicious journalism. The paper was hauled back before the committee. *Gazette* publisher Robert McConnell was unrepentant. He told the politicians that the *Gazette* not only had a right to publish the story, but also a duty to do so. Further, it was the *Gazette* that was being smeared by the politicians, not the other way around.

The committee eventually made its ruling, addressed to Mackasey, saying it found the Gazette's allegations about him unsubstantiated. The ruling also said, "the allegations reported by the Montreal *Gazette* have adversely affected the reputation of the honourable member for Lincoln and, through him, the privileges of the House of Commons."

There was one dissenter on the committee, NDP MP Rod Murphy, who issued his own report in which he wrote, "the rights of individual members of Parliament and of the House itself must always be balanced by the public's right to know and media's freedom to report. The House must never abuse its powers to condemn or censure the media without clear justification. Any attempt by Parliament to use its authority to limit coverage of its members or its activities should be restricted to those occasions where there is no or little doubt the media is abusing its powers and responsibility."

In an editorial afterward, the *Winnipeg Free Press* commented:

> The newspaper which blew the whistle has been ever-so-mildly reprimanded by the committee for damaging Mr. Mackasey's reputation. But the greater damage is that done to the reputation of Parliament by the privileges and elections committee. The world now knows that the committee's ethical standards allow it to look calmly at Mr. Mackasey's dealings with the Bank of Montreal and not bat an eye. . . . The damage to Mr. Mackasey's reputation arises primarily from the true facts established by testimony at the preliminary hearing. Complaint against the *Gazette* report, in the circumstances, is laughable.

Mackasey, of course, was delighted with the committee's report and made it a point to tell everyone he had been vindicated.

Marsden and his colleagues knew they hadn't been wrong, and they continued to pursue the story. Their public vindication came a year later in early 1984, after Mackasey had been appointed Canadian ambassador to Portugal. Robert Harrison was broke, disillusioned, and on the run from the police, facing perjury charges in addition to the fraud, theft, and conspiracy charges already laid against him. He was living in the tiny town of Feledelphia, Paraguay, "a dust bowl of bleached brick buildings," where he wrote down his version of the story. He contacted Marsden and invited the reporter to meet him in Miami, and proceeded to tell Marsden what the reporter had long suspected, that Marsden had been right all along. Harrison said the attack on the newspaper had been orchestrated from the beginning by Mackasey and a staff member in the Prime Minister's Office. Harrison said he met with Mackasey before and after the committee hearings in Ottawa and the court hearing before Judge Schecter so that they could keep their stories straight.

Harrison's job had been to play along with the committee, but the courtroom tape had made him vulnerable. After the tape was made public, the more Harrison talked, the weaker his story had become. He told Marsden that he went along with Mackasey's plan because he had no sense of disaster. "I just thought it [the committee hearing] was a bunch of parliamentary guys who wanted to have a big song and dance, a lot of publicity about this thing." It had all been like a game, Harrison said, and he believed he had done nothing unusual because "in Ottawa one hand always tries to help the other." If one chose to be moral or self-righteous about the law, he said, then he clearly broke the law. Marsden says that Harrison saw his role in the affair as the most undesirable of all – that of fall-guy.

Before publishing his story about Harrison, Marsden

attempted to get Mackasey to comment. Mackasey hid behind his lawyer, who threatened legal action should the story be published. The *Gazette* published the story anyway.

Harrison told his story again, in court, where Judge D'Arcy Asselin allowed the testimony to roam far and wide because, as he told Marsden later, the Canadian public needed to hear everything, once and for all. "It was a festering boil that had to be excised," Asselin said.

Harrison was convicted. Before he went to jail, he tried to expose other wrongdoings and other hidden and sinister connections, but his credibility was long gone. He formally dropped the two libel suits he had filed against Marsden and the *Gazette*.

Mackasey had also claimed libel damages from Marsden and the *Gazette*, which got him a fat headline in newspapers across Canada. After the headlines he never pursued the matter one step further, retiring from politics and disappearing into the anonymity of Verdun. According to Harrison, the libel suit had never been intended to do more than block the *Gazette* in its pursuit of the truth. Before Mackasey left the national scene, Barry Callaghan wrote a glowing profile of him in *Saturday Night*. There was no mention of the Les Ateliers affair; it was as if it had never happened.

With Harrison in jail, the Mounties closed the books on the investigation, which appalled the old commercial-crime cops back at headquarters in Ottawa – Stamler and Jensen. But there was nothing they could do about it; the rules had changed.

15

Changes at the Top

By 1986, the Drug Enforcement and Commercial Crime branches had each grown so large they were converted into full directorates. Earlier, Stamler had been promoted to chief superintendent, which meant he now reported directly to the deputy commissioner of operations, the second most powerful person in the RCMP. A year later, Stamler moved up to become assistant commissioner in charge of the Drug Enforcement Directorate.

Stamler had risen much higher in the force than he had ever aimed. "Once I'd reached superintendent, I really didn't care about the future," he says. "I knew I wasn't going to go any higher. I hadn't commanded a contract division and I only had B-level French. The first obstacle I could overcome, but no one was going to become commissioner unless he was fluent in French."

The issue of who was going to become the next commissioner was very much in the air in 1986. Robert Simmonds had been leading the force for almost ten years, the third-longest tenure in the force's history. He had taken over in 1977 when the RCMP was about to be scrutinized by the McDonald Royal Commission. Until the Security Service became a separate entity in 1984, he was all but consumed by the controversies it spawned. Other formidable political forces also had borne down on the RCMP: the new Constitution, the new Charter of Rights and Freedoms, stronger privacy legislation, restrictive court decisions, demands for racial and sexual equality, and increasing public pressure for civilian control of the police. The RCMP was forced to react quickly to these fundamental changes. Each of them threatened to tear the force apart. But none of them was as debilitating to the force as the changes in its reporting structure.

The McDonald Commission had recommended that there be political responsibility for the activities of the RCMP. Simmonds had interpreted this to apply to both the Security Service and the police force, although the intention, as articulated by Pierre Trudeau and Francis Fox, among others, was only for the Security Service to be strictly controlled.

Henry Jensen says, "After the McDonald Commission there was far more top-down vigilance, control if you would, of the force. There was detectable nervousness in the Commissioner's Office. I guess the politicians made almost compelling reasons for information to be drawn to the top. I think it led to information improperly being disclosed to political officials or to officials of the minister. To me, that's wrong. No one should know outside of the police who is under investigation."

The "detectable nervousness" of the commissioner had much to do with the fear of controversy. By its very nature, police work sparks controversy – people do not like being investigated, especially people with something to hide. "The police go out on a limb from time to time, but they do it because they believe they have to do it. They have to do it to live up to their oath of office," says Jensen. "The role of the police is not to please any one government. The role of the police is to live up to their obligations to society, to enforce the law."

Under Simmonds, the practice of providing the solicitor-general with information about investigations became formalized. There were two sets of briefing books, one for the commissioner and the other for the minister. Whenever a Mountie program director saw a headline in a newspaper relating to his area of responsibility, he had to write up a report on the matter, including possible questions that might be asked of the appropriate minister and suggested responses. There was even a liaison officer between the government and RCMP headquarters who handled the paperwork. The Mounties at headquarters thought that the liaison officer, although a Mountie, was acting like a ferret for the government as he often came back with further questions about a case. There was a constant flow of information up to the minister and his political staff.

Rank-and-file Mounties had been co-opted into acting as political advisers to politicians, but the police had no avenue of protest – Simmonds believed there was nothing wrong with the practice. "You know, being a deputy minister is a powerful position, without question," says Jensen. "And once you see in your mind that you're a deputy minister, it affects your role as a policeman. You cross the line." It was an intolerable situation for the police, and it continues to exist.

"First of all, the role of the solicitor-general is not supervision of criminal investigations," Jensen says. "It is the supervision of the administration of justice. Secondly, I believe that there is a great danger whenever information leaves the police force [and goes] to an elected body. There is always the potential that the information will get misused for political reasons, rather than legitimate law-enforcement reasons.

"Did the ministers ask questions because they wanted to know what was going on as much as possible? Or was it because they wanted to deal in a legitimate way with a question that was coming up?" Jensen says, "We would be told that the politicians expected a question on this or that case and urgently required background. We would provide the information, and then nothing ever happened. What really was going on was that the government was trying to head off embarrassment, while the Opposition was always looking for something to do just that to the government. It was a game being played by all the politicians, everyone was in on it. The integrity of police operations was being severely jeopardized."

It was in this context that the hiring of a new commissioner was undertaken. A decade or two earlier, based on the overall excellence of his performance, Stamler might have been invited to apply for the job. But times had changed, and no one gave him the go-ahead to put his hat into the ring. As successful as he had been, Stamler had taken chances and had made too many waves.

Four candidates were asked to compete for the post: Thomas Venner, Don Wilson, Norman Inkster, and Henry Jensen.

Venner, a well-respected career officer, had just retired as deputy commissioner and had served earlier as commander of the lower mainland division in British Columbia, which Jensen had once headed.

Wilson was the current commander of the British Columbia division and a former head of the Commercial Crime Branch.

Jensen was both the most successful policeman of all the candidates and the most controversial. He had set up the Commercial Crime Branch, had received the Mounties' long service and good conduct medal in 1972, the Queen's Silver Jubilee Medal in 1977 and, until 1981, had seemed to be a shoo-in for the commissioner's job. That year, just after being appointed deputy commissioner of operations, the country's chief criminal investigator, he made a decision that rocked the force. While Simmonds was off studying the McDonald Commission report, Jensen alone approved paying $10,000 into a trust fund each time serial killer Clifford Olson disclosed the whereabouts of one of his victims' bodies. Jensen's original plan to seize the money back was subverted by Olson's lawyer when the story became public. In 1985, Jensen was transferred from operations to law-enforcement services. The new job placed him in charge of identification services, forensic laboratories, and the Canadian Police College. Many in Alta Vista thought he'd been shipped out of sight for two years. Stamler, who has always admired Jensen, comments: "The law was the law to Hank. His first instinct was to do the right thing, even if it meant he'd be unpopular."

The Winnipeg-born Inkster had spent most of his time in the administrative ranks where he had risen to be head of personnel. In spite of his lack of investigative experience, Simmonds had made him deputy of operations in 1985, replacing Jensen. Inkster had the reputation of being an excellent delegator, or, as his critics thought, an excellent manipulator. Many Mounties were of the opinion that Inkster was not only ignorant about, but actually disliked, police work. One factor in his favour, however, was his complete fluency in both English and French.

The race was between three well-rounded and proven police officers and a well-groomed administrator. Most observers saw it as a battle between Jensen and Inkster. But in the end it wasn't much of a contest. Jensen lost. Perhaps because he was not afraid to speak his mind. Perhaps because Simmonds never got over the embarrassment caused by the Olson case. Perhaps because he wasn't fluently bilingual. Official bilingualism had been RCMP policy for a little more than a decade and had blocked the progress of many a well-qualified senior officer who couldn't master a second language so late in life.

On September 1, 1987, Norman Inkster became the eighteenth commissioner and the deputy solicitor-general. As compensation for losing, Jensen was returned to the powerful post of deputy commissioner of operations.

It was a strange mix: Jensen was now having to work closely with a man he didn't respect, and, from all accounts, Inkster didn't much like Jensen. Jensen was named acting commissioner whenever Inkster was away, and since Inkster knew so little about policing, some thought Jensen had actually won. In Jensen's mind, he was perfectly positioned to realize his lifelong dream and become commissioner next time around. But there was another scenario at work with a few twists in the script, which would result in a turbulent and disturbing end to the decade, and to his career.

Within a year of taking over as commissioner, Inkster had imposed his style. He saw himself as president of a large national corporation, not as chief constable of a police force. He was a deputy minister, appointed with the approval of the prime minister, not a cop. "Inkster didn't have the fine feel for police powers, for the positions the police must take and the need for independence a policeman must have in certain situations," says Stamler, echoing the observations of many Mounties. "Inkster wanted to be a manager, he wanted others to make the decisions. He wanted a trouble-free office with a clean desk, unlike Simmonds who had 450 files in his office through which he was always poring because he had to know everything."

Michael Shoemaker, a career public servant, was brought in as the first civilian deputy commissioner, in charge of corporate management. Many senior officers suspected Shoemaker was a political spy and treated him as such, although there was no evidence that he was.

The piles of files grew on the desks of Inkster's deputies. Meanwhile, he worked at implementing new policies, dealing with the politicians, hobnobbing with the élite, and travelling, always travelling, leaving Jensen to run the force. Almost from the outset, Inkster began campaigning to become the head of Interpol, an honorary position with no real function. He finally succeeded in 1992.

Inkster was a master of symbolism and grand gestures. He

pushed ahead plans for decentralization, first championed by J. Grant Glassco in 1962, and which had been political dogma ever since. Even if critics inside the force had serious reservations about decentralization, Inkster was not going to argue with the government. The critics thought that in some cases decentralization made no sense at all. For example, it was announced that "O" Division headquarters in downtown Toronto would be closed and moved to London in 1993, and the various investigative sections within the Toronto office would be scattered. The Commercial Crime section would be located where land was cheaper, far from the downtown core. Stamler shares the opinion of many, thinking the idea ridiculous: "The biggest financial market in Canada is in downtown Toronto. As a result, the centre for commercial crime in Canada is downtown Toronto. By putting commercial crime investigators forty miles away in Bowmanville, you are immediately cutting their effectiveness. Investigators report to their office before heading out to an assignment. When they were in downtown Toronto, commercial-crime investigators often could walk to their assignments. By placing them in Newmarket or Bowmanville, they will be fighting traffic heading into the city in rush hour and, when their day is over, fighting traffic in rush hour all the way back, with an hour for lunch in between. It's a minimum loss of two hours' work per day per officer. That makes sense?"

Under Inkster, education requirements for applicants were improved, hiring freezes were placed on white, anglophone men, French-Canadian officers were moved into key positions, some women were promoted, and Inkster championed the cause of Sikhs who wanted to wear turbans while on duty. Not one of them was a tough decision. It was all going with the flow, whether it was ultimately the right thing to do or not.

Appearances suddenly became very important. Many Mounties worried that public relations were becoming more important than real police work. The epitome of Inksterism in the RCMP is an heroic portrait hanging in the foyer of the RCMP "D" Division headquarters in Winnipeg. It depicts four Mounties in uniform: a black man, a Native man, a white woman, and an Asian woman. The painting is a calculated lie.

The force had become leaky with information under Simmonds, but Inkster's close relationship with the Conservative government turned the trickle into a steady stream. Not only was the solicitor-general informed about investigations, but unelected political aides began to hang around looking for, and often picking up, precious tidbits. Inkster demanded that briefing reports on important investigations be filed every week. Jensen and Stamler read this as a clear message from the Conservative government that there were to be no surprises. They were to avoid controversy at all costs. That was the message from Inkster.

Senior Mounties had the distinct impression that Inkster would have been perfectly happy if the RCMP never conducted another investigation and the entire force was turned into a full-time spectacular musical ride. Soon everyone was talking about the "good old days" under Simmonds. "At least Bob Simmonds knew what a policeman's oath meant," said one former senior Mountie, voicing the sentiments of a number of others, including some senior officers on the force today.

By the time Inkster was appointed commissioner, Stamler was already thinking about retiring, and Inkster's conduct in the following year only made Stamler think harder about retirement's merits. Then one day in early 1988, Inkster called Stamler in to his office and told him that Jensen had recommended that Stamler be transferred to the Economic Crime Directorate, the new name for the old Commercial Crime Branch. Stamler was initially dismayed at the prospect as it was a lateral transfer, but to a directorate with less money and fewer resources. Besides, he'd already worked in that area; there would be nothing new there for him. Still, he considered, if Jensen wanted him in

Economic Crime, there must be a good reason. Stamler's impression from afar was that the Economic Crime Directorate had become ineffective. Perhaps Jensen wanted him to revitalize commercial-crime investigation.

In June 1988, he returned to his old stomping grounds. If the grand plan was for him to whip the Economic Crime Directorate into shape, he would try to do as much as he could.

Stamler could sense major corruption in Ottawa. He could smell it. He could taste it. Intelligence reports pointed toward it, and there was plenty of talk about it in the newspapers and on the street. There were even real clues and complaints, but solid leads always seemed to fizzle out.

The Mounties in the Economic Crime Directorate were busy, but most of their cases the equivalent of the five-dollar marijuana busts Stamler had found were popular when he first moved into the drug branch. Meanwhile, the serious cases were getting lost.

When Tory MP Michel Gravel pleaded guilty and was sentenced in 1987 to a prison term for accepting bribes and for influence peddling his conviction was held to be a singular accomplishment. He was the first sitting federal politician to go to jail in twenty-five years. By pleading guilty, Gravel had prevented further examination of the Tories' curious fundraising activities. Stamler wished there was someone hungry enough to go deeper.

The allegations of the disgruntled former businessman Glen Kealey pointed to more corruption. Kealey had planned to build a $160-million office tower in Hull. To make the project work, Kealey needed government business. He claimed he was approached by Public Works Minister Roch LaSalle, who demanded $5,000 down and five per cent of the contract. But it was a case of Kealey's word against LaSalle's. No money changed hands; nothing could be proved.

Former minister Suzanne Blais-Grenier and others had also

spoken publicly about kickback schemes, but the Mounties never could find anything to substantiate their stories. Meanwhile, there was the matter of former Liberal minister John Munro, alleged to have directed federal grants through Native Indian organizations and into his own Liberal leadership campaign in 1984. The investigation had begun in 1985, and, for the next three years, a senior officer had interviewed people all over the country trying to make his case, which eventually failed in court.

As he reviewed the files, Stamler found much that disturbed him, both as a policeman and a taxpayer. Two recent cases stood out.

In the first, the giant U.S. aircraft-maker Boeing had complained about influence peddling and kickbacks in the $2-billion deal Air Canada had made in 1988 to purchase commercial airliners from the European consortium Aerospatiale. Unknown to the Mounties at the time was that pressure had been put on Air Canada by Prime Minister Brian Mulroney to pay former Newfoundland premier Frank Moores' company, Government Consultants International, a $5-million consulting fee for the deal, even though the deal had been completed without any input from GCI. Just as the Mounties started their investigation of Boeing's complaint, the government announced that it would allow Boeing to purchase the assets of de Havilland of Canada in an extremely controversial deal. Boeing withdrew its complaint and the police investigation had to stop. Stamler's gut feeling was that both deals probably required thorough police investigation, the kind that might have been undertaken in the early 1970s but was now impossible.

The second case concerned allegations that a substantial secret commission had been paid to a top adviser in Mulroney's office. The money was said to have been paid by Metropolitan Life Insurance to secure Canadian government leases at a Met-Life building at 50 O'Connor Street in Ottawa. The investigators learned that a key document, on which the signature of the Mulroney staffer appeared, was located at the company's U.S.

headquarters. As the Mounties could not exercise a search warrant in the United States, they had made arrangements for the U.S. authorities to get the document for them. Coincidentally or not, over the intervening weekend in August 1987, Canada signed the Free Trade Agreement with the United States. The document never arrived and the U.S. authorities never explained what had happened to it. The Mounties couldn't help but wonder if it had been used by the American negotiators as a bargaining chip at the eleventh hour.

In the thirteen years since Stamler had investigated the Hamilton Harbour fraud the world had changed dramatically. Computers, instant money transfers, and sophisticated offshore banking schemes had transformed the money-laundering business. In retrospect, the Liberals and their dredger friends looked as if they were running Mom and Pop political operations. Stamler suspected the Tories had gone hi-tech and that little actual money ever touched their hands in Canada, but he knew where to look and how to get there. Common sense told him that most, if not all, of the transactions were being conducted offshore; the documents in one country, the bank accounts in another. All he had to do was organize his force to tap into that system, but it would be no small task.

Stamler was distressed by the poor conditions and investigative abilities of many of his detectives. The directorate was bulging with officers – 450 across the country – but the time and talents of even the best were being wasted on other assignments such as returning to uniform to guard VIPs or foreign missions. The fact that so many politicians were under investigation spoke of a relatively open season for fraud, not only in Ottawa, but across Canada. Yet his investigators were working on dime-a-dozen cases. Commercial-crime officers prosecuting NSF cheque cases in Nelson, B.C. was a waste of an expensive federal program. There was a clear need for leadership, for someone to help investigators separate the worthwhile from the worthless.

But the more he poked and prodded his staff, the more

dismayed Stamler became. Too many of his Mounties looked good, sounded good, had the right letters after their name, were polite, courteous, and were so much the pride of the force he could almost see the regimental number tattooed into each one's hide. But they were not good investigators. One of his senior investigators, with twenty-five years' experience in the force, much of it in the Security Service, had never testified in court.

When Jensen had handpicked the commercial-crime officers in the late 1960s and early 1970s, he had looked for people with differing experiences and talents, a good education coupled with the will to learn more and, more important, the right look in their eyes – good cops who knew what to do in any situation.

By the mid 1980s, new personnel policies and cutbacks in training had filled the Economic Crime Directorate with a different class of police officer. Where in Jensen's day a university degree might be a bonus, now Mounties with a university degree were losing out in competitions to others with two or three degrees. Those who were fluently bilingual had a leg up on those who couldn't master French, and so on. Many had little, and sometimes no, experience in day-to-day police work.

In Jensen's view the new staffing policies were encouraging mediocrity and, unconsciously or otherwise, were weakening the chances that the Economic Crime Directorate would be successful in its work. He says, "Highly qualified staff were transferred away and, in many respects, were never replaced by competent staff. People ended up being in charge of units who didn't know anything about commercial crime. Well, if you want to have an ineffective squad, transfer in a mediocre individual. He won't know what he's looking for. The long-term implication is that you have a specialized squad with no specialized talent that will be ineffective in its work."

When Stamler had been assigned to monitor bankruptcy investigations in the 1960s, he had found that all the investigators were doing was building files. Once again, he found that his investigators were building files and that few of them could figure out how to make a case. "God, he was at their mercy," Jensen says. But Stamler's staff were far from being his worst enemy.

In his years in the Drug Enforcement Branch Stamler had learned two valuable lessons in how to succeed in difficult investigations that he now wanted to adapt to economic and commercial crime – a focus on money-laundering and on pro-active investigations.

Parliament was about to pass Bill C-61, which, when it was enacted on January 1, 1989, made money-laundering a crime in Canada. Stamler's plan for the Economic Crime Directorate to have its own team to investigate for money-laundering – an enterprise crime unit similar to the one that helped put teeth into the prosecutions conducted by the Drug Enforcement Branch. Stamler knew that seizing the profits of crime is a political winner.

The issue of active investigations was more complicated. A normal police investigation is reactive. That is, someone notices a crime and reports it to the police, who send out investigators. But economic crime is markedly different. These violations are almost always so surreptitious that they are virtually undetectable, especially when the victim is the taxpayer. With rare exceptions there are no witnesses, other than the perpetrators themselves. Another problem lay in locating the transactions. By the late 1980s, it was evident that not only were the proceeds of crimes committed in Canada increasingly being held offshore, but also many, if not all, transactions were being made offshore. It was getting nearly impossible for the police to find direct evidence against a suspect, even though there might be overwhelming indications of a crime, even formal complaints.

To mount an active investigation would mean using informants and undercover agents in an attempt to tap into a suspect's loop. From his years in the drug squad, Stamler knew the different roles agents and informants played in undercover operations. They were an acceptable and successful part of drug investigations, why not use them to fight economic and commercial crime? After all, crime was crime.

Another part of Stamler's plan was to reintroduce the concept of cases being investigated from the regional offices under directions from headquarters, not in a top-down fashion, but in a team approach. That way, Stamler felt, he could ensure that investigators were dealing with appropriate and important matters and could be guaranteed co-operation and co-ordination across the country.

Stamler needed a vehicle for his vision. He found it at headquarters in the Special Federal Inquiries Unit, a little-known operation, which had been set up informally in 1978. The unit handled investigations based on complaints made by Ottawa. Parliamentarians and their officials were always calling on the Mounties for investigations, and having such a specialized squad, knowledgeable about political procedures, was deemed useful.

Over the next few years, however, "A" Division in Ottawa was in a constant battle with Commissioner Simmonds, who wanted to move the unit into Alta Vista headquarters where he could "keep an eye on it." Jensen and others resisted him because they believed it was important to have the SFIU work out of the regional headquarters for two reasons: regional headquarters were equipped to handle operations, and Alta Vista wasn't; it was also a way of protecting the appearance of integrity in the investigations. It was better, they argued, for both the individual investigators and the commanders of the force that headquarters not know the details of individual investigations. Only in that way could it be argued that the investigations were free of any form of political influence.

The battle was lost in 1985, when Jensen was shuffled aside and personnel chief Norman Inkster was moved in as deputy commissioner of operations to give him some experience running police investigations. Inkster later told a Commons committee the SFIU was moved into headquarters because "many of the cases that they were investigating were not solely involved in the National Capital Region. In other words they were spinoffs to other parts of the country. Therefore, to avoid jurisdictional concerns and so on, we centralized it." The explanation never washed with knowledgeable Mountie insiders.

The SFIU had four senior investigators – two inspectors and two sergeants – and a public service clerk. Stamler's plan was to make the SFIU responsible for investigations of crimes against the Government of Canada and serious crimes committed by public officials. The SFIU would report directly to him. Stamler made his case and received approval from Inkster and Jensen.

Stamler was ready to move ahead. And he began almost where he had left off more than a decade earlier, investigating an influential senator from Montreal. Then it was Liberal Louis Giguère, now it was Conservative Michel Cogger.

16

A Chance Meeting with Mulroney's Best Buddy

Rod Stamler first met Michel Cogger in 1984, on an Air Canada plane flying out of London's Heathrow Airport. As Stamler settled into the business-class seat waiting for the doors to close he noticed a small, rather chubby man arguing with a flight attendant. He was demanding a first-class seat, and the attendant was insisting she could seat him only in business class. Stamler could see that the empty seat beside him was about to be filled. Some flight this was going to be, Stamler thought as he moved aside to let the man in.

Over Ireland the man introduced himself as Michel Cogger, a Montreal lawyer. Stamler had never heard of him.

"What do you do?" Cogger asked.

"I work for the federal government," Stamler replied, discreetly, "in the drug enforcement area." Cogger didn't press for details; he wasn't really listening anyway.

During the flight over the Atlantic, Stamler flipped through a

British sports-car magazine, since he had two such cars at home – a GT6 and a Triumph Spitfire, which he was restoring in his spare time.

"My partner, Walter, has all kinds of sports cars," Cogger said. "When you're done with the magazine, do you mind if I read it? I've got to learn more about these things, so that I can talk to Walter about them." Walter, Stamler learned, was Walter Wolf, a Canadian-born businessman who lived abroad for tax reasons.

Cogger chatted away. He had just been in London and had spent some time doing business in the Channel Islands, a place which immediately brought one thing to Stamler's mind – money-laundering. Soon Cogger had digressed into his business affairs in Montreal. At one point he mentioned the Montreal brokerage firm L. J. Forget, a name which tickled Stamler's ear. Cogger rambled on, dropping familiar names left and right. This is going to be an interesting trip after all, Stamler thought.

When Cogger finally stopped to take a breath, Stamler prompted him back to L. J. Forget, saying he remembered something about Irving Kott, the old Canadian Stock Exchange, and a scam pulled by Buffalo Oil & Gas in the mid 1970s. Of Kott Stamler said, "I used to deal with him in a professional sort of way." Cogger's eyes lit up and he began to tell Stamler what he knew about the old Buffalo Oil & Gas gang. Stamler was impressed that Cogger seemed to know everyone involved. Perhaps he had been the lawyer for an investor, Stamler thought, but he never got to ask the question because Cogger had moved on to his current affairs. He had been Brian Mulroney's campaign manager during the election two months earlier in which the Tories defeated the Liberals and claimed the largest majority in Canadian history. "I was the one who convinced Brian to run for leader," Cogger bragged, adding that he and Mulroney went back a long way. That was true; Cogger had studied law with Mulroney at Laval, was an usher at Mulroney's wedding, was with the Mulroneys the night their first child was born, and had convinced Mulroney to run in his unsuccessful bid for the Conservative leadership in 1976.

"I owe a lot to Brian," Cogger told Stamler with such reverence and affection that the Mountie didn't doubt him for a moment. In fact, Cogger boasted, he was responsible for Joe Clark being knocked off as Tory leader in 1983. Cogger outlined how he and Walter Wolf had set up a bank account in Bermuda, financed to the tune of $50,000 by Wolf, secretly to fund Mulroney's campaign.

Banking in the Channel Islands and Bermuda, too? Soon, Cogger began to talk about his current problems. "I'm on the block when I get back," he said. He was going to be interviewed by Jim Reed, from the CTV show "W5." The story was a big sensation, Cogger said. Had Stamler heard about it? The Mountie said he must have missed it, so Cogger reached into his briefcase and pulled out a two-week-old copy of *Maclean's* magazine.

Stamler, who had been out of the country when the story broke, read that there had been break-ins at two Montreal offices – one belonging to Roger Nantel, a Mulroney adviser, and the other at the Conservative Party headquarters. Strategy notes and Mulroney's personal papers from his 1976 leadership bid were missing from Nantel's office.

The *Maclean's* story went on to speculate that the intruders might have been looking in the party's offices for a list of election campaign contributions to compare with the official list scheduled to be published the following month. "Somebody may also have been trying to find out who bankrolled Mulroney's campaign for the party leadership eight years ago or his successful bid in 1983." At the end of the piece Stamler read that the Montreal police were complaining about lack of co-operation from Tory officials. " 'The break-ins were a high priority for us when they happened,' a policeman said, 'but now they [the party officials] don't seem to care, so why should we?' " Stamler couldn't help but think of another famous political break-in – Watergate.

Cogger than talked about meeting with the RCMP and the new solicitor-general, Elmer MacKay, to discuss the break-ins. Stamler wondered why Cogger was telling him all this and curious why the solicitor-general was involved. If it had been anyone else but MacKay, Stamler might have been more concerned, but he had faith in the Tory politician since his role in the Sky Shops affair. Nevertheless, Stamler knew that no matter how well-intentioned MacKay might still be after two months in power, he would soon learn to appreciate the realities of Canadian justice – Watergate-type prosecutions aren't allowed in Canada.

Upon their landing in Montreal, Cogger offered Stamler a lift in the helicopter he normally used to commute between his farm in Quebec's Eastern Townships and Ottawa. Pretty expensive way to travel, thought Stamler, once the owner of his own airplane, and he refused the ride. The last thing he wanted was to be caught taking a freebie from the prime minister's right-hand man, especially one who appeared to be up to his eyeballs in manure. All in all, it had been a memorable trip. On the way back to Ottawa, Stamler made notes of the conversation and sent them to the deputy commissioner of operations on his return.

The next day, November 5, *Maclean's* published a new story about the break-ins, headlined "A Deepening Tory Mystery," with a picture of Cogger illustrating the piece. The story focussed on a third break-in, this time at the offices of Voyageur Marine Construction in the Montreal suburb of Pointe-Claire. The firm was an offshore oil-and-gas equipment leasing company in which Cogger was a director and Wolf was a one-third owner. According to *Maclean's*, the thieves had stolen a photocopy of a cheque from Wolf for US$82,000 (it was actually for US$80,231), and Cogger hadn't reported the break-in until police stumbled upon evidence of it during their investigation of the other two break-ins. *Maclean's* theorized that the break-ins had something to do with the financing of either the party or Mulroney's leadership campaign; perhaps someone was looking for documents that would link Wolf and Mulroney. Mulroney was on record as denying any knowledge of Wolf's contribution to his leadership campaign.

Three weeks later, on November 25, "W5" broadcast its story, which Stamler watched with amazement. Host Jim Reed started by outlining the story: "For months now, rumours have circulated that some of Brian Mulroney's campaign donations may have come from Walter Wolf, a mysterious Canadian businessman who lives in Switzerland. It certainly would be illegal, but the suggestion with all such rumours is that the contributor hopes for some economic benefit in return. 'W5' looked into the story and found no evidence to support any of the rumours." Reed introduced Cogger as a man who had once been close to Mulroney, but who recently and inexplicably had withdrawn from the centre of power "for personal reasons." Paraphrasing Cogger, Reed added, "He has also said that one factor in his decision was a business relationship he felt might prove embarrassing to the new leader." Reed was talking about Wolf. On camera, Reed asked Cogger to describe the relationship between Wolf and Mulroney.

"Well, not much more than a passing acquaintance, I should think. Walter is not very often in Canada, anyway. They met, I guess, through me – you know, most of the time I would have been present – several times over a period of five or six years," Cogger said.

"Did you ever approach him and say, 'Walter, we're old friends, Mr. Mulroney's going to need a lot of money for this campaign. We're certainly going to expect you to kick in?' Did you ever do that?"

"No," Cogger said. "No, the furthest I went was to say to Walter, 'Look, my friend Brian is going to be very active in politics, and I'd like to get active again. So, I'd like to be free to spend my time there as opposed to doing corporate stuff.'"

Tory back-roomer Dalton Camp was then introduced and queried about his suspicions that Wolf had indeed been Mulroney's secret benefactor. Camp talked about offshore bank accounts being used in Clark's defeat. Then Wolf himself was asked about a quote attributed to him in 1984 that he had spent $25,000 on the anti-Clark campaign. Wolf admitted only to paying approximately $25,000 in "a director's fee" to "people that have been associated with Mr. Mulroney. As director of services, they worked for me and they were directors of the company." Wolf was referring to Cogger and former Newfoundland premier Frank Moores. There was nothing political about it, Wolf said. (Moores later denied being paid anything by Wolf.)

Reed then confronted Wolf with allegations that Voyageur Marine was nothing but a money-laundering operation, and that the stolen photocopy of the $80,231 cheque from Wolf was evidence of this. Wolf shot that one down by producing another copy of the cheque as well as the president of Voyageur Marine, Sandor Koscic, who described the money as Wolf's down payment on a one-third interest in the company. Finally, Reed said of Cogger, "His treatment by the press has wounded his pride, but left him unbowed. Regardless of the controversy and the concern about political financing, Cogger firmly believes that no one could buy influence with the prime minister."

Cogger had the last word, "I think that the record will show as it evolves that Mr. Mulroney will be very much his own man and make the right decision, regardless of friends or buddies or acquaintances."

The story Cogger had told him on the plane was so different from the explanation on "W5" that Stamler decided he had to speak up. The next day he raised the apparent discrepancies with a deputy commissioner, and eventually he submitted an A-5 report – an internal intelligence memo – on his conversations with Cogger on the airplane. But he wasn't going to worry about it; investigating politicians wasn't his job in 1984.

On October 26, 1988, in Montreal, Japanese businessman Takayuki Tsuru swore a sixty-six-page affidavit before a commissioner of oaths. In it he told the story of how he and his Japanese partners had been duped out of $39 million in a complicated series of financial manoeuvres by Senneville businessman Guy Montpetit (not the same Guy Montpetit named in Chapter 9). Among Tsuru's allegations was a charge that Michel Cogger, by this time a senator, had received $114,000 from a Montpetit company. Within days, the Montreal *Gazette* was tipped to the existence of the case, and the chase began.

Cogger told a reporter that the money was for legal services, but documents filed with the affidavit indicated that Cogger was acting on Montpetit's behalf and lobbying the federal government for a $45-million contract. In return, Cogger was to serve on the board of directors of a Montpetit company, GigaMos.

Tsuru's affidavit was a direct hit into Mulroney's bunker, especially since it came just four weeks before the November 21 federal election, and Cogger was the Conservative Party's campaign co-chairman.

Montpetit's own lawyers immediately fired back, not so much defending Montpetit but, tellingly, Cogger. They threatened a lawsuit against Tsuru for making "defamatory and malicious" statements about the senator. Mulroney rejected demands that Cogger be suspended from the campaign and told *Gazette* reporter Rod MacDonell that Cogger was only one of thirty legal and professional advisers on the campaign. When Stamler heard the news he decided that the Mounties should investigate Tsuru's complaint.

Investigators were assigned under Inspector Tim Quigley, but the Mounties immediately ran into problems – within the force itself. About a week later, while Stamler was away from the office on other matters, a telex signed by Jensen was sent from Alta Vista to investigators at "C" Division in Montreal, ordering them to discontinue the Cogger investigation immediately.

Today Jensen insists that he never sent the telex: "Never, absolutely never. I would never stop an investigation." He might have been hungry for power within the force, but he would never let politicians direct his work.

Stamler agrees that it was unlike Jensen to stop an investigation. "His name was on it, but to this day I don't know who really sent it."

No matter who sent the Cogger telex, the moment was the darkest of Stamler's career in the Mounties, the first time he had experienced interference from within the force in a case.

Then it happened again. During the days leading up to the election, the Economic Crime police were investigating the case of Tory backbencher Richard Grisé. On November 15 – six days before the election – investigators in Montreal determined that there was enough evidence to seek a search warrant against Grisé for fraud and breach of trust involving his duties as a parliamentarian. At the time, most of the RCMP brass, including Stamler, were out of the office, Jensen and Inkster in Thailand at an Interpol meeting. The assistant commissioner sitting in for Jensen that day, Marcel Coutu, decided to sit on the application for a search warrant until November 21, the day of the election. Jensen didn't learn about Coutu's decision until two weeks after the election.

The fear of being accused of political interference on the one hand, and of angering or embarrassing the Mulroney government on the other, seemed to extend to the media, as well. The *Globe and Mail*, which had been in the forefront of writing about the petty and not-so-petty corruptions of the Tories, had its own Grisé story ready for publication prior to the election. However, after much internal wrangling, the paper made the decision to hold off until after the election, on the grounds that it didn't want to influence unduly the outcome of the campaign in Grisé's riding by providing an unfair advantage to his opponents.

Mulroney and the Conservatives won the election with a reduced majority, but a majority nonetheless. And Grisé won in his riding. Within days of the election, Mulroney caused another controversy by granting a banking licence to the giant American charge-card company American Express, in defiance of Canadian rules. The move was made quietly and quickly, and some thought it was a deal that the police should investigate. But there was no opening or complaint, so the Mounties could take no action.

Grisé was eventually charged and, like Michel Gravel before him, pleaded guilty. He was sentenced to one day in jail and fined $20,000. He resigned his Commons seat. Once again, the public was deprived of finding out what was really going on.

While Stamler was manoeuvring his department into position, some of its members learned about a bizarre series of money transfers. Members of the Islamic sect of Ismailiya had been detected using armoured cars to move about $1 million a week in cash across the U.S.A. and Canada. Simultaneous and separate investigations were being conducted on both sides of the border. Through its sources the Special Federal Inquiries Unit knew the money was taking a circuitous route from Dallas to Seattle, over the Canadian border to Vancouver, by Brink's Express to Toronto, then to Switzerland, where it was being deposited in secret bank accounts. It smelled like money being moved through a laundry.

Almost as if on cue, police informant Paul Vidosa popped out of the woodwork to talk to RCMP Constable Brian Sargent and Sergeant Ray Elrick, at first to tell them of other matters before telling them he knew something about the Ismailis and their government contacts. Stamler knew about Vidosa from his years in drug enforcement, where Vidosa had been one of the force's best informants. Then, in 1980, on behalf of the RCMP, Vidosa had infiltrated a major Colombian drug-smuggling ring in Canada. During the operation, Vidosa was arrested in Colombia on espionage charges. He spent thirty-nine days in jail where, he says, he was tortured and beaten unconscious before being rescued by the Mounties. Difficult to control at the best of times, Vidosa went public in 1982 about his role with the Mounties, and Robert Simmonds promptly issued a prohibition against using him again as a source.

Stamler was approached by the investigators to use Vidosa on the Ismaili case, however. It was a tough call. There was a new proceeds-of-crime law, the Enterprise Crime project was ready to go into action, and the Ismaili operation looked like as good a first case as any to pursue, but using Vidosa could prove embarrassing. Stamler revisited the Vidosa cases and met with Jensen, since Inkster was away on one of his many trips. Jensen, too, was nervous about using Vidosa, but gave Stamler his permission as long as Vidosa was employed in a limited way.

Vidosa wanted a contract for two years at $1,500 a week. This was considerably more than Stamler's $50,000 signing authority, so Stamler included in the contract a two-stage payment, depending on whether criminal activity was detected, and a clause allowing the RCMP to cancel the contract with a week's notice. Any payments over $50,000 would have to be approved by at least the deputy commissioner of operations, Jensen. The contract was signed in January 1989.

Project Albus, as it was called, was doomed from the start. Stamler's plan was stymied within the force when members in his old fiefdom, drug enforcement, refused to co-operate with him. The new masters in the directorate thought Stamler was overstepping his boundaries by getting involved in undercover work and anti-profiteering. Also, they didn't trust Vidosa.

As Stamler's investigators were getting organized, the Mounties learned that a drug ring was intending to import 500 kilograms of heroin into Canada. Vidosa was asked to make contact with the group. He did and was sent to Hong Kong where he identified key members of the ring. However, the trip came close to disaster. In booking Vidosa into a hotel, the Mounties' liaison officer in Hong Kong, eager to save the government money by claiming the lower corporate rate, described Vidosa as an employee of the government of Canada. It was the kind of inexcusable mistake that could get an agent killed. Vidosa, rightly so, was furious.

In January 1989, customs officials at a border crossing south of Vancouver found $1,080,000 in American bills in a routine check of a courier – suspected Ismaili money. Stamler's budding Enterprise Crime Unit lobbied to have the money released so they could trace it to its ultimate destination. But Drug Enforcement's anti-profiteering arm, Stamler's good idea a few years earlier, moved in, claimed jurisdiction, and froze the money, which sat unclaimed for years. The anti-profiteering cops called their action a victory, while the commercial-crime investigators shook their heads over the short-sightedness. In the end the police could never prove exactly what the Ismailis intended to do with the cash.

In the summer of 1988, Michel Cogger's activities once again came to the attention of the Mounties when the force was asked to investigate possible bid-rigging in the tendering of a $160-million communications system for the Department of External Affairs. The RCMP carried out two short preliminary investigations, but did not interview one of the complaining bidders, who was concerned about possible political influence being exercised by Cogger and another senator. In late December 1988, Pierre Ducros, the president of one of the unsuccessful companies, came forward to complain he had not been interviewed by the police. Ducros said Cogger had told him that if he wanted to get the contract, he would have to "play ball" with Cogger and another senator. Ducros had lost $4 million on the bidding process and was upset.

The next month, the SFIU's two inspectors, André Beauchemin and Tim Quigley, met with Ducros. Stamler wasn't present. Ducros said he wanted revenge, "almost insisting something be done," Quigley wrote afterwards. Beauchemin and Quigley felt they had no alternative but to attempt to cultivate Ducros as an agent, but he refused. As eager as Ducros was to complain to the police about Cogger, at the same time, the police figured, he didn't want Cogger to know about his betrayal. Ducros was likely scared off after he was warned by the police that they couldn't guarantee his anonymity because recent developments in the law might force them in court to reveal his identity as a confidential source.

Nevertheless, the two Mounties prepared an operational plan, code-named Sack, and discussed it with Stamler. Cogger was already the subject of a multi-pronged investigation sparked partly by Tsuru's civil suit in Montreal. There were already two aspects to Cogger's involvement with Guy Montpetit, one being influence peddling, another, a curious French-language translation project in Saskatchewan, Gigatext Translation Systems, which had resulted in a significant financial loss for the provincial government. Now there was Ducros' case, which the Mounties code-named Cosics.

Based on complaints and on their own observations, the police believed that, under the Tories, it was difficult for companies to get federal government contracts unless they had good political connections and made hefty contributions to the party. Cogger seemed to figure in these dealings and was operating with impunity, as if he knew the police would not investigate him. Stamler wondered if this was the opening the Mounties needed to determine whether institutionalized corruption existed within the government.

Based on the testimony and complaints that had come to them, the Mounties had enough evidence to satisfy them that Cogger may have committed a crime. They could have used what they had to seek search warrants, but Stamler didn't think that was a good idea. Once a search warrant is executed, everything stops; the police can investigate only what happened prior to the moment the search warrant was served. Stamler wanted to know more about Cogger's activities. Cogger was so prominent and well connected that Stamler knew the police would need much more evidence than normal to convict him. The cases that had already been investigated had shown the Mounties how difficult it was for them to detect political pressure being applied. As such delicate matters were never discussed in the open, it seemed there was only one alternative – the introduction of an agent. The Mounties debated whether they should go after both senators or just Cogger. They chose to ignore the other senator because he was named only in Ducros' complaint. "The object of the exercise," Stamler told his men, "is not merely to confirm evidence of criminal activity but to confirm or dispel it. At all times we must act within the law. We must ensure that we do not proceed without reasonable and probable grounds."

Everyone was to act at all times within his authority, Stamler told them. It was a highly sensitive case that very well might lead right back to the prime minister himself. He would make every attempt to conduct a proper investigation, even if it flew in the face of political will. Stamler didn't want to create the appearance of a massive investigation, which would serve only to invite more scrutiny and possible interference by the commissioner and his political masters. If there was evidence of criminality and the investigation was to be escalated, it would be done slowly and deliberately, without alerting the élite.

The Mounties' plan was for one agent to make contact with Cogger and introduce a second agent. The first agent would then disappear from the scene. "If the first step doesn't work, that's the end of the matter," Stamler told Beauchemin and Quigley. Quigley says, "Stamler agreed there was a risk of criticism to the RCMP, but that was not a valid reason to fail to do an investigation. There are consequences whether things go right or wrong."

The Mounties turned to Vidosa, who was floundering on the Ismaili investigation. Vidosa would contact Cogger and ask him for help in recovering the US$1,080,000 seized by customs. Stamler hoped that Cogger would be as talkative as he had been on the plane all those years before. It was a long shot that didn't come close to paying off. Cogger rebuffed Vidosa. So the Mounties continued with a more conventional investigation of Cogger.

Eventually Vidosa was assigned to a murder investigation in Vancouver. That failed, too, after a battle between the different factions within the force over Vidosa's protection. In May 1989, after five months of paying Vidosa $1,500 a week for little more than nothing, Stamler ordered that the RCMP cancel his contract with the force. It had been an investigation that could not be continued, no more, no less. But Vidosa, once again, was back on the streets without a job, mad as hell at the Mounties and ticking like a time bomb.

Strange things were happening within the force. If many of the Mounties had danced a jig when the "business-minded" Tories came to power, by the late 1980s they were dancing at the end of a string.

The body politic had insisted that the police change the way it did things. Most progressive-minded Mounties, particularly Jensen and Stamler, agreed that many of the changes were necessary improvements, part of an evolutionary process. They had long ago proven themselves to be innovators and agents of change.

But Jensen and Stamler were also among many in Ottawa who worried about what had really happened to the Mounties. They feared that the majority of Canadians had little or no idea about the extent to which the police had been co-opted by the political process. The balance of power that most Canadians assumed existed between the country's major institutions – Parliament, the courts, and the police – was largely an illusion. Rather, political manipulations and intrusions had served to undermine the integrity of the supposedly independent judicial system.

Jensen and Stamler were among those who believed that the police, as the agents of the law, had lost too much independence, which meant they could not uphold the law equally for all Canadians. The powers of the police had been slyly subverted by duplicitous and self-interested politicians. The real down side was that, unless the situation was recognized and corrected, Canada was headed down the road to the kind of institutionalized corruption endemic to Third World countries.

Throughout Mulroney's tenure, rumours about political

interference within the force were rampant. The fact that the police were being ordered to disclose the details of their cases up the command structure to their political masters was seriously jeopardizing the integrity of some critical investigations. Not only was the federal solicitor-general of the day seeking information, he had also deputized his assistants, special assistants, and God knows who else to do the same. When the Mounties wouldn't co-operate, they were sometimes subjected to harassment from either the politicians or their agents. While no current or former Mountie, including Stamler and Jensen, would talk about the specifics of any such conversations that they might have had about such problems with Commissioner Inkster, it seems evident that several Mounties took their complaints about political interference directly to Inkster.

For example, three Mountie investigators conducting a search one day in the late 1980s came across an interesting and important document during a search of files at one federal department. The police officers had deliberately left the document in place, then applied for a search warrant specifically for it. By the time they returned, the document had been removed from the files. The Mounties suspected that information about the new search had been leaked from within the force to the suspect.

There were other stories about senior officers going directly to Inkster to complain about the unseemly pressure and close relationship between the government and senior members of the RCMP. In each case the police were worried that they were getting too many requests from the government for information about investigations, that the force was giving up too much information, and that senior Mounties had to be more careful about their dealings with politicians and bureaucrats.

But on such occasions, the Mounties say, Inkster took few or no notes about the complaints and seemed largely unconcerned. As one Mountie who met with Inkster put it: "It would be fair to say that Norman would remind everyone that the legislation says the Mounties have to report to the minister, and that he was only following orders."

To some of the seasoned investigators, it was evident that Inkster, the former personnel chief of the force, had no real idea about the intricacies of criminal investigation work, the need for confidentiality, and the very good reasons why investigators need an independent leader. At the same time, some Mounties believed a more serious concern was that Inkster was just as oblivious to the long-term implications and damage being done to the country's social fabric, security, and institutions by the RCMP's almost total obeisance to the government of the day. The Hollywood image of the Mounties as dedicated police officers who always got their man was, apparently, so much fiction. Modern Mounties knew all too well that men and women with the right connections are out of the reach of the police. Over the years, with the possible exception of the early 1970s, the RCMP had come to believe in the rule of law only as long as enforcing the laws didn't upset the government of the day, its friends, family, and benefactors.

Just as Stamler was ready to leave the force, Henry Jensen got caught up in a high-profile dispute once again. On April 26, 1989, Global Television news chief Doug Small held up a pamphlet containing details of the federal budget to be released the next day. The disclosure on the dinner-hour news broadcast sent Ottawa scrambling. The budget was hurriedly read into the record that evening and the Mounties were brought in to investigate the leak. A war room was set up at Alta Vista to manage the investigation of what Mulroney publicly called a criminal act.

Jensen was determined to lay a charge against Small. He believed that Small, despite his protests to the contrary, had paid for the documents, and knew that they had been stolen, a *prima facie* criminal act. "I didn't think the media should be treated any differently from anyone else," Jensen said afterward.

Although Stamler always had a high opinion of Jensen, and still does, he says he disagreed with his friend in the Small case. On balance, Stamler thought, it wasn't in the public interest to charge Small. In fact, Stamler believed Small was acting in the public interest by publishing the document. Just as the police did not owe a duty to the government, neither did the media; they were both there to protect the public interest.

In any event, Jensen relented and, based on the evidence and his belief that an offence had been committed, ordered that a charge be laid. On May 29, 1989, Small was charged with possession of stolen goods, and two others were charged with theft.

"Hank was a police officer to the core and, for those who knew him, what he did in the Small case was typical of him," Stamler said afterward. "Hank never ran away from controversy. Even in the Clifford Olson case he did something unpopular because he believed it was the right thing to do. In the Small case, he believed a law had been broken, so he had a charge laid. That was his duty as a police officer. There was no compromise."

That the Opposition and the media immediately retaliated with allegations that the charges were politically motivated set off another storm of anxiety at Alta Vista. Even Inkster, certain that he was about to be strung up for exposing the government to ridicule, sent out feelers to a bank and a multinational company about moving into the private sector himself.

17

A Letter to Glen Kealey

After Stamler came up to him and shook his hand on Parliament Hill during the Doug Small–budget leak investigation in 1989, Glen Kealey was perplexed about the Mountie. Stamler was the head of the Economic Crime Directorate, but he was encouraging Ottawa's leading protester to "keep up the good work." It didn't make any sense.

Kealey had turned himself into a one-man clearing house for Canadian scandals and conspiracies, committed to being a perpetual thorn in Mulroney's side. Taking up what had seemed to be a cue from Stamler, Kealey wrote to the force's public complaints commissioner, asking him about political corruption and interference in police investigations. A few weeks later, Kealey read a newspaper story that Stamler was leaving the force to join Peat, Marwick, the huge international accounting firm. Kealey was dismayed. Then, almost two months later, he received a reply to his letter, dated July 12, 1989. It read:

This letter is in response to your correspondence dated April 14, 1989 addressed to the Royal Canadian Mounted Police Public Complaints Commission.

With respect to your allegations of political interference, the Royal Canadian Mounted Police has conducted a number of investigations involving political figures and charges have been laid when sufficient evidence existed. I am not aware of any political interference in these investigations. Should you be in possession of evidence to support your allegations, I urge you to contact the "A" Division, Commercial Crime Section at 400 Cooper Street, Ottawa, telephone number (613) 993-6884 and divulge this information.

Yours truly

R.T. Stamler, Assistant Commissioner
Director,
Economic Crime.

Kealey was devastated by the response. "I thought that [Stamler] was really honest, and the letter proved to me that he was not," Kealey says. Two days later, Kealey picked up the letter and looked at it again. Although Stamler's name was on it, it had been signed by someone else. He couldn't make out the signature. The letter had actually been prepared by an analyst and sent through the system. It had been signed by a superintendent who was sitting in for Stamler.

Kealey decided to track down Stamler. He called Peat, Marwick in Ottawa and was told that Stamler was still at Mountie headquarters. In fact, Stamler was cleaning out his office that day. He had combed through his files and his case-books gathered over the years, and had packed his personal papers. The dozens of plaques he had been awarded were stuffed into a couple of boxes. It could have been a teary moment, but the force had long ago squeezed any sentimentality out of him. The

RCMP he was leaving was not the RCMP he had joined and had been so proud to serve. Stamler says he left the RCMP on good terms and that Inkster had even offered him the opportunity to serve as deputy commissioner after Henry Jensen moved on, but Stamler wasn't interested in serving as the commissioner's functionary. In any event, after thirty-three years in the RCMP, he was ready for something different.

Stamler was looking forward to his new career as a partner in Peat, Marwick, working with Robert Lindquist, the firm's chief of forensic accounting. When he had made up his mind about leaving, Stamler knew nothing about Lindquist. But while attending a meeting in Newfoundland, Stamler had talked with Frank Barbetta, the former deputy chief of the Metropolitan Toronto Police force. Stamler thought Barbetta had been the best cop in Canada before he was squeezed out of the Metro force. Barbetta told Stamler about Lindquist and that Peat, Marwick was expanding its forensic accounting business. It would be like police work – tracking down white-collar criminals – but in the pay of the private sector. Stamler joked that he certainly could see the need for the private sector having to pay for its own policing. The Peat, Marwick partners hired Stamler as soon as he approached them. It had been that easy.

Stamler's phone rang. Glen Kealey was on the line.

"Mr. Stamler," Kealey said, introducing himself. "I'm totally confused here. I get a letter from you, not signed by you, at a time after you were supposed to be retired and you're still at your desk. What's going on?"

Stamler explained that although his retirement was official at the end of July, he hadn't been at work for some time. He was using up his holiday leave.

"But you sent me this letter," Kealey said and then read it to him.

"I did not write, I did not authorize, I did not send you a letter."

"But it's in your name."

"I signed over responsibility for the operation as a matter of procedure, and the standing policy of the force is that, even though you hand over responsibility, you are effectively the boss until you retire. During that period, the force is legally entitled to use my name," Stamler explained.

By the time the short conversation ended, Kealey had regained his high opinion of Stamler. "It became clear to me that Stamler was extremely perplexed about what was going on. He seemed to be a distressed, honest cop."

Stamler tried to forget the letter. He didn't know what Kealey had written and hadn't been briefed about the response to it. A picture had been painted of Stamler's mind for a member of the public which misrepresented his real concerns – and there was nothing he could do about it. It had all been done by the book.

Stamler admired the tenacious Kealey, not because he believed everything Kealey said, but for the fact that Kealey wasn't just sitting back. He was speaking out, trying to wake up the public, something the press was failing to do. Under Inkster, the force had become paranoid about reporters. Only reporters who could be trusted to get out the police's side of the story were cultivated and given nuggets, which they often published without question as "scoops."

Stamler had always genuinely liked reporters, but he found that by the late 1980s there were in his opinion less than a half-dozen solid news reporters left in Canada. "The trouble with reporters is that there are only a few of them who understand that they have to deal with the issues," Stamler says. "The rest want to make everything sensational. They don't want to go into details and tell the real story. They say they haven't got the time or the story's too complicated or too long. They seem to think only in headlines. I'm not saying they mispresent the facts at all. They may, in fact, take it up to the key issue, but they don't tell the whole story. What happens is that half the story is lost. In historic events, the background is left out, which at a later date may be the most important part of the story. But it's all lost."

That's why Glen Kealey impressed Stamler. On Parliament Hill, he was a pre-Gutenberg town crier. At home, he was a postmodern propagandist, wickedly effective with his fax machine, flooding Canada with his views. Kealey, at least, was digging for something.

"I thought he was on the right track in terms of being upset," Stamler says, "but he was on the wrong track in terms of his own case. He was wrong on some of the evidence, but he was sort of a hero-like individual who stood up and said, 'I'm not going to take it anymore.' For that, I admired him."

Kealey had tried everything to get the justice system to listen to his complaints. He had failed in Hull, where Crown prosecutor Valmont Beaulieu found there was no evidence of corruption against the Tories.

On July 17, 1991, however, Ottawa Justice of the Peace Lynn Coulter ruled that Kealey had "reasonable grounds to believe a crime had been committed" and allowed him to proceed with private charges against thirteen top Tories and three top Mounties – Inkster, Jensen, and civilian Deputy Commissioner Michael Shoemaker.

The Tories Kealey was accusing were Sports Minister Pierre Cadieux; Senate Speaker Guy Charbonneau; Senator Michel Cogger; former ministers Roch LaSalle, André Bissonnette, and Michel Côté; former Mulroney aide Bernard Roy; former senator Jean Bazin, former cabinet aides Pierre-Claude Nolin, Pierre-Paul Bourdon, and Michel Deschênes; and businessman Gervais Desrochers. "This is Canada's Watergate," Glen Kealey declared at a press conference.

The charges befuddled most Canadians, who had little idea about how the justice system worked. In fact, charges laid by private individuals are no less serious than those laid by the police. In theory, the right to lay such charges is a fundamental underpinning of common law.

Coulter heard seventeen days' worth of evidence from more

than a dozen individuals, including two former Tories and five RCMP officers. Stamler was one of them, but won't comment on what he said at the hearing. Kealey, however, says he testified about the MetLife deal, a drug case involving a member of the Prime Minister's Office, and the allegations about kickbacks in the Airbus case.

From the moment Kealey laid the charges, the federal government signalled its displeasure with Coulter. "I am sure that any investigations will prove that there is no foundation to the charges," Solicitor-General Doug Lewis was quoted as saying. It was the kind of careless comment that did little to persuade Canadians that the justice system was fair to all.

A month later, at a closed hearing in an Ontario courtroom, a Crown prosecutor dropped the charges against the three Mounties, saying Kealey had no evidence that they had obstructed justice. Charges were also dropped against twelve of the remaining thirteen politicians. The Ontario prosecutor called Coulter's decision to issue a process "a miscarriage of justice."

Only charges against Roch LaSalle, of conspiracy to defraud the government and seeking a bribe, were allowed to stand. All the evidence – fifteen hundred pages of transcript – was kept secret, despite protest.

The Ottawa *Citizen* wrote:

> Agreeing that such a closed hearing violated the constitutional guarantee of freedom of the press, the Ontario Court of Appeal nonetheless reasoned... that the infringement was justified because "all subsequent proceedings will be in public and the public will then be able to learn about the allegations of the accused."
>
> But what if there are no "subsequent proceedings" ... then the evidence would remain secret. This is not good enough. These are serious allegations against powerful individuals. If the justice system keeps that evidence secret

through a combination of court rulings and prosecutor discretion, many in the public will suspect the worst.

For the good of all concerned, the affair must come out into the open through a preliminary inquiry.

There never was a preliminary inquiry. An OPP investigation foundered, and Kealey, disheartened and convinced of a massive conspiracy, continued with his crusade.

In the heat of the Kealey affair and in its aftermath, four people in key supervisory or prosecutorial positions were appointed to judgeships, including Valmont Beaulieu, who in 1991, at the age of thirty-one, was made the youngest judge in Quebec. Other new judges were Douglas Rutherford, who had been the assistant deputy minister of Justice, Ontario deputy minister Mary Hogan, who supervised prosecutor Douglas Trafford, and, finally, Trafford, himself, on Brian Mulroney's last day in office, June 24, 1993, St. Jean Baptiste Day. Kealey said they were all protectors of power and suitably rewarded.

Stamler felt sorry for Coulter, the justice of the peace, who had been placed in a difficult position. "The J.P. is the entry level to the justice system. Her role in the system is to pursue an information based on her reasonable belief that an offence against the Criminal Code has been committed. If the evidence she received was good and she believed the evidence, she had no choice but to issue a process. That is her duty, but few seemed to understand that. Instead, she was criticized. It was unfair to criticize her. She was only carrying out her responsibilities under the law."

What happened next concerned Stamler even more. In almost every province in the country, attorneys-general, through their representatives, had managed to insert themselves into the justice system through administrative regulations. That is, charges could not proceed unless they were approved by the Attorney-General's Office. The rationale is to prevent spurious actions being brought by private citizens against prominent individuals.

"There is no provision in the Criminal Code for the attorneys-general or their representatives to approve charges. That is not their role under the law," Stamler says. "For the courts to be equitable, everyone must be allowed free access, without fear of political interference. The justice of the peace system was devised as a check against abuse of power. What has happened in Canada, and gone largely unnoticed, is that the justice system has been undermined and subverted. In the name of order and justice, control of almost every lever of power within the justice system has been carefully placed under the authority of the attorney-general. It has the publicly approved means to protect itself from serious investigations. Every time a government finds itself in a difficult situation, it takes control of areas that the law never intended politicians to take control of, because they feel they are better judges of what is good for the public." The result is a two-tiered justice system – one for the rich and powerful and another for the rest of us. A latter-day Family Compact.

18

A Kick to the
Horsemen's Head

It was probably one of the most effective and influential comments ever made by a prime minister to the Mounted Police. Brian Mulroney walked up to the car carrying his RCMP security detail and let go a swift, angry kick to the door, denting it. The shocked Mounties didn't make out everything Mulroney barked at them, but the phrase they quoted in their A-5 memo, "You dizzy, stupid bastards," stunned the brass at Alta Vista.

Mulroney's outburst seemed to have been triggered by a front-page story in the Ottawa *Citizen* on January 19, 1990. Its headline read: COGGER "STING" TARGET: AGENT. For the second time in his career as a police agent, Paul Vidosa had gone public with his complaints about the Mounties. It had been eight months since he had been dismissed by the Mounties, but Vidosa had been waiting to get his revenge. He had gone to the press saying he had been hired by the Mounties to target Senator Michel Cogger in an undercover sting operation. He said the Mounties suspected that Cogger was one of a number of high-ranking Canadian politicians involved in offshore money-laundering.

Vidosa told *Citizen* reporter Stephen Bindman he had felt so bad about trying to entrap the senator that he had contacted Cogger just before Christmas 1989, and had told him what had been going on. "I feel it was wrong what we were doing to him," Vidosa said. "Maybe they had good reasons, I don't know. Whatever reason they had, they never told me."

At the time Vidosa came forward with his story, Cogger was under great police and political pressure. He had just been forced to resign from the Tory caucus after the RCMP and a special Senate committee began investigating allegations that he had accepted money for lobbying and had received payments from a government agency after becoming a senator. With Vidosa on his side, Cogger could now really kick up the dust.

Inkster responded to Vidosa's splash by immediately calling for an internal review to determine the "propriety of the activities of the members of the force." It would be only a file review, not an inquiry, and conducted by Superintendent John L'Abbé.

Within days, Montreal businessman Pierre Ducros emerged, claiming that the Mounties had tried to enlist him, too, as an agent against Cogger and two other Quebec senators, but failing to point out that it was he who had first gone to the bureaucrats and police with his complaints about Cogger.

Four weeks later, on February 13, 1990, Cogger rose in the Senate on a question of personal privilege. For months he had been trying to negotiate his way through the turmoil around him. In a previous speech he had called the House of Commons too partisan to consider his case, but had said that he had faith in the RCMP. The force was the most impartial, professional, and non-partisan arbiter one could find, he had told his fellow senators. Now he told them that he had come to realize he had been naive. The RCMP was out to get him; Vidosa had told him so:

He was given the job of tying me to a money-laundering ring when the RCMP, by its own admission, had no reason to believe that I was involved in any criminal activity. . . . The RCMP was determined to destroy me, no more and no less. . . . Entrapment, odious and repugnant as it is, remains an accepted method of police investigation which is recognized by the courts, provided that there are 'reasonable grounds.' For lack of reasonable grounds, the above-mentioned actions are nothing more or less than criminal plots by members of the RCMP against me.

In an emotional outburst, Cogger portrayed the Mounties as being out of control, undisciplined, unprofessional, untrustworthy, and prone to leaking word of its investigations to the media. They had a dirty tricks squad, he said, using a phrase that evoked memories of the Security Service's barn-burning escapade of the early 1970s. The individual investigators, Cogger went on, "have shown the highest degree of bias and prejudice – indeed, they may be guilty of a criminal conspiracy." Vidosa had told him that one of the Mountie investigators had described Quebec MPs as "all crooks anyway," and that there was plenty of work for Vidosa in investigating them. Cogger continued, on the verge of tears:

The facts are troubling and the allegations are serious. The problem is more widespread and goes deeper than what we have seen so far. . . . I am talking here about my fundamental right – not as a senator but as a Canadian citizen – to be able to live my life, to carry on with my profession, to pursue my career like everybody else, free of malicious prosecution, entrapment, undue suspicion, and police harassment. I am referring to my right not to have my telephone conversations tape recorded; my right to carry on my business or profession with other Canadians who are not paid by the police to entice me into criminal activities. Honourable senators, like most of you, I want the right to travel on an airplane and not to have to worry whether my seatmate is a plant of the RCMP.

If true, his allegations were a damaging indictment of Stamler and the force, but the Mounties were confident they had done nothing improper. There had been reasonable grounds to suspect Cogger – in spades – and, so, it had been their duty to investigate him.

Cogger would not repeat his allegations outside the protection of the Senate, nor did the police expect him to do so. They had heard it all before. From Gilles Grégoire's taunts and Jean Marchand's allegations of racism to Bryce Mackasey's charges of police harassment, when the heat was on, the politicians started blowing smoke. History had shown they would say and do anything in an attempt to relieve the pressure by deflecting it onto the backs of their pursuers. Inkster, the ex-personnel director turned commissioner, seemed to be the only one who had not heard of this reaction. Not only that, but based on what he did next, it appeared that Inkster was the only Mountie who believed every word Cogger mouthed in the Senate.

The Mountie investigators were faced with a political obstacle course that was certain to wear them down. For his internal review, Superintendent L'Abbé interviewed all those involved and soon submitted his report to Inkster. It was clear to those intimately involved in the Vidosa file that L'Abbé was unfamiliar with the force's policies and practices regarding undercover operations. To a man they said L'Abbé had difficulty comprehending that undercover operations are conducted in stages and that Vidosa had been only the first stage. Vidosa's role had been to make contact, introduce a highly trained member of the force, then disappear. Once in position, it was up to the Mountie to determine if there was criminal behaviour as suspected and, if so, to gather evidence for the laying of charges.

In his report L'Abbé pointed to some errors in the handling of Vidosa, but at the same time he couldn't find anything really wrong. Stamler and his men had been careful to do everything by the book. As best he could, L'Abbé tried to take the middle road, although those Mounties being investigated thought L'Abbé had manufactured his minor allegations of supposed questionable behaviour to please his own master, Inkster.

Inkster seemed furious with L'Abbé's report. He told senior Mounties that he was convinced Cogger was right, the Mounties were wrong, and that there would be a public perception that the force was covering up. To that end, Inkster drafted a strong letter to the solicitor-general, but his deputies intervened and urged him to tone it down. "You can't be seen to be taking sides," one deputy told him. Inkster then revised the letter and told the solicitor-general that he would be setting up an independent inquiry.

On March 15, 1990, Inkster announced that former Ontario judge René Marin would conduct a one-person board of inquiry into Cogger's allegations in the Senate. Judge Marin was an experienced inquirer; in the early 1980s, he had investigated the Post Office and had recommended against its having its own peace officers. Later, he had conducted an internal review of the RCMP for the commissioner. At the time of his latest appointment he was a member of the government-appointed external review committee, which monitored the force's behaviour.

Stamler was astounded by Inkster's move. "It was the biggest undermining of law enforcement and authority under the law in living memory," Stamler says. "It was absolutely unheard of to have an inquiry being conducted by a judge into an investigation when the investigation was still ongoing."

Stamler was clearly the target of the Marin inquiry, as he had masterminded the Vidosa operation. Stamler smelled a rat. He believed the inquiry had been set up to smear the Mounties and stop the momentum of their investigation of Cogger. Stamler was no longer with the force, but he was still a policeman at heart, so he decided he had to defend himself in the hope that he could protect both himself and the investigation.

In preparing notes for an affidavit in support of a motion to derail the inquiry, Stamler laid out what he believed were the fundamental errors in Inkster's decision.

Stamler wrote, in part:

> In my experience as a police investigator, RCMP officer and supervisor of undercover investigations for over 30 years, I can see no difference between the complaint of Mr. Cogger and other complaints the force has received over the years and rejected as unfounded or self-serving. It has never been RCMP policy to subject the RCMP investigators to a Board of Inquiry to examine their ethics whenever an undercover operation is exposed; on the other hand, if this case has been singled out, I am not aware of any RCMP law, rule, policy or precedent which would justify it.
>
> It is an important principle of police conduct that a criminal investigation is recognized as the most intrusive and coercive step a state can make in relation to the life of an ordinary citizen. For this reason, once the decision is made to begin it, until the investigation into the individual's conduct has been completed, no other inquiry can be held or should be held which might jeopardize that investigation.

Stamler's lawyer decided against using this statement in filing a motion with the court, saying it was not legally relevant in the circumstances. So Stamler challenged Marin on a number of other grounds, including his belief that there was no legal authority for Marin to "assess and advise on the ethical conduct of RCMP members" and ex-members. The inquiry served no useful purpose, Stamler also argued. He challenged Cogger's statements and the fact that neither L'Abbé nor anyone else had been able to corroborate Cogger's allegations in the Senate. Marin denied the motion, and made it clear he had scant regard for Stamler's lawyer, former Ontario deputy attorney-general Rod McLeod.

When Cogger eventually testified before the Marin inquiry he admitted that he could not substantiate any of his allegations against the Mounties. He even indicated he didn't believe in some of what he had said, but had simply felt that he had to say it. The reason for the hearing had just been declared nonexistent but, nevertheless, Marin trundled along, examining all parties, as per Inkster's orders, in an attempt to determine if the members had acted ethically.

In April 1991 – a little more than a year after he was appointed – Marin tabled his findings in thirty-five recommendations. Marin found no wrongdoing by the force, but no one could tell that by reading the newspapers. When the report was made public in June 1991, the *Globe and Mail*, for example, headlined the story, REPORT CRITICIZES MOUNTIES' JUDGMENT: INQUIRY FINDS OFFICERS WERE MANIPULATED IN COGGER CASE BY UNDERCOVER AGENT. The lead paragraph of the story, however, adequately summed up Marin's findings: "An inquiry into the RCMP investigation of Senator Michel Cogger has concluded that the force 'as individuals, acted ethically, although their judgment was on occasion flawed.' "

Stamler was dismayed that not one reporter in the country had the energy to chase the real stories from the Marin inquiry: that the RCMP had behaved properly; that Cogger could not substantiate his claims in the Senate and, in fact, didn't believe them himself; and, most important, that the lengthy inquiry had served to derail the multifaceted Cogger investigation.

During the Marin inquiry several officers quit, retired, or were transferred. "What was most disturbing," Stamler says, "was that there were three or four other cases being investigated, which were all part of the original police affidavit filed in Montreal. Those other cases were allowed to fall by the wayside. All that was left was the easiest one to pursue, which fell directly out of the Tsuru civil suit, was public and controversial, and which couldn't be ignored by the police."

Stamler regretted his decision to hire Vidosa, but not much. Informants were a tricky business at the best of times, and Vidosa had proved himself to be valuable in the past. Stamler still feels he had no choice but to approve the investigation. "If I had to do it all over again, with the evidence that was before us, I would have approved the same kind of operation. When a police officer believes serious crimes are being committed, it is his duty to investigate. That's the law."

For Stamler's lawyers there was another harsh outcome from the Marin inquiry. Although the RCMP had agreed to pay his legal bills for the inquiry, the force tried to change its mind and eventually paid less than half the amount. Meanwhile, Marin recommended that the government pick up the entire tab for Cogger's lawyers, even though he couldn't back up his charges in any way. The government swiftly acceded to Marin's request.

One of Stamler's lawyer's, Andrew Roman, complained to Inkster, writing in part, "Look at the justice in this case. The man who raises the false complaint is left at the end of the day with virtually no legal bill to pay, whereas the man who has always been helpful and co-operative, but blameless, is left with an outstanding legal bill. That is a grossly unfair situation which no bureaucratic argument can excuse."

It took a year for the Mounties to reply to the letter. The force rejected the claim, and Stamler's lawyers eventually absorbed the balance of his legal bill.

In September 1991, Cogger was charged with influence peddling for accepting $212,000 in illegal benefits during his dealings with Guy Montpetit. This was the case that arose from Tsuru's civil suit. Stamler thought it was a token effort by the Mounties to show they were on the job.

The matter finally went to trial in Montreal in spring 1993, and the outcome was no surprise to Mounties with experience of the Quebec justice system. Cogger benefited from possibly the most bizarre procedures ever allowed in a serious criminal case in Canada. The prosecution agreed that it would call no witnesses, not even a police officer, to testify against Cogger. It relied only on documents to make its case. The defence also called no witnesses. There was no cross-examination, no digging to get to the truth. In June 1993, the judge, Jean Falardeau, acquitted Cogger on the grounds that while a crime had clearly been committed, there was no evidence that Cogger "has a corrupt state of mind." Falardeau argued that there was no evidence that a Canadian senator could exercise influence on the federal bureaucracy. The Crown launched an appeal of the decision that has not yet been heard.

Cogger, like Giguère, Mackasey, and the others before him, then did what seems *de rigueur* for the politicians. He complained that his life had been ruined by both the Mounties and the media, specifically the Montreal *Gazette*, for their "malicious" attitudes and unseemly behaviour in "wrongly" pursuing him.

Cogger got off, and Stamler probably paid another price for initiating the investigation – out the window went any chance Stamler might have had of being named to the Order of Canada, an honour for which he had been nominated. It seems that controversy, no matter how tiny or maliciously motivated, outweighs merit when it comes to the awarding of laurels in Canada.

Henry Jensen's demise came in two steps.

When the Doug Small case went to preliminary trial, Mountie Sergeant Rick Jordan testified that he believed the charges against Small were politically motivated. He said that Jensen was trying to please Mulroney, who had called the budget leak a criminal act right from the start.

Jensen denied that and was put in the unusual position of having to defend himself against allegations from one of his own underlings. He argued that Jordan had lost his objectivity and "was not prepared to look at the various aspects of the law."

Today, Jensen says the police had to pursue Small because they believed Small had bought the document from men who had stolen it from the government printing plant, an allegation that was never proven or disproven. Secondly, Jensen alleged, when the police visited Small, Jordan took a legal copy of the document from the reporter. Afterwards, the police had had to retrieve the stolen version, which had been printed upside-down.

The case was a debacle from beginning to end. Jensen survived, but barely. Then he was done in by Inkster, and in public. The venue was the Standing Committee on Justice and the Solicitor-General. On June 6, 1989, in the heat of the storm over the charging of Doug Small, Inkster and Jensen were summoned before the committee to answer questions about, among other things, political interference. At one point, Liberal MP Robert Kaplan tried to ask Inkster about the case of disgraced Tory MP Richard Grisé, but he fumbled the question so badly that it went unanswered. A week later, on June 13, NDP committee member Andrew Brewin stated that the RCMP had admitted that it had delayed laying criminal charges against Grisé until after the November 1988 election.

Inkster leaned over to Jensen, who whispered that Brewin was wrong. The charges had not been delayed.

"The charges were delayed relative to the ongoing investigation," Inkster said. "They were not delayed at all. It was a matter of carrying on with the investigation. . . . The coincidence of the election had no impact in one way or the other in terms of that particular investigation."

"A mere coincidence," Brewin mused.

It was apparent that the opposition parties had a mole somewhere in the Mounted Police, but their information wasn't right. The charges hadn't been delayed.

"I did not call the election," Inkster said, "and I am certain that [the government was] not telling me how to do my investigation, so I can only conclude it was a coincidence."

The following December, Inkster was getting ready for another appearance before the standing committee. The issue of

Grisé was bubbling beneath the surface, once again. Jensen went to Inkster and told him that he now knew a decision had been made to delay obtaining search warrants against Grisé until election day.

On December 12, 1989, Inkster went back before the standing committee and apologized for "inadvertently providing inaccurate information" in his answer the previous June. Inkster said,

> I wish to note that it was a delay in the obtaining of search warrants, not their execution or the laying of charges, that was at issue. Evidently, it would have been possible to make application for search warrants on November 15, 1988, but judicial authority was not sought and obtained until November 21, the day of the election, and the search warrants were executed on November 22. I believe this to have been an appropriate exercise of discretion and was not unprecedented. The officers involved, after careful deliberation, concluded that the processes of the criminal investigation would not be jeopardized; that what evidence might be available was not all in Mr. Grisé's possession, and that, on balance, injury that might be done to the electoral process on the eve of an election or to the individual concerned, should it subsequently be determined that he was innocent, outweighed any possible risk to criminal procedures.

That was fine, but then Inkster went on to add that he had been provided inaccurate information and had only recently been alerted to the discrepancy. "I recognize this situation as being unacceptable, and as commissioner responsible for the control and management of the RCMP, I will take that action which is necessary to rectify the situation."

He didn't have to do a thing. Jensen decided it was time to take his pension. "That first meeting," Jensen says, "I remember when Inkster turned to me. The question was loud and clear: "Were the charges delayed?" I answered no, which was true. Did he expect me to play devil's advocate and get into a debate in front of the committee about the search warrants? In the end, Inkster hung me out to dry. I did not do anything wrong. Inkster even asked me to stay, but I clearly could not in those circumstances."

For almost a decade Jensen had hovered a heartbeat away from the commissioner's job. He had always tried to do the right thing, but in the end found that he just didn't have the fine-tuned political touch required. His personal disappointment didn't concern him as much as what had happened to the force. He was devastated by what had become of his beloved RCMP. It was as if all he had fought for over the years had been lost.

Inkster's obsequious performance before the standing committee stunned long-time members of the force. Strong leaders such as George B. McClellan or Maurice Nadon, who had no fear of controversy, would not have willingly given up precious ground that they did not have to cede, especially when it affected the rule of law. They would have and did tell the politicians to mind their own business. But Inkster was a different breed, even going as far as attending private parties with the prime minister and other politicians.

Inkster, instead, tried to heal all rifts between the politicians and the police, and to show the world what a wonderful and sensitive man he was. That day's committee hearing was one of the more ignominious moments in RCMP history, far worse in its implications than the transgressions of the Security Service in the early 1970s. Inkster told the committee he wanted to "clear the air about the appearance of political interference" in some of the force's criminal investigations. He talked about how Robert Simmonds and he had a dedicated policy of ensuring RCMP accountability to civilian authority, and then went on to say:

> Ironically, however, there is a growing trend to interpret this changed relationship with government not as an

enhancement and a further contribution to the development of public policy, but rather as a growing intimacy which allows the force to respond to political pressures and influences. Any interpretation of this changed relationship which infers that the force can be used as a vehicle for political partisan purposes is sadly inaccurate and one I find totally unacceptable.

Since 1985 the force has investigated over 30 cases involving persons appointed or elected to Parliament. Each of the investigations has the potential for serious political embarrassment, and this embarrassment has touched all parties. Most of these investigations have been carried out amidst great public debate. Yet in each case I can find no evidence that members of the force did other than their duty without fear, favour or affection of or towards any person. The RCMP enforces the law and should not be subject to criticism from those who wish to deflect their embarrassment or use the force in an attempt to further embarrass a political opponent. Political partisanship may be an essential feature of representative government, but it is not essential to discredit the RCMP to serve partisan political purposes.

Inkster had done the unthinkable; he had told the politicians exactly what the police were doing. Leaking sensitive information had become so routine for the force that the commissioner was now doing it in public. Naturally, there were follow-up questions to his stunning revelation that there had been thirty investigations of politicians since 1985. In his reply, Inkster blithely disclosed, "There are approximately fifteen ongoing investigations involving members of Parliament. I do not think it would serve any purpose to say which party they came from." But the suspects knew who they were and had now been given ample warning to destroy evidence or run for cover.

While some parliamentarians waxed indignant about the number of investigations being mounted against politicians, an Ottawa *Citizen* editorialist saw Inkster's revelations in the same light as most police officers did:

> Announcing investigations of his political masters in order to show that the RCMP is not in the government's pocket is a rather dubious way to restore the force's lost credibility.
>
> It has been RCMP policy not to say an investigation is taking place until it becomes public. This policy makes sense since not all who are investigated are charged.
>
> Good policing that results in convictions against those who commit crimes, whether they are Tories, Liberals or New Democrats, however, would be a better way of showing how credible the force is. . . .
>
> We must not lose sight of the fact, either, that Inkster is not the only question mark in this affair. All RCMP investigations are not whimsical; there are elected officials who abuse their office and are convicted because of it.

Inkster survived this controversy, too. But in February 1994, Inkster made a surprise announcement of early retirement.

19

Controlling the
Intersections of Power

"The message is clear. The political system and its institutions are essentially sound. Canadians are neither cranky nor difficult. Rather, they are disillusioned and dismayed by the behaviour and the legacy of the Mulroney government," wrote veteran Ottawa civil servant Brooke Jeffrey in her 1992 book, *Breaking Faith*. Jeffrey's is a familiar refrain in Canadian politics: the institutions are sound, it's just that the people in them are a bit wonky and suspect. But are the institutions sound?

Stamler, Jensen, and many others in the justice system think otherwise. Over the years they have witnessed corruption first hand. They've seen the RCMP's independence eroded, and the courts become crassly politicized as politicians insinuated themselves. It had been bad enough at the federal level under the Liberals, but the Conservatives seemed coldblooded in their determination to promote their particular agenda. Fresh into their second majority term, the Mulroney government showed it would brook no opposition to its plans. The government might not be able to place its people in every position of power but, at the very least, it could control the key intersections of power and influence. Within government, within the public service, and, some argue, even within the private and public media, the Tories flexed their considerable political muscle.

The Mounties were largely under control, as much as a wilfully compliant commissioner could keep them without being unseemly about it. But they continued to be pests, however, mainly because of their oath as police officers. They still had to investigate crimes and, when they held a reasonable belief that an offence had been committed, they had to lay an appropriate charge. Throughout the Tory years, the one place the police kept getting complaints about was Parliament Hill. Mounties such as Henry Jensen were dismayed by the larceny of the parliamentarians, especially members of the Conservative Party. "There was so much petty thievery going on, it made you sick."

Some members of Parliament were using their discretionary allowances to fly party stalwarts to Mexico. Others conspired to hire each other's relatives on their staffs. The hidden staff rarely if ever showed up for work, but still collected their paycheques, the members of the Special Federal Inquiries Unit found. To get to the politicians the police now had to cross through a key intersection. Throughout the Tory reign it was patrolled by Marcel Pelletier, law clerk and legal counsel to Parliament.

The soft-spoken Pelletier had worked within the bureaucracy for twenty-five years, but he was virtually unknown outside the parliamentary precinct, except for a brief stint in the limelight during the Mackasey affair in the early 1980s. Most of Pelletier's public appearances were at the clerk's table when the House of Commons was in session. Among his many responsibilities was the job of providing legal advice to members of Parliament and helping to draft legislation. Pelletier's boss was the Clerk of the House, the immediate adviser to the Speaker of the House.

Whenever the Mounties came to the door of the House of Commons with a search warrant in hand naming a member of Parliament, Pelletier stood behind the sergeant-at-arms when he answered the knock. A summons, search warrant, or subpoena cannot be served on a member within the walls of Parliament without the prior permission of the Speaker. When the Speaker gives his authorization, he does so on behalf of the House and acting as the guardian of parliamentary privilege. Throughout the first six years of the Mulroney reign, the niceties of parliamentary privilege aside, the Mounties seemed to be executing a blizzard of search warrants.

Members of Parliament, unsurprisingly, attacked the Mounties. One Liberal MP, John Nunziata, went as far as to suggest that the reason the politicians were being investigated was because the RCMP didn't like Parliament criticizing the force. The police couldn't fight back and the politicians knew it.

By 1989, the politicians had created a dilemma for themselves over the questionable and illegal spending of discretionary funds. Many politicians believed that how these funds were spent was nobody's business but theirs and that any violations of the rules were matters of interpretation and should not be the subject of criminal investigations.

At the same time, however, they didn't want to be self-regulating. They refused to set up an independent committee to monitor such spending because, they argued, a committee would infringe on the independence they require to carry out their duties as elected members. They wanted neither administrative scrutiny of their spending nor did they think they should be subject to the Criminal Code. The compromise struck between the government and the two opposition parties was that ways would be explored to get better legal control of the police in matters affecting politicians – Bill C-79, it would be called. To that end, a special all-party committee was set up in late 1989 to review the Parliament of Canada Act.

Marcel Pelletier participated in those hearings and shivered at what he believed was the evil the Tories had wrought on the operations and integrity of Parliament. It had begun with a subtle alteration to the Board of Internal Economy in 1985. Since Confederation this board had overseen the expenditures of Parliament, including salaries and other contingent expenses. Traditionally, the board had been chaired by the Speaker and consisted of four ministers. Under Mulroney, the governing Act was amended to enlarge the board's membership to nine. The number of cabinet ministers was reduced to two, and the other seven members were backbenchers and representatives from each of the opposition parties. The board continued to meet in secret. Its records were not published.

Pelletier is one of many who believes that, by bringing the opposition parties onto the board, the Tories slyly co-opted the Liberals and New Democrats. In matters of great dispute, they could all end up on the same side of an issue, and not necessarily on the side of the public interest.

Now, the special committee reviewing the Parliament Act had one overriding intention: to devise a method whereby parliamentarians could decide for themselves whether police search warrants were valid. No outsider would be allowed into the loop. The plan was for the Board of Internal Economy to vet all police search warrants to be served on politicians.

To Pelletier this was outrageous, evidence that the politicians were determined to set themselves above the law and, by doing so, to block due process. "To me that goes contrary to any normal police investigation," Pelletier says. "If the police are after someone for wrongdoing, whatever it is, they certainly won't warn the chap ahead of time, 'Hey, be careful, fellow. I'll be in your office investigating your behaviour in two weeks.' That doesn't make sense."

At the committee hearings, Pelletier says, the politicians also made wild allegations about the Mounties, which couldn't be substantiated in any way. And none of it conformed with Pelletier's own experience. In his many years of dealing with Mountie investigators, he had found that they had always conducted themselves professionally and with respect for the rules of Parliament. He was impressed that most had been senior investigators. "They never really pushed their way in or tried to overpower the institution, if you wish. As far as I know, they kept their place."

Whenever the Mounties sought to conduct a search within the walls of the House, Pelletier would first check their warrant to ensure that it was proper and legal. Then, in the company of the sergeant-at-arms, he would visit the Speaker's Office and explain the situation, the nature of the investigation, and make a recommendation to the Speaker. If the documentation was found to be proper and correct, Pelletier's recommendation was always to proceed with the inquiry, to let the Mounties do their search. Otherwise, the Speaker could well have been accused of interfering with the administration of justice. "That's certainly something that Parliament should not be doing," Pelletier says. Finally, Pelletier would accompany the Mounties during their searches to ensure that they seized only relevant documents. The police were only doing their jobs. Pelletier was certain of that.

During the special committee hearings that began in late 1989, Pelletier, among others, was alarmed by how out of touch with the real world the elected members seemed to be. As they wrestled with issues of conflict of interest, breach of trust, parliamentary privilege, fraud, they argued, almost to a person, that there should be no scrutiny of the $165,000 each was allowed in discretionary monies.

The official minutes of the meetings confirm Pelletier's impressions about the politicians. They show Pelletier giving his calm, cool advice, gently trying to educate the members about the rule of law. Meanwhile, the politicians seem all but oblivious of the concept that all Canadians are equal under the law, and they blithely ignore suggestions that they are trying to place themselves above the law. Their questions betray a breathtaking lack of understanding of the system, as they struggle to give themselves the widest leeway to spend public money.

Pelletier believed that ninety per cent of politicians were honest and upright, yet the Board of Internal Economy was determined to protect the other ten per cent from the police. "Why?" he asks. "It seemed like a strange thing to do."

In May 1991, Bill C-79 was hurriedly proclaimed as law by the Tories, the day before the opening of a preliminary trial into fourteen charges of breach of trust against Tory MP Gabriel Fontaine. The law gives the Board of Internal Economy the exclusive authority to decide whether Commons funds are being spent properly and allows the RCMP to ask the board for an opinion during an investigation of an MP's spending. Fontaine tried to use the new law in his defence but his arguments were rejected by Quebec Judge Laurent Dubé, who ruled that MPs do not have immunity from the ordinary criminal laws of the country.

The ruling didn't surprise Pelletier. He had learned that when it came to playing by the rules, the Tories were always ready to ignore the rules or make up new ones to suit their purpose, seemingly without much regard for the integrity of Parliament. The Bill C-79 debate was only one part of the fundamental problem afflicting Parliament, Pelletier believes.

In 1988, Robert Marleau was appointed Clerk of the House, which carries with it the rank of deputy minister. Marleau, a former teacher, had no legal training, but was believed to be close to the Tories. During his reign, each time police showed up with a search warrant for a politician's office, Marleau attended the meeting. This action was unprecedented.

Inevitably, Pelletier said, Marleau would side with the interests of the government, advising caution. "We don't want to do things which are wrong since, perhaps, these members might really be innocent. We don't want to do damage to them,"

Pelletier and a number of Mounties quote Marleau as saying on several occasions.

Pelletier didn't think Marleau's intervention was proper: "The Clerk's role was administration of the House. The search warrants were strictly legal matters, which should not have concerned him. Sure, there may have been ramifications for the administration, but only after the investigation proceeded." Like the police themselves, Pelletier was nervous that the information contained in confidential search warrants was being leaked out, but there was nothing he could do about it as Marleau was his boss.

It seemed to Pelletier that the Clerk's Office had ceased to be entirely independent. Instead of making recommendations based on what was good for Parliament, the interests of the government were often given more weight. Within the Speaker's Office, the catch phrase was: "Rule to Please."

The disintegration of standards continued in other areas. Pelletier witnessed Speaker John Fraser, Marleau, and the government House leader of the day occasionally discussing strategy in the House, contrary to all the traditions of Parliament. The Speaker was supposed to be neutral, and the Clerk's responsibility was to Parliament, not the government.

Pelletier had learned about Parliament studying under masters who were long on memory and knowledge and high on ethics. He felt honour-bound to uphold Parliament's traditions, and he refused to play the new game. "Watching what was happening with government was very demoralizing," Pelletier says. "There was no vision and no real philosophy at work. All they were doing was taking advantage of one situation after another, as if they knew that tomorrow they might not be there and, therefore, they had to make the best of it. The best of it happened to be a mess."

Pelletier's position had afforded him one of the most beautiful offices in the Commons, overlooking the Ottawa River and the

Gatineau Hills. One day in early 1990, Pelletier was told he would have to move his office off Parliament Hill to a nondescript block on Sparks Street. He had four days to make the move. The space was needed for other purposes. To move the law clerk off Parliament Hill was unprecedented, and Pelletier didn't need a map to figure out was happening to him. He dutifully took up the new office space and continued on with his work. Soon afterward, Mary Anne Griffith, who had lost out to Marleau for the Clerk's job, was moved into Pelletier's office, as Marleau's deputy.

In October 1990, before the Bill C-79 committee was done with its work, Pelletier was fired by Marleau because, in Marleau's words, "There was a lack of chemistry." Another intersection had been commandeered by the politicians. Pelletier could have slunk away and licked his wounds, but he chose to fight back. In the wrongful-dismissal action he launched, he sued not only Marleau and the government, but also Brian Mulroney. It was an unusual tactic, but Pelletier believed Mulroney had been directly responsible for his dismissal because he had made it clear to the Tories he would not be part of their team. "My loyalty was to Parliament," Pelletier says.

The case was settled out of court. The government chose not to tackle Pelletier, but forced him to agree not to disclose the size of the settlement. Pelletier found himself out on the street and, according to the old saw about being fired, without a voice. "They are wrong if they say I am bitter," he now says. "I am not bitter about what happened to me. I am bitter about what happened to Parliament." In the end the only regret he had was that he didn't get the chance to say goodbye to friends and workmates he had known during his quarter-century of public service. "When the chef from the parliamentary restaurant left at about the same time as me, Mulroney threw a black-tie dinner for him," Pelletier says. "That tells you more about the government's attitudes than anything."

20

Fighting for the Rule of Law

Being a police officer had given Rod Stamler a special privilege, the ability to peek occasionally behind the élite's curtain of respectability and view its hidden secrets. He had seen some of Canada's most important businessmen and politicians cavorting, innocently and otherwise, with some of its most questionable and despicable characters.

By the time Stamler left in 1989, the rule of law had deftly been usurped by the rule of politics, just as Pierre Trudeau seemed to fear might happen during his impassioned speeches prior to the McDonald Commission hearings. Stamler lamented that the public had lost touch with its political and legal institutions, or the other way around. He believed that the institutions had been allowed to become sick, diseased, rickety, and there seemed to be few effective checks and balances governing Parliament, the judiciary, or the police. There were still honourable men and women but, Stamler thought, too many of those who wielded power had

301

become addicted to it, more loyal now to their careers, pension plans, and creature comforts than to the public interest. Powerful political and business leaders had gained the ability to protect themselves from threatening police investigations and, if they failed there, to neutralize or derail any subsequent prosecution.

In the Mounted Police, the rule of politics arrived through a change in management fashion to a top-down autocratic system. The commissioner was made politically accountable, but political accountability saw him become a deputy minister, directly responsible to the prime minister and not the justice system. Staff were chosen more for their compliance and eagerness to please than for their creativity or ability to meet a standard of excellence. Where individuals once made decisions, committees stood in their place. Where there was once competition between police forces in enforcing laws, an *ad hoc* system of checks and balances, as it were, business-school notions of efficiency have dictated that there be little or no overlap in police jurisdiction. The result, Stamler believes, is a nurturing atmosphere for the systematization of corruption.

Along the way, innovation and ingenuity had been replaced by consensus and acquiescence, and the key intersections of power often seemed clogged by design with the weakest and most inept people, who were guaranteed to follow the orders of their insecure leaders.

In difficult investigations this came to mean that many peace officers were forced into the most difficult moral and ethical situations – having to betray the police oath to uphold the rule of law. What police believed to be true came to matter less than what their superiors within or outside the force wanted them to believe. The inevitable result was that Canadians were no longer being treated equally under the law. Rather than a beacon shining into all corners of society, the light of the law had been seized and turned into a spotlight, leaving those who controlled it hidden in the darkness above.

Many good, well-meaning men and women in policing and

the public service had met their demise trying to uphold the rule of law, trying to ensure that all were treated equally.

At the beginning of the 1970s, Cliff Kennedy had told Stamler about what was happening in Ottawa, about the lack of controls on the public purse and the virtually open invitation to criminal behaviour – thanks in part to the innovations of the Glassco Commission. The politicians had called it reform, bringing business sense and practices to the bureaucracy, and Canadians accepted their word that this was a good thing.

Stamler had quickly learned that Kennedy not only was right, but also that, as bad as things were then, they were far worse now. Trudeau had been one of the few politicians who seemed willing to support the rule of law, but he was defeated and his vision repudiated by the Mulroney government.

There was another constant that Stamler and his cohorts were quite familiar with: the labelling of the police as corrupt, inept, out of control, and dangerous, especially when the very same police appeared to be on the verge of penetrating some inner sanctum of the élite. Stamler realized that many Canadians, confused by the politicians and by the rhetoric of the times, had become disoriented.

Canadian politics had been reduced almost entirely to symbols and illusion, serving to confuse and confound the public. What the political and business leaders said they were doing more often than not seemed out of step with what they actually did. They said they were going to open up the political process, but fundamental deals such as free trade treaties were negotiated in secret. They said they were fighting government spending and intent on bringing down the public deficit, but they did precisely the opposite. They said that they were opening up the political process, but it was evident that the only open doors were reserved for the friends and cronies of the governing party and the establishment. The politicians promised to fight crime, but then deftly weakened the ability of the police to do so.

As French philosopher Yves Simon once wrote: "the thing

which is never ethical and never political is insincere, unfaithful, apparent and not real – in short, treacherous – transmission of power."

The treachery of the Mulroney government did not go entirely unnoticed.

On November 8, 1993, the Canadian public administered the most devastating punishment ever to a ruling party. The electorate reduced the once-mighty Conservatives to a two-seat rump under a Liberal majority. Much of the Conservative vote outside Quebec swung to the Reform Party, led by Preston Manning, which promised a return to ethics and integrity in government.

What had helped to bring down the Tories were the very same things Stamler would have been trying to pursue had he remained a Mountie.

The Conservatives insisted on purchasing $5-billion worth of state-of-the-art helicopters. The deal didn't make sense either in its timing or scope. The intransigence of the Tories in defending the deal reminded Stamler of other curious business dealings he had wanted to investigate in previous years – Aerospatiale and Oerlikon, to name just two. The helicopter deal was cancelled as one of the first acts in office by incoming Prime Minister Jean Chrétien.

Mulroney and his successor, Kim Campbell, tried to force through without tenders the giveaway sale of Toronto's Pearson Airport, the country's most profitable airport. The buyers were a group of mostly wealthy Conservative supporters, including a former president of the party and a former cabinet minister. A number of bureaucrats who tried to block or stall the sweet deal until after the election were removed from their posts under direct orders from the Prime Minister's Office. Jean Chrétien quickly killed that deal, too.

These were only two questionable deals. What else was there that the public didn't know about? Stamler wondered what lay behind a lot of political decisions that had made no sense to the average Canadian, such as the extension in 1993 of patent protection to major pharmaceutical companies. There were rumours in Ottawa that as much as $38 million had been paid offshore to high ranking Tories to push the legislation through. In fact, Mulroney's office personally saw to the drug-patent legislation being enacted.

Based on his experience, Stamler knew that where there was smoke in the political process, there was often fire. But at the same time, there was little will among the political élite of the police to detect the flames. At most, they'd go through the motions, file a report, and do little else. Controversy had become anathema for the police.

Therein lay Stamler's major concern: the integrity of the Canadian justice system and the manner in which the country is being policed.

The great, abiding fear of civil libertarians and other interest groups has always been of a police state – intrusive, racist, biased, out of political control, and anti-democratic. To assuage these voices, new laws had been quickly promulgated, administrative controls rushed into place, and politically correct staffing changes made.

Stamler believes that for all their energy and doggedness the mostly left-wing watchdogs of the police and the justice system can't see the fallout for the snow – they inadvertently have helped to create and enforce another brand of police state – entirely insidious, strategically in political control and thoroughly anti-democratic. "It is a system of justice designed at its heart to protect the political and economic élite from police investigations and prosecutions," says Stamler. "We clearly have a two-tiered justice system in this country, and I don't think that's what Canadians expect or want."

That is a real issue Canadians must address, Stamler thinks. As dark as he thinks the times might be for the justice system, he has remained a peace officer to the end, loyal to his oath to the rule of law. In allowing his story to be told, he felt it was his duty to take one more tough stand. That is why he decided to speak up about what he saw, experienced, and most importantly, about what he believed.

Index